D1807433

05/07

UNIVERSITY OF
WOLVERHAMPTON

Harrison Learning Centre
City Campus
University of Wolverhampton
St Peter's Square
Wolverhampton
WV1 1RH
Telephone 0845 408 1631
Online renewals:
www.wlv.ac.uk/lib/myaccount

ONE WEEK LOAN

Telephone Renewals: 01902 321333 or 0845 408 1631
Please RETURN this item on or before the last date shown above.
Fines will be charged if items are returned late.
See tariff of fines displayed at the Counter.   (L2)

Aging by the Book

SUNY series, Studies in the Long Nineteenth Century

Pamela K. Gilbert, editor

Aging by the Book

The Emergence of Midlife
in Victorian Britain

KAY HEATH

SUNY
PRESS

Published by
State University of New York Press, Albany

For information, contact State University of New York Press, Albany, NY
www.sunypress.edu

Production by Kelli W. LeRoux
Marketing by Michael Campochiaro

Library of Congress Cataloging-in-Publication Data

Heath, Kay, 1953–
  Aging by the book : the emergence of midlife in Victorian Britain /
Kay Heath.
      p. cm. — (Suny series, Studies in the long nineteenth century)
  Includes bibliographical references and index.
  ISBN 978-0-7914-7657-4 (hardcover : alk. paper)
  1. Middle-aged women—Great Britain—Social conditions.   2. Middle-aged women—Attitudes.   3. Great Britain—Social life and customs—19th century.   4. Great Britain—History—Victoria, 1837–1901.   I. Title.

HQ1059.5.G7H43 2009
305.2440941'09034—dc22   2008017370

10 9 8 7 6 5 4 3 2 1

For Hope and Laura, with all my love

Contents

Illustrations

Acknowledgments

I began this book at Rice University where I was fortunate to have the expert advice and friendship of Helena Michie. Bob Patten was an unfailing resource with far-reaching connections and compendious knowledge of all things Victorian. Marty Wiener provided many helpful insights on historical matters. The former Dean of Humanities at Rice, Judith Brown, generously supported two summer research trips to England. The women in my writing group, Annie Tinnemeyer, Carolyn Dorow White, Janet Myers, and Louise Penner, continue to be a much-appreciated source of support and friendship. I especially am grateful for continued collaboration with Janet and Louise as fellow Victorianists.

I have benefited from the collections at the following libraries as well as from the help of their staff: Julie Anne Lambert, Josie Lister, and Samantha Townsend at the John Johnson Collection, Bodleian Library, Oxford University; the British Library; Stephen Lowther and Rachael Cross at the Wellcome Library; Erin Blake, LeEllen DeHaven, and Bettina Smith at the Folger Shakespeare Library; and Dale Neighbors at the Library of Virginia. Without the generous borrowing policies of the University of Virginia libraries, I could not have completed this book.

An earlier version of chapter 4 appeared as "Marriageable at Midlife: The Remarrying Widows of Frances Trollope and Anthony Trollope," a chapter in *Frances Trollope and the Novel of Social Change*, edited by Brenda Ayres, pp. 85–102, © 2002 by Brenda Ayres, and is reproduced with the permission of Greenwood Publishing Group, Inc., Westport, Conn. An earlier version of chapter 5 appeared as "In the Eye of the Beholder: Victorian Age Construction and the Specular Self" in *Victorian Literature and Culture* 34.1 (2006): 27–45, © 2006 Cambridge University Press, and is reprinted with the permission of Cambridge University Press.

SUNY Press has been a delight to work with at every stage of the project. I especially would like to thank my editor James Peltz, as well as Allison Lee, Marilyn Semerad, and Kelli W. LeRoux. I also appreciate insightful and encouraging comments provided by Teresa Mangum and two anonymous readers.

I have received constant support from many wonderful friends during the years I have worked on this book. My office mate at Virginia State University, Donna Crawford, makes the challenges delightful and motivates me with her dedication to all good causes. Renée Hill is compassion personified and an inspiration in our writing group as well as on all spiritual matters. Thank you both for your invaluable friendship. Sara Leland's open heart has enlivened many days of writing. Oliver Hill has been an excellent meditation teacher. Many thanks to my colleagues and students at VSU's Institute for the Study of Race Relations, who have educated and supported me throughout writing this book. Thanks to the entire Bickley clan for opening their family and their beach house to me. Lara Smith's pithy hilarity never fails to provide sanity. Scot Pedin often challenges my brain and my spirit. I am grateful to the members of the Sangha. Thanks to Ann McClain for being more than a cousin.

Michael McClure's literary insight, encouragement, and love have left their mark on these pages. Emily McClure has an enthusiasm for my work that inspires me, and Tieran McClure's bountiful intelligence has been a ceaseless source of delight.

My sisters, Bobbi Heath and Susan Heath, are an unfailing source of strength and have provided much-needed relaxation on many sisters' trips as well as innumerable hours on the phone, just listening. I would also like to thank my parents, John and Helen Heath, for teaching me how to work and how to dream. Inez Batson Heath has been an example to us all.

I am grateful to my son-in-law, Dave Johansson, for loving me and my loved ones so well. I will always be thankful to Samuel Toby Johansson and Nathaniel David Johansson for turning me into a grandmother. You are the delight of my life. I can never adequately express my gratitude to Hope Johansson and Laura Egliht, best of daughters, for being there no matter what. You will forever be at the center of my heart and life as the kind of women I want to be. The words "I love you" are truly inadequate.

Chapter 1

Introduction

The Rise of Midlife in Victorian Britain

A man rakes his fingers through his beard as he peers into a mirror, startled by the possibility that a gray hair may have materialized on his face (figure 1.1).[1] Such images punctuate our daily lives to the point that we only half attend, barraged by advertisements and commercials that peddle the latest age preventative to our commodity-addicted culture. In this case, however, the familiar scene is Victorian, a *Punch* cartoon by John Leech published in 1852. Its comedy rests in the gazer's quandary about age identity as he jumps back and forth between relief and alarm: "Good gracious! Is it possible?—No! Yes! No!—Yes! Yes, by Jupiter, it's a grey hair in my favourite whisker!" The sketch's title, *Tempus Edax Rerum*, which appropriates the classical line "Time, the devourer of all things," lends a tragicomic air to the sufferer's plight, his fate hanging upon the appearance of a single hair. We are all too familiar with this dilemma. We know that the first gray whisker symbolizes much more than just loss of melanin, announcing the onset of a deterioration that leads first to old age and ultimately to death. And, from the perspective of our current youth-adulating consciousness, the prospect of facing the former can appear almost more difficult to endure than the latter.

Though this picture may seem routine to our early twenty-first-century eyes, it encapsulates an idea that emerged with great force in the Victorian era and changed Western concepts of the life course: the belief that the middle years begin an inevitable and calamitous decline.[2] As the cartoon pokes fun at aging, it also registers an anxiety about early signs of senescence that gained enough cultural authority in the nineteenth century to generate a new term, the word "midlife" first appearing in an English-language dictionary in 1895. "Middle age" had been a feature of the life course for centuries before the Victorian era, based on the Aristotelian notion of *akme*, the peak and "prime of life," dubbed "the perfect age of man's life" or "ripe age" in medieval Britain and often gendered male (Dove 6,

TEMPUS EDAX RERUM.

"Good Gracious! Is it Possible?—No! Yes! No!—Yes! Yes!
By Jupiter, it's a Grey Hair in my favourite Whisker!"

Figure 1.1. Cartoon. *Punch* (1852): 216. The Library of Virgina. Reproduced by permission.

29).[3] This concept differs strikingly from our construction of "midlife" as decline, the inception of loss and a sense that time is running out. The view of midlife as the beginning of the end, an inevitable slide into deterioration, is now commonly associated with the term "midlife crisis" first articulated in 1965 by French psychologist Elliott Jaques.[4] In *Aging By The Book*, I explore the nineteenth-century roots from which this theory grew.

Leech's cartoon points to several issues of identity which form the territory of this study. The gazer is a typical British citizen according to Victorian notions of subjectivity, a white, middle-class male. Gender is a key component both to his age anxiety and this book—after all, the gray hair appears in his beard, a secondary sexual characteristic that is decidedly male.[5] What if the midlife sufferer had been a woman? How would a cartoon represent the first manifestations of her aging, and would such a joke have been considered funny in the same way? The man's clothing and surroundings suggest neither wealth nor poverty—how important is his middle station to the concern he feels? And, what if the man had been designated ethnically "other" in Victorian terms—perhaps Indian or African—would his race have any bearing on his concerns about age? The most uniquely midlife aspect of this cartoon and the feature most basic to my project, however, is the man's uncertainty, his sense of existing tenuously in an ambiguous, uncharted zone of the life course, a nervous need to understand his position in a liminal space between youth and age.

In order to answer the questions both explicit and implicit in this sketch and the cultural issues Leech suggests, I draw on sources such as medical literature, demographic data, and advertisements, but I center my attention most extensively on Victorian novels. The characters I examine are white and middle- or upper-class Victorians created with and depicted as possessing particular assumptions about gender, race, nationality, sexual orientation, and social class. I consider ways in which these suppositions shifted and were shaped by the notion of midlife, an aspect of subjectivity intersecting with and complicating all other categories. *Aging by the Book* explores the rise of midlife in Victorian Britain as a new way of understanding the human life span, an age ideology that was fully deployed by the fin de siècle. Our current sense of midlife decline emerged in the nineteenth century, a credo that has only continued to gain power as Western cultures become ever more youth-oriented, increasingly devalue aging, and push back the years of danger to earlier stages in the life course. I argue that today's hyper age-consciousness, with its aura of a fate worse than death, is a dogma we have inherited from the Victorians, our predecessors in midlife trauma.[6]

I.

In the latter decades of the twentieth century, academic studies in the humanities began to explore race, class, gender, sexual orientation, nationality, state of health, and other such concepts as central to individual and collective identity. At the same time, healthcare specialists, social scientists, and historians began to consider the importance of age, but literary and cultural theorists have been slow to enter the discussion.[7] Helen Small's recent book *The Long Life* is a welcome exception to the scanty literary analysis of aging. As she points out, though many literary texts deal with the later years, it is "surprising that so few critics have read these works *for* what they have to say about age" (5). The few age-related studies of the Victorian era are almost completely confined to explorations of child-hood and old age, and in this field as elsewhere, midlife has been "the last portion of the life span to be 'discovered,'" as anthropologist Margaret Lock insightfully comments about her own field of study (45).[8] To exclude the concept of age is not only to ignore, but also to deny, its pervasive influence on the way culture constructs our identity as humans and by such denial to remain unconscious of and therefore vulnerable to age's hegemonic intensity.

Discussing midlife as a creation of certain twentieth-century cultures, age theorists point to its absence in many non-Western societies, a gap that makes obvious the culturally constructed nature of life stage theories.[9] We tend to view age uncritically as an unvarying and inevitable process, a stable element of being that is biologically determined in a uniform progression, occurring in virtually the same way in all places at all times. Only recently has age's malleability begun to be recognized (Lock 47). Age is universal, a fact of existence for all living things, but one understood differently by each society and era. As sociologists Mike Featherstone and Mike Hepworth argue, we must look beyond viewing age as something "reducible to biologi-cal processes of physical decline which take place in some vacuum sealed off from social life" ("Images" 308). Culture prescribes how age should be and often is experienced—both biologically and behaviorally—through life course paradigms. As Margaret Morganroth Gullette points out, "what-ever happens in the body, humans beings are aged by culture first of all," placed by age expectations into categories that prescribe possibilities for identity (*Declining* 3). While a grandmother's wrinkle in China is inter-preted by her granddaughters as a marker of increased status, the same wrinkle in the West is read as a sign of lost youth and a proof of decay (Featherstone and Hepworth, "Images" 306). Western cultures place great stress on chronological years, and transition from one life stage to another often is discussed in terms of significant birthdays—are we "over the hill" at thirty? . . . forty? . . . fifty? Some cultures emphasize other factors. For example, progression through social roles according to community status, including alterations in the lives of one's children, may be more significant than chronological age or biological symptoms (Shweder xi).

Though meanings assigned to age are culturally determined, in any study of age we must also acknowledge the physical body. Age theory always exists in a tension between biological essentialism and cultural cues. Kathleen Woodward argues that "a position of pure social constructivism" is not possible, because "[w]e cannot detach the body in decline from the meanings we attach to old age" (*Aging* 18–19). Gullette, however, wants to do exactly that, at least as far as possible, asserting, "I would like to be at a point equivalent to that argued by Judith Butler in *Gender Trouble*, interrogating aging as a 'natural process' altogether, but I think that the most age studies can do now is to urge a radical social constructionism that pushes 'the natural' out of context after context" (*Declining* 245–46).[10] Though we cannot escape the body altogether, we must be vigilant to examine formulaic interpretations, scrutinizing cultural assumptions. Only when we question what we see as "natural" about aging do we become aware of the ways in which our perceptions are fashioned by cultural cues. Though aging occurs in the interplay between physical facts and socially constructed meanings, any experience of its biological aspects is always filtered through how we have learned to perceive them.

The concept of midlife itself especially is difficult to define because it lacks clear cultural or biological markers of onset and cessation. Certain bodily changes may be associated with middle age, but none conclusively initiate or end this stage. Though theorists have attempted to use menopause as the inception point for women, it has proved an unreliable index, occurring as it does across a wide range of ages (Levinson et al. 24).[11] Key events in family and community status usually associated with the middle years—one's children growing up and leaving home, parents dying, or grandchildren being born—can be unreliable indicators, because familial rites of passage are chronologically inconsistent and individually variable, such as children of older parents who are still young when their parents die, or parents past middle age raising teenagers (Woodward, *Aging* 186). Some cultures mark the advent of midlife by significant life passages. For example, Sudhir Kakar reports that in semirural India, one enters the Hindi stage of *burhapa* or abstinence at fifty (79), and when the first child marries the parents begin a "psychological transition . . . into middle age" (78). Some may even cease their sexual relationship, because "It is thought to be polluting and undignified for two generations to copulate under the same roof" (Shweder xi).

While biology and society may suggest certain midlife boundaries, none are conclusive and all are contingent upon interpretation, factors such as gender, class, and age cohort influencing how people define midlife. Surveys have shown that in late-twentieth-century Britain, men and the middle class were considered to enter midlife later than women and the working class (Benson 7). Women and men may define middle age differently, each group having one paradigm for itself and another for the other gender. In addition, as the adage goes, "old" is always twenty years beyond your current age, definitions tending to exist on a sliding scale determined by one's own position. One example is a study by psychologists Margie E. Lachman and Jacquelyn Boone James that found people in their twenties locate midlife onset between ages thirty and fifty-five, while those in their sixties and seventies believe it occurs much later, in the forties to seventies (3).

Because middle age is most often defined as the chronological middle of the life span in Western cultures, changes in life expectancy should produce alterations in ideas about its onset and cessation. Lachman and James believe that midlife is not a recognized stage in cultures with shorter life spans and early onset of certain key life events, but as life expectancies rise, what was once considered old age becomes midlife (2). Jon Benson reports this phenomenon in Great Britain: between 1901 and 1930 middle age was believed to begin at thirty-five, but by 1950 a popular periodical claimed, "While it is true that people are living longer, it also certain that they retain their youth much longer. A woman at forty is not middle-aged now as she was in Victorian times" (11). By the mid-twentieth century, the general consensus in Great Britain was that midlife began at age forty and lasted until sixty, a shift of a decade from census figures in 1851 and 1871 that defined midlife as between thirty and fifty (Benson 9).[12]

As Gullette contends, the inception of midlife cannot reside in a particular age or date, but is contingent upon our personal application of societal norms: "The middle years begin when the culture gets you to say they do" (*Declining* 159). Changes in health care and technology that enable us to increase longevity could, at least theoretically, push midlife back further and further. Obviously, neither chronological, biological, nor sociological factors alone are sufficient for defining midlife (Levinson et al. 322). Only by placing various aspects of midlife within a cultural context can we begin to understand its spectrum of meanings, the project of this book in regard to Victorian Britain.

II.

What makes the Victorian era so important in the history of midlife? After all, "middle age" was not a new concept but for centuries had designated the apotheosis of adulthood. Medieval writings "exalt and glory in a middle age which . . . was represented as being possessed of exuberance, strength and maturity" (Dove 3). From the medieval period to the nineteenth century, steps-of-life drawings represented the life course with "remarkable consistency" as an arched stairway that accords with Aristotle's principle of *akme* or prime occurring after seven periods of seven years (Covey 18; Dove 28). A male stands on the top step labeled fifty while younger and older versions descend on his left and right in drawings that became the "standard bourgeois image of a lifetime" from 1500 to about 1850 (Cole 19).[13] As the examples in figures 1.2 and 1.3 illustrate, separate depictions appeared for men and women during the seventeenth century, emphasizing a proper gendering of the life span with an apex at fifty (Cole 28).[14] In the

Figure 1.2. Anon. Engraving. c. 1630. Folger Shakespeare Library: ART Box A265, No. 1. Reproduced by permission.

Figure 1.3. Pieter Nolpe. Engraving. c. 1660. Folger Shakespeare Library: ART Box A266, No. 2. Reproduced by permission.

nineteenth century, Americans Currier and Ives issued twin drawings that moved women's peak back to thirty, while men's remained at fifty (Cole and Edwards 260), but other nineteenth-century artists, such as the British James Baille, retained fifty as the high point for both genders (Covey 16–17). Though Peter Joerissen and Cornelia Will's *Die Lebenstreppe*, the definitive collection of steps-of-life images, contains examples produced throughout the twentieth century, the popularity of these prints waned in the nineteenth century. Chris Gilleard attributes this demise to rising levels of unemployment and privation among the elderly that moved decrepitude to earlier years during the Industrial Revolution (156).[15]

Susannah R. Ottaway argues that the eighteenth century was an especially crucial period in the history of age because demographic changes such as lengthening life span, earlier, more fertile marriages, and the emergent Industrial Revolution affected definitions of old age (6). The elderly began to be seen as a separate cohort in the overall population, age came to be defined chronologically rather than by functional capacity and fitness, and the concept of elders as dependents or "burdens" on society developed, setting the stage for nineteenth-century pension schemes (Ottaway 13). Due to the secularizing influence of Enlightenment thought, philosophical texts were less oriented around "the good death" and focused more and more on how to age well (Troyansky, "The Older Person" 51–52). Since the early modern period, longevity literature had focused on ways to extend a "green old age," which included lengthening life, preventing disease, and forestalling signs of age, but in the eighteenth century, "green" aging was addressed by a proliferation of new texts that detail methods of diet, exercise, sleep, and even proper breathing (Ottaway 24–25).[16]

While most theorists locate the genesis of apprehension about middle age in the twentieth century, midlife anxiety became fully expressed as a regular part of the life course in the nineteenth century.[17] Several factors shifted the problem of aging from longevity to midlife decline during this period. Rising life expectancy was a key component. During the preceding century, the life course had changed from a religious pilgrimage to a secularized journey, and age became a scientific issue with technical solutions (Cole 5). In the past, British people had not kept track of exact age, rounding the number to the nearest decade (Ottaway 45), but as the Enlightenment increased literacy in the eighteenth century, more emphasis was placed on record keeping, and ages became known with greater accuracy (Ottaway 53).[18] As Victorians compiled data at an unprecedented rate, the life course became a uniform system, and statisticians recorded significant demographic changes that affected concepts of midlife. The first census occurred in 1801, and a population surge across the century increased the count from eleven million in 1801 to thirty-seven million in 1901, a rise of

300 percent (Soloway 617). Longevity literature lost popularity when new demographic data, including insurance statistics, made its excessive claims seem "fanciful" to this growing populace (Katz 62).[19] Life expectancy also grew steadily—while the average life span in 1801 was thirty-six years, by 1901, males were living on the average forty-eight years and females fifty-two, an increase of over a decade for men and a decade and a half for women (Laslett 19). These numbers give a somewhat false picture of how long an adult in Victorian England expected to live, however. Though the average life expectancy may have been in the upper forties by the end of the century, this number must be corrected for a high incidence of infant and child mortality. Death rates for both males and females were extremely high from birth to age four, and although numbers climbed in midlife, they did not reach levels comparable to those of early childhood until sometime in the sixth decade (Mitchell 38–41). Most people who survived into adulthood lived at least into their fifties, and, if they had means, they could expect even more, as Victorian physician John Gardner points out: "The rich, or those exempt from the cares and anxieties of business . . . live longer than the middle classes, or the poor" (9).

When did midlife occur for Victorians? The greatly expanded life course affected the timing of middle age, but determining a chronological definition is a complicated process. Some nineteenth-century writers attempted to describe middle age as the exact numerical center of life; for example, an 1830 pseudo-medical treatise by "an Old Physician" claims that at thirty-eight half of life has been lived, which specifies a seventy-six year average life span (257), well above the census figures of forty-one years for 1831 (Laslett 19). This disparity between words and figures can be understood, however, in terms of personal experience rather than life expectancy averages. Despite what statisticians reported, Victorians knew individuals regularly lived to become octogenarians, and some even nonagenarians or centenarians. In addition, while the compilers of the 1871 census defined middle age as the period of years between ages thirty and fifty for both men and women (Benson 9), statisticians' clear, gender-neutral, and seemingly definitive statement is challenged by fiction which indicates a much more complicated scenario.

As I show in chapters 2 and 3, literary evidence consistently demonstrates that women were aged into midlife earlier than men, due in particular to the concept of spinsterhood and medical theories of reproduction. The nineteenth-century novel routinely relegates single, thirty-year-old women into spinsterhood, a paradigm inherited from the eighteenth century when a woman was pushed across "the threshold from marriageable girl to old maid" at thirty, with a radical shift in status (Ottaway 43–44). Early in the nineteenth century, Jane Austen indicates the boundaries of female marriageability when Frederick Wentworth comments in *Persuasion* (1818), "Yes, here I am . . . ready to make a foolish match. Anybody between fifteen and thirty may have me for asking" (86). Elizabeth, the eldest Elliot daughter, feels "her approach to the years of danger" at age twenty-nine (38), because she had, after all, been on the "market" for almost fifteen years. That spinsterhood automatically associated women with middle age is evident in Dinah Mulock Craik's *Hannah* (1871) when the protagonist, at thirty, is described as both "an old maid" (27) and a woman "on the verge of middle age" (16).

While Victorian novels depict women nearing middle age at thirty, they present equivalent men as still young. When Jane Eyre first meets Rochester she notes that he "was past youth, but had not reached middle age: perhaps he might be thirty-five" (114). Craik's *Hannah* says that "men are young still at thirty" (21), and Lady Laura in Anthony Trollope's *Phineas Finn* (1867–69) observes that a "woman at forty is quite old, whereas a man at forty is young" (1.74). In contrast to women, men also remain marriageable in their forties. In *Phineas Finn*, the narrator specifically points out that Robert Kennedy at forty has all the requisites of a good husband: "Mr. Kennedy was an unmarried man, with an immense fortune, a magnificent place, a seat in Parliament, and was not perhaps above forty years of age. There could be no reason why he should not ask Lady Laura to be his wife . . ." (1.55–56). In Trollope's *The Way We Live Now*, Roger Carbury at forty is "still regarded . . . as a young man. They spoke of him at the county fairs as the young squire. When in his happiest moods he could be almost a boy" (1.130). Though Hetta Carbury joking calls Roger "old," she specifically states he is marriageable, asserting, "Men a great deal older get married every day" (146).

As I discuss in the next chapter, Victorian novels depict male midlife onset in the forties. Arthur Clennam, forty at the beginning of *Little Dorrit* (55), describes himself as "in middle life" (59) and as having "lived the half of a long term of life" (86), Mr. Broune in *The Way We Live Now* is called middle-aged at fifty (1.287), and Mr. Maule, Sr. in *Phineas Redux* (1873–74) is described as "hardly beyond middle life" in his mid-fifties (1.183–84). Victorian fiction makes a finer distinction than the census designation of thirty to fifty, specifying a decade's difference for men and women, with middle age occurring for females in their thirties to late forties and men in their forties and fifties.

Novels also depict men as at the height of their attractions in middle age while women are past their prime. Caroline Norton begins *Old Sir Douglas* (1868) with high praise for midlife men that contrasts with a critique of women: "There is no example of human beauty more perfectly picturesque than a very handsome man of middle age," with his "air of customary command, of mingled majesty, wisdom, and cordial benevolence" (1.1). However, "with the other sex it is different," because, she explains, "bloom is an integral part of woman's loveliness, and every day that brings her nearer to its withering takes away something of her charm" (1.2). As Amy M. King argues, Victorian female beauty was assessed by the botanical metaphor of "bloom" that assigned value to women in reproductive terms as sexually ripe and fertile (8). When women near the age of menopause, which was considered to occur in their mid-forties, they are described with images of lost "bloom," withering, and fading, past their reproductive prime.[20] In his autobiography, Anthony Trollope implies that women in their fifties are elderly. Though his mother Fanny's first novel came into print when she was fifty, he records that "till long after middle life she never herself wrote for publication" (*Autobiography* 20).

In addition to identifying midlife onset, it is essential to make a distinction between midlife and old age instead of conflating the two under "aging." This fusion locks age studies into a binary of young versus old and frequently elides the middle years from the discussion altogether, while the concept of midlife questions and complicates such essentialism. Paradigms of old age also are vital to any discussion about the middle years, because the two are inextricably linked, as midlife is deeply influenced by a culture's attitude toward generalized aging. However, determining when midlife gives way to old age is not a straightforward issue. Recent work in the history of old age reveals that onset of elderliness has been determined by a variety of means. Lynn Botelho and Pat Thane describe three common methods of assessing elderliness in the British past: "chronological" old age, "functional" assessment of physical ability, and "cultural old age," a combination of these measures along with other factors (4). Thane stresses that agedness was measured on an individual basis in preindustrialized Europe, by "appearance and . . . capacities rather than by age-defined rules" ("Social Histories" 98), though she also identifies sixty as the age most commonly associated with old age onset throughout British history (*Old Age* 16). Shulamith Shahar argues that during the Middle Ages and Renaissance, people were considered to enter old age at some point between sixty and seventy, though function was a more significant criterion than chronology (43). Ottaway confirms that sixty serves as a good average age of entry into elderhood during the eighteenth century, though "individual circumstances rather than strict cultural standards were the final determinants of when the decline of life began" (54). Janet Roebuck contends that before the nineteenth century, function was a more important age marker than chronology for poor law authorities, who considered the indigent elderly to be those who could no longer support themselves and also looked old (419). However, with the establishment of pension and retirement age in the late nineteenth century, chronological age became more important as an official marker of elderhood.

For the most part, women not only aged into midlife earlier than men in Victorian England, but also were considered elderly sooner, an assessment that historical evidence suggests has been the rule since at least the Renaissance (Ottaway 35). Lynn Botelho identifies old age onset for women in the sixteenth and seventeenth centuries at around age fifty, due to physical signs of menopause such as "the wrinkled face and gobber tooth, the hairy lip and squinty eye, the stooped back and lamed limbs" (60). Ottaway, however, has not found similar associations of menopause and old age onset in eighteenth-century British women (40) and views markers of age as remarkably similar for both genders, but she adds that depictions of older women were more critical than those of older men (44). Teresa Mangum reports that in the nineteenth century, men were relegated to elderhood when they were unable to work, but women became "old" when they could no longer reproduce—which would have constituted a much earlier old-age onset for females ("Growing Old" 99).

Mike Featherstone and Mike Hepworth identify a shift in the imagery of aging in Great Britain and the United States in the middle of the nineteenth century, when the elderly were categorized for administrative purposes, and a new stigma was attached to the aging process ("Images" 322–23). In the eighteenth century, though some pensioners began receiving benefits as early as age fifty, sixty was the most common age used for the inception of age-based subsidies (Ottaway 59). The development of poor law benefits and pensions during the nineteenth century necessitated establishing an official number for the beginning of old age. Janet Roebuck reports that responses to the Poor Law investigators of 1834 indicate that most local authorities considered people old if they were unable to support themselves and were fifty or older (418), but commissioners set sixty as the age at which special considerations were given to the inmates of workhouses (419). The Friendly Societies Act of 1875 established fifty as the demarcating year for old age, but that number was amended by the Royal Commission of 1895, which substituted sixty-five for fifty (420). Sixty-five was chosen to be the official pension age by the Old Age Pensions Committee in 1898 (421). The continual reassessment of old age onset by these commissions suggests not only the enhanced importance of chronological definitions for statistics-obsessed Victorians, but also an increased attention to aging in general, as the line of demarcation between midlife and old age was repeatedly refined.

III.

The distinguishing characteristic of Victorian middle age in fiction that delineates it from old age is liminality. Whereas old age is depicted as a final stage increasingly associated with the end of certain activities and identities—lessened marriageability, waning sexuality, and retirement from work—midlife plots stress the possibility that character's fortunes may go either way, from acquiescent decline to a sustained youthfulness. This border aspect of midlife is the subject of my project—examining a life passage whose tenor is determined by a combination of individual and cultural meanings—as subsequent chapters demonstrate.

Several cultural shifts in Victorian England had a significant impact on age construction, causing new apprehensions about decline. As I explain at greater length in chapter 2, revised concepts of masculinity increased age anxiety for men, a devaluation that affected aging for the entire populace, because until quite recently "the universal person" has been gendered as male in Western cultures (Butler 9). Early in the century, gentlemanliness was based on breeding and manners, and hallmarks of high social class determined a man's place in the masculine hierarchy (Tosh 86). These qualities were possessed for life—whether at eighteen or eighty, one could be the consummate gentleman—but this measure of a man became outmoded. As the Reform Acts of 1832 and 1867 brought middle- and working-class men into the electorate, more respect and authority were conferred upon work as a man's identity, whether in the "professions" or by physical labor (Tosh 74–75), and manliness became the ideal, earned on an individual basis rather than bestowed by hereditary right (Tosh 86). Muscular Christianity began to take hold of the British imagination by mid-century, and manly muscle joined middle-class respectability as prime characteristics of manhood, including the first organized sports in public schools which stressed physical prowess over intellectual achievement (Vance 166). Elite males who lived off of inherited land and wealth appeared effete next to the hardworking householder, and independent self-reliance became important attributes of the true man (Tosh 86–87). The autonomy and physical strength required of the manly man are attributes compromised by aging, however, and while those at the height of vigor might have been able to fulfill the requisites of the new masculinity, as their bodies began to wane, men had reasons for age anxiety. The more that manliness became associated with physicality, the greater the threat to a midlife man's sense of mastery.

By the end of the century, age-based emasculation had increased further. Retirement schemes formalized the idea that a man lost power and status as he grew older, and men whose identities were invested in work saw their standing wane as they were pensioned out of professional identity.[21] The scramble for Africa and anxiety about Britain's ability to maintain control in India put manhood on the defensive, because empire was considered a theater for the "making" of men (Tosh 209), a test of national "virility" (Tosh 193), and physical strength and endurance were considered necessary to maintain colonial rule (Tosh 195).[22] The New Woman's increasing autonomy also suggested that men were not able to retain gender-based authority (Tosh 205). For midlife men, the first signs of age could signal encroachments on their ability to meet the increasing demands of manliness as courageous adventurers in the colonies and masters over their womenfolk at home.

The fin-de-siècle preoccupation with degeneration in individuals and the general population also increased age anxiety. Age itself could be considered definitive evidence of degeneration as the human body began to devolve before one's eyes, a miniature version of the regression of the populace which was becoming feared.[23] This was exacerbated by the furor over homosexuality reflected in the Criminal Law Amendment Act of 1885, which made private homosexual acts illegal, as well as Oscar Wilde's trials in the 1890s that created concern over increased effeminacy in the population and caused a new reserve about "too much effusiveness or physicality" between men that could be misread (Tosh 115). Some saw homosexuality in the populace as a sure sign of waning masculinity and rising degeneration (Hamilton 67). Midlife men who felt their sexual powers decreasing had even more reason to worry in a culture becoming increasingly focused on virility. The novels I consider in chapter 2 evince an increasing anxiety in midlife men about whether aging makes them lose masculinity and marriageability. By the fin de siècle, the physically tough younger man has a clear advantage over an older rival.

Two aspects of women's lives had special significance for midlife aging: an emphasis on reproductive function as the defining characteristic of womanhood and increasing legal rights. For centuries, aging women routinely had been maligned, but in the nineteenth century, as Linnaean botany inspired writers to characterize young nineteenth-century women with metaphors of "bloom" that emphasized their sexual ripeness and, therefore, marriageability (King 8), women were relegated to spinsterhood at thirty and typified by images of withering and sexual desiccation. Women's value came to be defined by their reproductive function, the growing science of gynecology characterizing female generative organs as vulnerable and diseased, completely different from those of males. Because women were considered hysterical beings governed by a wayward and pathological reproductive cycle, we might guess a logical corollary would be increased worth at menopause when this chaotic fertility ceased. However, all females were seen as "potential mothers, actual mothers, or retired mothers," whether they had children or not (Jalland and Hooper 5), and therefore the postmenopausal woman depreciated. She was expected to become sexless and focused only on fostering the younger generation's search for a mate. From their mid-forties, when they were considered menopausal, women were depicted as increasingly less valuable.[24]

As women gained more rights during the second half of the nineteenth century, however, the position of the aging female was also enhanced, at least to a certain extent. Married women obtained legal means to divorce and retain wealth with the Married Women's Property Acts of 1870 and 1882, securing new authority and respect (Tosh 117). Though women still were denied equal status with men in many areas, including the vote, as their rights increased, fiction began to depict some as independent, with more options for their lives. For example, as I explore in chapter 4, Arabella Greenow in Anthony Trollope's *Can You Forgive Her?* is allowed to marry the "wild" man for romance and frank erotic attraction rather than the "worthy" man who is moneyed and stable, while the younger women in the novel must make the less exciting, latter choice. Though Victorian fiction represents women as denigrated for aging, especially when their reproductive function ceases in midlife, sometimes their lot is improved by new freedoms, though they continued to be more harshly judged for aging than men.

Another important nineteenth-century development that influenced age ideology is a change in conceptions of time. As Mark W. Turner describes it, "the whole idea of 'time' was a problem for the Victorians," because it both "slowed down" when considered in light of new discoveries that placed humankind at the very end of eons of geologic time but also "sped up" with emerging technology such as railway travel and the telegraph ("Telling" 122). Despite rising life expectancy, the expanded geologic time introduced by Lyell's and Darwin's theories created consciousness of a relatively short, insignificant, vulnerable human life span, transforming time from "a relatively stable continuum" to a volatile quantity in short supply which must be carefully attended (Murphy 10, 11–12). In the traditional agrarian economy, daily routines had been conducted according to natural cycles of day and night determined by the seasons, but in industrialized Britain, life became a scheduled round dictated by the clock (M. Turner, "Telling" 128). The exigencies of the railway demanded that people follow standardized schedules, and time-telling devices, both public and private, became a staple of Victorian culture, from the installation of Big Ben in 1859 to the increased availability and use of inexpensive watches (Murphy 13–14). Time was standardized throughout Great Britain in 1880 and demarcated by international time zones in 1884 (M. Turner, "Telling" 123). These new ways of thinking about time as a limited commodity formed the basis for a new anxiety, that at midlife one's time and therefore opportunities were running out.

Thomas R. Cole and Claudia Edwards suggest several reasons why nineteenth-century industrialization contributed to a more pessimistic picture of aging. Social reform called attention to the harrowing plight of the aged poor, and artists' renderings of "ordinary people" were published widely in burgeoning nineteenth-century periodicals, often depicting their suffering as frightening (220). Because it was more difficult to be poor in the city than the country, when an agrarian populace moved to industrialized urban centers, the troubles of the lower class were worsened, especially the aging who were unemployable in new markets (Cole and Edwards 217). In addition, increased opportunities for wage-labor gave aging parents less control over their offspring as adult children became less financially dependent on their parents. Parental control over family inheritances waned, and the middle-aged lost power (Cole and Edwards 224).

Changes in material production and distribution of goods in the nineteenth century also had an impact on midlife ideology in a new commodification of the body. As the life span lengthened and mass produced and marketed products proliferated across Britain, manufactured goods became a means of age resistance, as I explore in chapter 6. The Crystal Palace exhibits transformed British subjects into consumers ready to educate themselves about and purchase the wide array of goods that had become available (Richards 5, 64–65). By the last decades of the century, an advertising boom metamorphosed age remedies from patent medicine quackery to credible beauty products, and the British populace embraced consumerism as a way to put into practice their growing belief that midlife is a decline that can and should be prevented.

As the idea of a predetermined life course gave way to a new preoccupation with forestalling outward manifestations of age, the medical community focused its attention on the physical aspects of aging, and aging became a "clinical problem" (Katz 66).[25] The elderly became subjects of medical study, and aging was medicalized, signs of age classified as either "morbid" or "normal." What formerly had been seen as normal effects of age, conditions such as thrombosis caused by thickening of the arteries, were listed as disease (Cole and Edwards 244). Though gerontology and geriatrics did not emerge as medical specialties until the twentieth century, Victorian physicians began to feel the need of such experts. Dr. John Gardner notes in the 1875 edition of *Longevity, The Means of Prolonging Life After Middle Age*, that "a distinct class of physicians" was now necessary to deal with the problems of the elderly, and he mentions several who had attained recent prominence (19). When Elie Metchnikoff coined the word "gerontology" in 1908 during the course of his work at the Pasteur Institute in Paris (Achenbaum 23), he gave a name to aging as a problem that required specialized medical intervention, an idea that had been rumbling across Europe for several decades. As aging became medicalized, midlife increasingly was understood to be a time of incipient danger, an embattled frontier between youth and elderhood that announced the first onslaughts of decline.

IV.

Tamara K. Hareven delineates three phases that new life stages go through as they are "discovered": in the beginning, "individuals become aware of the specific characteristics of a given stage of life as a distinct condition among certain social class or groups," a concept that next is "publicized in the popular culture" and taken up in professional discourse. Finally, the emerging life stage is "institutionalized" and becomes the subject of policies and legislation specific to the needs of the new group (121). Because aging is a capacious, multifaceted aspect of identity with indefinite boundaries, I have chosen to focus this book on specific textual representations of Victorian midlife as manifestations of a new life stage in Hareven's second phase, a decline ideology about the middle years that became increasingly evident in and popularized by print culture. I begin each chapter with an artifact of print culture—a cartoon, an advertisement, a poem, an essay—that serves as an example of the larger issue taken up in that section. Chapters 2 through 5 contain a series of chronologically ordered close readings of novels that demonstrate an increasing concern with and anxiety about midlife, while in chapter 6, I turn to advertisements as texts that reveal fin-de-siècle anxiety about the middle-aged body. By focusing on these genres, I am not claiming that a new midlife ideology emerged exclusively in novels and advertisements, nor am I saying that the few texts I explore in themselves provide conclusive evidence of a shift in age conscious. However, I do offer these examples of "aging by the book" as representative of many more texts that present a similar preoccupation. As I have presented parts of this project at conferences over the course of several years, one of the most frequent comments has been the suggestion of yet another novel to include. This multiplicity of possibilities demonstrates that midlife is a Victorian issue so ubiquitous it would not be feasible to cover even a fraction of eligible texts here and points both to the need and rich resources for further age studies of the nineteenth century.

Novels and advertisements are unique and provocative vehicles for age studies. Cultural construction of the life course lends itself to both genres, because, as Gullette has observed, "Age ideology assails its victim in narratives and images" (*Aged* 79). An advertisement is a "carrier of culture" (Loeb viii), a circulating text that echoes and generates current ideas.[26] Novels and advertisements often appeared in proximity, because promotions for hair-restorers and youth-enhancing soaps were printed in the back of periodicals such as *The Graphic* that contained serialized fiction and also were bound into novels published in parts.[27] I consider representations of middle age in both genres not only as reflections of how Victorians viewed midlife, but also contributors of new ideas that augmented midlife redefinition.

Novels are problematic bearers of cultural freight. As many literary critics have noted, though fiction reflects culture, we cannot naïvely assume that novels provide a faithful mirror, because they also simultaneously introduce new concepts to readers and their world. Perhaps the single "fact" of which we can be certain is that fictive imaginings become culturally available upon publication, whether as new ideas or reflections of what is already there. In *How Novels Think*, Nancy Armstrong explains ways in which "the history of the novel and the history of the modern subject are, quite literally, one and the same," especially in British fiction where modern, individualized identity came into being and then spread throughout Western culture, "reproducing itself not only in authors but in readers, in other novels, and across British culture in law, medicine, moral and political philosophy, biography, history, and other forms of writing that took the individual as their most basic unit" (3). Elaine Showalter points out that fictional characters "become part of our cultural mythology" after having "leapt out of the pages of their books into popular culture. We know them whether or not we have read the books in which they first appeared" (15). Novels often are conduct books of the imaginary, tutoring readers in how to act, but also inspiring them about possible dreams. Though Lily Dale professes in *The Small House at Allington* (1862–64), "a novel should tell you not what you are to get, but what you'd like to get" (460), fiction fills both functions for real readers, instructing us about what we are as well as to what we may aspire.

In *Aging By The Book*, I focus in particular on midlife decline as a concern of the marriage plot, a primary structuring device in most Victorian novels (Dever 160).[28] Marriage is one of the primary methods used by Victorian characters to establish identity and attempt social mobility, the story of young lovers meeting, falling in love, and marrying on the final page a plot "so familiar as to seem 'natural'" (Dever 161). Countless nineteenth-century novels repeat this pattern, a fairly youthful male protagonist and his always younger female counterpart achieving "perfect happiness" in early adulthood, the remainder of their lives merely a decline from an early apotheosis. Though the middle-aged usually appear as supporting figures within stories about the continuing stream of young marriageable couples, they do appear as brides and grooms in nineteenth-century fiction, however, in subplots of midlife romance. Though young love may be considered normative and primary, I explore the alternatives offered in these secondary tales.

The "texts" I examine—novels, and particularly advertisements—focus on representations of the midlife body. Victorians believed that the body should represent a person accurately, an idea with a long history in British culture, as evinced by medieval and early modern sumptuary codes. An important aspect of the respectability so dear to Victorians was "being what you seem," and, in novels, secret histories serve to prove a character's flaws, from Willoughby's hidden history of seducing young women and the clandestine Fairfax/Churchill engagement early in the century, to Dorian Gray's covert debauchery at the fin de siècle. "Being what you seem" included displaying a body that registered a subject's social worth and marriageability, upon which not only gender, race, and class but one's age was made clearly evident. At the same time, however, Victorians became increasingly interested in preventing signs of age. Taking charge of age not only can seem liberating but also may produce great anxiety about disjunctions between seeming and being. The nineteenth-century novel is caught in a tension between desire for clearly read signs of age and a perhaps greater need to avoid such signs. Victorian fictions, including those purveyed in advertisements, record the psychological, emotional, and sociocultural history of an emerging decline ideology and its repercussions.

For this study, I have chosen novels that represent midlife aging as an essential aspect of a character's subjectivity, even if only in subplots. Though I frequently turn to Dickens in these pages, and other novelists also play a part, as I've searched for nineteenth-century plots that feature middle-aged characters who struggle with the repercussions of age, I've returned again and again to the works of Anthony Trollope, both those that have received wide critical attention as well as one that has remained relatively unknown. Of all Victorian novelists, Trollope shows most interest in and sensitivity toward midlife issues. Trollope has long been identified as a realist writer—Nathaniel Hawthorne described his novels as "a great lump of earth hewn out and put on display," a characterization Trollope calls "true in its nature" (*Autobiography* 96). His descriptions of numerous midlife struggles provide detailed and telling portraits of Victorian thought about age and its intricate relation to other concepts of identity. Though I've limited extensive analysis to only five of his forty-seven novels—*Can You Forgive Her?*, *Phineas Finn*, *Phineas Redux*, *The Way We Live Now*, and *An Old Man's Love*—I have found a wealth of material with which to work.

V.

As the masculine ideal became the hardworking, physically fit man of business and empire builder, novels register a new awareness of age-based decline for men, the subject of chapter 2, "No Longer The Man He Was: Age Anxiety in the Male Midlife Marriage Plot." Fictive midlife men ask themselves whether their "time of love has gone by," anxiously questioning their ability to retain erotic and affective power in their middle years, a scenario that appears repeatedly in Victorian novels that feature aging men who court much younger women. In the 1830s and 1840s, Frances Trollope and Charlotte Brontë created plots in which the suitor's age is at issue, but class is a far more significant factor of marriageability. At mid-century, Charles Dickens registered a change, focusing on male aging in several successive novels. Often the older suitor fails in his romantic quests, and only after experiencing an intense bout of age anxiety can he become the worthy husband of a younger woman. In the next two decades, Caroline Norton and George Eliot addressed the aging suitor in stories that reveal how much cultural capital he is losing, even, in Norton's case, when the author sets out to prove his desirability. In the last decades of the century, Anthony Trollope depicted middle-aged men as increasingly inadequate in two novels with plots of age that echo each other. The midlife man fails to make a conquest in either, but the latter text increases age devaluation and suggests a far greater stigma as older men compete against a younger manly ideal. The progression in these novels from worthy midlife husband to rejected, superannuated father figure shows an increasingly diminished status for aging men in Victorian marriage plots.

Nineteenth-century medical theorists such as Edward Tilt constructed male and female sexuality as entirely different, due to a new concept of incommensurability of the sexes that had serious implications for gendered aging. Menopause became increasingly linked to physical and mental illness, and postmenopausal women were seen as sexless androgynes. In the third chapter, " 'The Neutral Man-Woman': Female Desexualization at Midlife," I use this theory to posit a Victorian paradigm of sexless service that requires menopausal women to relinquish sexuality and foster reproduction in the next generation in order to be deemed worthy midlife matrons. This model appears in several Dickens novels of the 1830s to 1860s in which midlife mothers are satirized as inappropriate love objects when they attempt to flirt and develop their own romantic possibilities instead of subsuming themselves in their children's marriage market quests. Charlotte Brontë valorizes a widowed mother who orients her life around her daughter's marital fortunes, but she protests against spinsters being obliged to practice the same self-sacrificing behavior. Elizabeth Gaskell upholds the sexless service paradigm for single women when she requires two elderly sisters to serve the next generation's mating while denigrating the marriage of a middle-aged widow. Margaret Oliphant indicates the extent to which the menopausal paradigm had become expected behavior by comedically switching the roles of the marriageable young woman and the mentoring matron. At the end of the century, H. Rider Haggard expresses a terrified response to the older woman who disguises herself with youth, refusing to age out of desirability. Taken together, these novels indicate that sexless service was a common convention of Victorian womanhood that required "women of a certain age" to become sexually extinct or be condemned as, at best, unworthy and at worst, horrific monsters.

Marriageable heroines in Victorian fiction are, almost without exception, young, but midlife women do function as protagonists in subplots dealing with the exceptional case of the remarrying widow. In the fourth chapter, "Marriageable at Midlife," I compare Frances Trollope's infamous Widow Barnaby with widows in three of Anthony Trollope's Palliser novels, showing how notions of decline could give way to increasingly progress-oriented narratives for Victorian women in midlife. The Widow Barnaby is a buffoon who suffers setbacks and glories in triumphs on the marriage market. Anthony Trollope, Frances's son, appropriates his mother's humorous heroine by rewriting her as Arabella Greenow. Initially a silly flirt, Arabella is transformed into a wise and practical midlife bride who, because she is a woman of experience instead of a virginal neophyte, can choose the wild man for pleasure instead of the worthy one out of duty. He continues this depiction of the middle-aged woman when Madame Max Goesler changes from a vamp to an independent woman who marries her equal. These novels reveal a Trollopean empowerment of midlife women that affords them greater freedom than usually is granted to Victorian heroines and challenges nineteenth-century stereotypes of female middle age.

When characters in Victorian novels speculate about age and marriageability while looking in a mirror, they reveal psychological aspects of how fiction instructed Victorians to think about growing older. The fifth chapter, "In the Eye of the Beholder: Victorian Age Construction and the Specular Self," examines fictive Victorians who influence their own marriage market success or failure by their attitudes as they gaze at their mirrored faces. I make use of Kathleen Woodward's concept of the mirror stage of old age in which she argues that association with or dissociation from the signs of age can influence how one ages. In three of his novels from the 1860s and 1870s, Anthony Trollope depicts midlife women whose experience of aging is determined largely by whether they identify with or resist signs of age in the mirror, no matter what their actual chronological age. In the 1890s, Oscar Wilde and Thomas Hardy portray a similar pattern for men, but in hyperbolic forms that simultaneously indicate wider margins of age acceptability for men and heightened devaluation of older males at the fin de siècle. I frame this chapter with a Hardy poem that repeats the age anxiety resonating through the novels I consider, a poem that suggests ways in which Hardy's personal struggle with decline appears in his textual representations of age.

As the previous chapters of this book demonstrate, Victorian novels depict midlife as an increasing cause for concern, but discourses of age proliferated throughout society in a variety of mediums, not just fiction. Chapter 6, " 'How To Keep Young': Advertising and Late-Victorian Age Anxiety" examines how midlife devaluation was exacerbated at the end of the nineteenth century when advertisements made use of degeneration fears. During the last two decades, soap companies contributed to an unprecedented boom in advertising, one result of which was to give a greater cultural momentum to age anxiety by exploiting decline apprehensions for commercial profit. In a heated competition for new national markets, Pears' and Sunlight Soap, in particular, used anti-aging promises as one of many ploys to attract the British consumer. Their campaigns put youthfulness before a mass audience as an imperative of midlife, using decline fears about race, gender, and class to raise the profile of anti-aging as an important component of the middle years. In this chapter, I explore ways in which soap advertisements both expose and accelerate late-Victorian age anxiety by projecting fears of national decline onto the commercialized, midlife body.

VI.

While middle age had been considered the prime of life for hundreds of years before the nineteenth century, as a greater percentage of the population survived into old age, concern about longevity shifted to apprehension about midlife. As a result, Victorians relocated the dangers of aging backward in the life course. Age anxiety has continued to accelerate into a major crisis about identity in the West and, increasingly, throughout the world. The Aristotelian prime of life and medieval celebration of "the perfect age of man's life" contrast markedly with our current preoccupations, as we anxiously seek to thwart the earliest encroachments of decline and prevent and repair the slightest wrinkle, gray hair, or sagging flesh. Though longevity remains an issue of interest in Western societies, youthfulness has become a mania, especially in the middle and upper classes.

Of course, I am not immune to these cultural phenomena and have written this book while negotiating my own "coming of age." In *Aging*

and Its Discontents, Kathleen Woodward notes an autobiographical phenomenon that has swept academia: "In the recent practice of literary and
cultural criticism of difference—gender, race, ethnicity, and postcolonial
discourse—it has become almost axiomatic that one's body should resemble
the subject of one's research" (22). Cultural critics often are drawn to
investigate discourses with which they have a personal identification, and
I am no exception.

I began research for this project during graduate school, a "returning" or "nontraditional" student in my early forties. As I sat in seminars
pondering culturally-constructed subjectivities—often the oldest person in
the room, older even than several of my professors who had young children
while mine were finishing high school—I began to realize how often age
complicated my identity, my usually unmentioned yet obvious difference.
I was never sure how many of my graduate school anxieties were caused
or exacerbated by ageism. Was I marginalized by others? Did I sabotage
my own performance with insecurity about age? While I raised teenagers
and worried about the frantic pace at home ("Mom, if you'd get your head
out of the nineteenth century and into this one, things might go smoother
around here!"), and as I struggled with difficult hallmarks of age—midlife
divorce, death of a parent—I pressured myself to perform. I tried never
to miss a class, to reel out dissertation pages at a respectable pace, fearing
I would appear to lack seriousness, a middle-aged mother only playing at
returning to college, overly invested in her personal life, unprofessional. As
I negotiated a very tight job market for Victorianists, a look around the
interview room at MLA Convention after MLA Convention confirmed that
I was significantly older than the competition. Some repercussions of age had
benefits for my career: while many of my younger colleagues were timing
their children's births around dissertations and tenure requirements, I had
more time and new freedoms as my daughters graduated from college and
started independent lives of their own. Through the entire process, however,
like someone confronting the more subtle forms of racism, I could suspect
but never know how much ageism—in others as well as myself—affected
the outcome of my search.

This book is, in many ways, a product of my own midlife makeover,
a project I have pursued not only as a late twentieth- and early-twenty-
first-century American academic looking across an ocean and over a
century to Victorian England, but as a person whose subject position has
motivated and contributed to my academic interpretations of age. With
these words, I attempt to follow the advice of Gullette who urges cultural
critics to abandon "the pretense of maintaining an impossible neutrality"
("Midlife Discourses" 34) and instead overtly "expose" and "repudiate"
decline ideology (*Declining* 5). I am not "neutral" about midlife but have

a personal stake in overcoming ageist stereotypes, both those around and within me. In *Aging By The Book*, I interrogate age anxiety as a ubiquitous force, attempting to unmask and confront the power of midlife decline ideology by examining its origins. Only when we understand the culturally constructed nature of age can we expose its stealthy influence in our world and on ourselves, questioning not just the subjectivity of fictive Victorians but what we think we know about our own, time-bound lives.

Chapter 2

"No Longer the Man He Was"

Age Anxiety in the Male Midlife Marriage Plot

In 1907, George R. Sims used his own portrait to advertise the "great hair grower" Tatcho (figure 2.1).[1] Abundant locks combed sleekly against his head, he challenges British men with the bold headline, "Bald, grey or sparse of Hair: what are your chances in life?" He asseverates that baldness "is a touchy subject with most men," because age can be determined by hair rather than years: while a shiny pate makes one "old at thirty," "with a good head of hair" a man "may look young at fifty." Though this ad is a mere speck on the ocean of printed ephemera that flooded public and private spaces at the turn of the century, Sims's words reveal an entrenched cultural anxiety about male midlife aging, the belief that a man who in the past may have been in his prime at forty or fifty now was debilitated, his "chances" of success in every area of life threatened by signs of age.

The male decline ideology evident in this Edwardian advertisement resulted from nineteenth-century revisions to masculinity with significant repercussions for aging. As concepts like occupation and physical prowess replaced traditional notions of privilege to determine the measure of a man, masculine aging took on new meanings, a cultural shift registered in nineteenth-century fiction. This difference is readily apparent in the contrast between an early-century ideal and later Victorian male protagonists. We need look no further than Jane Austen's Darcy or Knightley for Regency examples of highly esteemed fictional heroes, propertied gentlemen whose masculinity resides in their superior qualities, including gentility and high character. Later in the century, however, the essence of manliness changed, evinced by Trollope's male characters in *The Way We Live Now* who struggle in a world transformed, where the landed gentry has lost sure footing, and a competitive, industrialized nation is controlled by corrupt industrial giants and unstable financial markets. At the fin de siècle, fictive men wrestle sensationalized threats, from Dorian Gray's struggle with macabre corruptions of spirit and body to Horace Holly's exertions

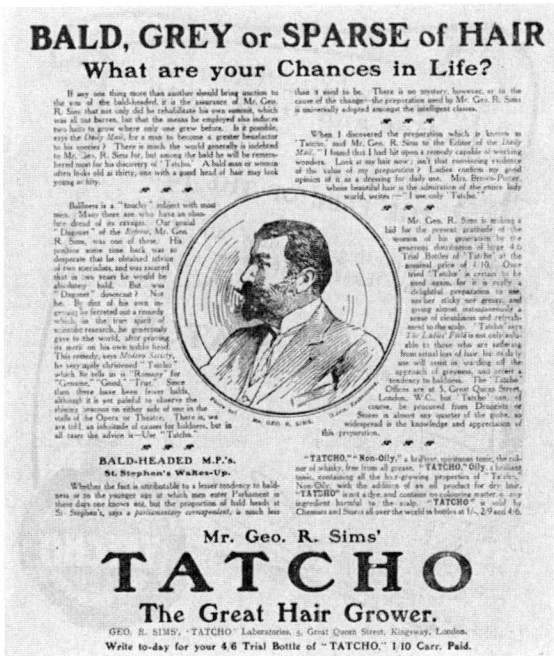

Figure 2.1. Tatcho advertisement. April 1907. The Bodleian Library, University of Oxford: Beauty Parlour 1. Reproduced by permission.

against exoticized geographies of the Earth and his own quailing heart. By century's end, fictive masculinity is besieged with troubling challenges, and an uncomplicatedly good man is much harder to find.

In this chapter, I trace a history of intensifying loss for aging men chronicled in Victorian fiction. After first considering how changing concepts of masculinity in a newly industrialized Britain increasingly stigmatized midlife as a time of danger, I then follow an accelerating age trauma both disclosed by and developed in novels that feature aging men on the marriage market. Written as whether "the time of love has gone by," nervousness about loss of erotic and affective power appears repeatedly in male midlife plots that define the middle years as a liminal space that contests marriage-ability, where the difference between superannuation and success is tenuous and in which the aging man is increasingly devalued. During the 1830s and 1840s, Frances Trollope and Charlotte Brontë created midlife romances that deal with suitors' age as a concern, but ultimately they determine marriage-ability by class and gender rather than age. These earlier, less complicated portrayals of male aging contrast with an accreting apprehension apparent in more and more complex depictions of age angst. Four Dickens novels from the late 1840s and 1850s include aging as a significant factor, their midlife suitors undergoing crises about whether they are too old for love, a theme continued by Caroline Norton in the 1860s and George Eliot in the 1870s as older husbands marry young wives. Two novels by Anthony Trollope from the last decades of the century detail the struggles of midlife suitors more and more unfit for love as a recurring motif that evinces increasingly diminished status caused by late-Victorian revisions to masculinity. Taken together, these fictive accounts reveal an escalating denigration of aging males who risk the vicissitudes of midlife romance, a trend of major consequence for subjectivity, because when males, as normative humans, lose status, a cultural shift in the life course occurs for all Victorians.

I.

In the eighteenth century, masculinity was understood in terms of gentlemanliness manifested by elite upper class status obtained at birth, highly polished manners, and proper social conduct, but during the nineteenth century, "manliness" became "the most clearly articulated indicator of men's gender" (Tosh 2). The opposite of surface sociality and upper-class politesse, "manliness" contrasts with the earlier and more hierarchically oriented "gentlemanliness" (Tosh 86). The manly man was domestic and respectable, possessed physical strength and prowess, and displayed autonomy and self-discipline (Tosh 87). While J. A. Mangan and James Walvin argue that this ideal was adopted mainly by the middle and upper classes (6), John Tosh concludes that "physical vigour, courage and independence were manly values which transcended class, and which informed the standards by which one man judged another, whatever class he belonged to" (94).

The move to manliness as the gold standard of masculinity had major consequences for the way Victorians constructed aging. When masculinity was determined by rank and property, age made little difference to status. The old-style gentleman was a gentleman for life—whether eighteen or eighty, he retained the social class and breeding that made him genteel. In fact, aging could even increase position in a patriarchy that esteemed wealth and experience, because older men maintained authority over the next generation's inheritance. Under the rubric of "manliness," however, an assault on masculinity began at midlife. When masculine status was no longer an assured matter of class and became determined instead by personal qualities such as energy and autonomy, even the first sign of senescence was a threat, and aging challenged men's ability to maintain mastery and therefore masculinity.

One of the amendments to masculinity most significant for aging was a major shift in the meaning of work. The influential texts of Thomas Carlyle and Samuel Smiles promoted the "gospel of work" that elevated industriousness and eschewed idleness as "a threat to the self" (Tosh 93). Tosh locates the rise of this ideology between the Reform Acts of 1832 and 1884 when privilege became increasingly distrusted, replaced by faith in individual autonomy (96). Labor, known as "occupation," was democratized and dignified by the Reform Acts as well as moralized by evangelicalism, which formed the basis for "the modern secular notion that a man's masculinity is vested in his working identity" (Tosh 75). An economy based on land ownership was replaced by industry and investment in financial markets, and the rise of the professional man and development of the "career" unsettled traditional ways of life that had been handed down from one generation to the next (Adams 5; Tosh 63). Increasingly, education fitted sons for careers rather than inheritances of income-producing land (Adams 5).

As manliness became defined by profession and capacity to work, waning strength and a sense of unfitness for new times feminized older men, excluding them from power. Trollope's *Barchester Towers* (1857) provides a mid-century example as the odious Obadiah Slope opines to Septimus Harding, "things are a good deal changed . . . not only in Barchester . . . but in the world at large" (111), because "a new man is carrying out new measures. . . . Work is now required from every man who receives wages. . . . New men . . . are now needed and are now forthcoming in the church, as well as in other professions" (112). Though Slope is perhaps the most reviled character in the book, his words accurately describe a reality to which Harding, perhaps the most loved, ultimately yields when he refuses the deanship at Barchester. He states not only that he is "too old for any new place" but also confesses that "The truth is, I want the force of character which might enable me to stand against the spirit of the times. The call on all sides now is for young men, and I have not the nerve to put myself in opposition to the demand" (479). Abandoning the job in favor of his daughter's young fiancé, Harding acts on his conviction that, as an older man, he is no longer a viable worker.

At century's end, formalization of retirement programs augmented the idea that a man could age out of occupational fitness. Jill S. Quadagno describes the usual financial pattern for a prosperous middle-class man: while he invested in "business capital" early in his career, at around age fifty, he switched to "rentier" investments that provided fixed income and would permit him gradually to retire (151). With the emergence of the professional man came a new formulation of the middle years as a time to prepare for superannuation, not a consideration for the traditional landed gentry who held property and status until death. For the working-class man, the situation was even more pronounced. In the past, elder support was provided by family members and patronage, though the majority of the working class remained employed in some function until death. Public debate about creating governmental old-age pensions for the working class began in the 1880s, and the necessity of establishing a pension age came to associate even the middle-aged with retirement in some occupations (Roebuck 420). For example, the Amalgamated Society of Carpenters and Joiners established fifty as retirement age, and Lancashire's Union of Glass bottle Workers paid pensions to workers after forty (Roebuck 420). By the 1890s, it had became common practice to pay older industrial workers less than younger ones (Quadagno 140–41), and if a man of fifty became unemployed, he knew he was likely to remain so for the rest of his life (Roebuck 420). Retirement became increasingly common, acknowledged officially in the 1891 census when retired persons were listed as a separate category instead of under former occupation (Quadagno 151), and at the fin de siècle and into the new century, census figures reported steady increases for England and Wales, especially in men over age 65.[2] Historians have attributed this trend to the change from an agrarian economy that could employ older workers to an industrial environment with no place for the elderly (Quadagno 162), as well as to competition from younger workers and rapidly changing technology that made traditional skills obsolete (Quadagno 154). Personal autonomy and self-reliance, hallmarks of Victorian manliness, were challenged in this new world where age caused both the middle- and working-class man to face impending unemployment, putting him at risk for dependency and, as a result, lessened masculinity. Midlife men began to feel the need to prepare for an inevitable waning of authority and productivity associated with employment, and age came to mean abdication from the masculinizing arena of work.

The nineteenth-century development with perhaps the greatest impact on aging men was the new focus on physical toughness that emerged at mid-century and continued to gain momentum through the fin de siècle. Norman Vance argues that the ideas behind "muscular Christianity," with its emphasis on physical brawn and skill, evolved early in the Victorian era, in the climate of "emerging individual possibility" created between the 1832 and 1867 reform bills (166). Most notable in this movement were the "democratic notions of Christian manliness" in Charles Kingsley's writings and sermons, as well as the meteoric success of Thomas Hughes's novel *Tom Brown's School Days*, first published in 1857 (Vance 166; Adams 108).[3] The world of sport and games came to epitomize notions of masculinity, and the public school ideology of manly strength first advanced by upper-class educational institutions soon was promoted by a variety of scouting and sports organizations.[4] Public school boys were subjected to harsh regimens intended to toughen them into men (Mangan 143). By the 1860s, a "games-playing 'cult' " had seized the British populace, and the young athlete was considered a hero (Park 7). Consequently, physicality replaced spirituality as the quality most cultivated in boys (Newsome 26). Because the muscularity movement was associated with educating adolescents, the new manly ideal was embodied by youthfulness, and the emphasis on muscularity in the training of apprentice manhood made stamina and strength essential qualities for all men. If masculinity is measured by physical ability at its youthful height, then waning vigor severely challenges aging men. As muscle took precedence, the older man increasingly was pushed to the margins, and aging became more and more debilitating and effeminizing.

Imperialism exacerbated Victorians' preoccupation with masculine physicality (Adams 109). As Britain struggled to retain colonial power, a strong empire came to be seen as a mark of the nation's virility (MacKenzie, "Imperial" 178). Qualities essential to colonial conquest such as stamina, strength, and sacrifice for the team were taught on the playing field (Walvin 250). Empire became heavily associated with hunting and the new craze for sport, a masculine domain in which a man could prove himself. The colonies were dominated by adept hunters and naturalists who possessed "virile" qualities such as "courage, endurance, individualism, and sportsmanship . . . resourcefulness, a mastery of environmental signs and a knowledge of natural history" (MacKenzie, "Imperial" 179). According to James Walvin, by the late nineteenth century, the new "cult of sporting manliness" had replaced Britain's history of abolition as proof of her superiority over other nations, and empire became the "arena" where such manhood was proven (246). The rigors of empire, increasingly associated with sports, hold requirements aging men could be hard-pressed to meet.

Older males also were especially subject to late-century anxieties that degeneration was causing weakness and earlier aging in the British populace. As I will discuss at greater length in chapter 6, Victorians feared that humanity was degenerating, devolving into a more primitive and feeble form. Apprehension was directed especially toward the male physique; for example, in Henry Rumsey's 1871 essay, "On the Progressive Physical Degeneracy of Race in the Town Populations in Great Britain," he reports that the health, including height and weight, of military recruits was on the decline (Childs 1). By 1900, thirty percent of the 20,292 men who volunteered for the British army were considered physically unfit to serve (Walvin 254). J. A. Mangan and James Walvin point out "the mounting concern felt about the physical, and later the psychological, condition of a highly urbanised plebian life where physical and social deprivation was widespread" (4). Max Nordau reported in his widely known text *Degeneration* (1892) that the enervating effects of modern, industrialized living exacerbated aging, causing earlier onset of baldness, vision impairment, heart conditions, and "nervous complaints" (42). He concludes that "[o]ld age encroaches upon the period of vigorous manhood" to the extent that "[d]eaths due exclusively to old age are found reported now between the ages of forty-five and fifty-five" (42). Degeneration theory was widely accepted by late-Victorians, beliefs that projected an accreting anxiety onto the aging male body.

Victorian gender ideology also placed new burdens on aging masculinity by opposing and hierarchizing male and female. Manhood was defined in opposition to "a powerful sense of the feminine 'other' " and grounded in an increasing emphasis on sexual difference that developed during the first half of the nineteenth century (Tosh 91). Tosh argues that the concept of "manliness" resulted from what Thomas Laqueur has termed the "two-sex model," the idea that the genders are opposite, in contrast to earlier beliefs that the female was a weaker, inverted form of the male (Tosh 91; Laqueur 149–50). As Tosh points out, though some have objected to certain aspects of Laqueur's argument, few would contest that nineteenth-century science explained sexual difference in unprecedentedly hyperbolic terms that envision males as sexually normative and females as their diseased and hysterical opposites (91). Because manliness was defined by its womanly inverse—"rationality as against emotionality, energy rather than repose, constancy instead of variability, action instead of passivity, and taciturnity rather than talkativeness" (Tosh 69)—qualities understood as masculine were presented as "natural or God-given," necessary for all males (Tosh 69, 92). Masculine identity came to be seen as stable, normative humanity that was based on natural and scientifically provable difference, and men's bodies were understood to be more highly evolved than those of women (Hamilton 77). While men were seen as large and healthy, "femininity was characterized by small size, weakness (both moral and physical), and illness" (Hamilton 75). Because some amount of deterioration is an eventual result of aging, no matter how healthy the body, when man is gendered as strong and opposed to enfeebled woman, the aging male is placed in a position of increasing feminization. As Lisa K. Hamilton describes it: "To be a man in decline was to become like a woman" (75).

Aging masculinity also was affected by women's gains in the nineteenth century. Newly empowered women were seen as a threat to male employment, because, as Mary Poovey argues, separately gendered spheres protected men's jobs by keeping women out of the workforce (10–11). W. R. Greg's 1862 article "Why Are Women Redundant?" expresses a deep fear of the "hundreds of thousands of women" in all social classes "who have to earn their own living, instead of spending and husbanding the earnings of men" (436). While he finds that the problem of "redundant women" is most severe among the educated and upper classes, he also suggests that female labor, though often preferable because cheaper, must be monitored to prevent depletion of male jobs: "If, indeed, there were only a certain fixed and unaugmentable quality of work to be done, and too many hands to do it . . . then it *might* be wise to employ men to do it, and let the women, rather than the men, sit with their hands before them" (456).[5] Tosh notes that in 1891, northern industrial centers such as Birmingham reported women holding over twenty percent of office clerk posts that traditionally had been filled by working-class men looking to rise, and in 1901 over ten percent of all such positions nationwide were staffed by women (204). At a time when older and even middle-aged working-class males faced retirement, ambitious women were becoming more and more evident in the workplace, a situation that stressed decreasing authority for aging men in a world where they were becoming obsolete, quickly superseded by the young and further emasculated when their successors were female.

According to Tosh, late-nineteenth-century culture was "permeated by images which expressed a fear of female power," an assault with special consequences for aging men (188). Elaine Showalter describes two fin-de-siècle responses to women's authority—"an exaggerated horror of its castrating potential" along with "intensified valorization of male power" (10)—both evident in late-century novels of empire and masculine quest filled with anxiety about "manly decline in the face of female power" (Showalter 83). The New Woman of the 1890s especially seemed to indicate "a failure of masculine authority in the most intimate areas of life" that threatened male virility (Tosh 205). Critics, both Victorian and modern, have contrasted the new woman with the "old" man, using the word "old" to designate all men, who, resistant to the liberated new woman, define themselves and live by standards that predate her emergence.[6] If even younger men are called "old" for adhering to obsolete gender paradigms, then the truly chronologically older man is even more out of touch, the denizen of a past era, devalued by antiquated values characteristic of his age.

During the nineteenth century, virility became an increasing concern for Victorian men, an anxiety that affected constructions of male aging. Not only the new woman but also the gay man was seen as a sure sign of degeneration in the culture and the body, and anxiety about homosexuality placed an emphasis on proving virility, a requirement that an aging man could find harder and harder to meet. Michel Foucault famously has traced the history of the "medical category of homosexuality" to an 1870 article by Carl Westphal that initiates a new, pathologized identity for same-sex desire (43). Homosexual subculture, as well as efforts to eradicate it, grew in the 1870s and 1880s.[7] Oscar Wilde's trials, in particular, created a new fear of effeminacy embodied in the decadent male and redefined as a degenerate tendency that should be feared (Hamilton 67). The uproar over homosexuality increased pressure on the midlife male to prove virility, an opportunity for new worry about waning sexual ability.

Apprehension about virility had been growing due to other factors as well. After 1850, the age of first marriage steadily rose, the average middle-class man in the mid-1880s delaying nuptials until after thirty (Tosh 106; M. Anderson 34; Adams 5). Simultaneously, birth rates also dropped, a trend which has been attributed to higher living standards and the rising costs of supporting a large family, as well as women's desire for more independence (Banks, *Prosperity* 6). If virility was proven by producing "a quiverful of children," as Tosh describes it, the declining birth rate in the last half of the century challenged masculinity (105).[8] With later marriages and smaller families, a man's virility, the "traditional test of masculinity," could be called into question, even if only subconsciously (Tosh 106). Escalating fears about waning sexual potency in relatively young men provided an even greater impetus for older males to become increasingly nervous.

The science of sexology that took shape in proliferating Victorian medical literature also increased focus on aging and virility. As I will discuss in the next chapter, women were considered more sexually complicated than men, prone to disease, and sexually obsolete after menopause. In contrast to the vicissitudes of female fertility, the dominant Victorian model of male sexuality presented libido and fertility continuing uninterruptedly from puberty through old age.[9] However, while physicians theorized that male sexuality could function throughout life, they also stressed moderation, especially with age.[10] William Acton set out a detailed regimen for aging men in his influential *The Functions and Disorders of the Reproductive Organs in Youth, in Adult Age, and in Advanced Life*, published in six editions from 1857 to 1875.[11] Though the first edition addresses physicians and deals with male sexual anxiety, later editions were oriented toward and became popular with lay audiences (Mason 191–92). Acton argues that moderation is necessary for all men, no matter their age, but he issues special warnings for those who are aging: "if a man in advanced life would preserve his intellectual faculties, health, and vigour, and would enjoy long life, he ought to look for only very moderate indulgence of the sexual passion" (48).[12] The book stresses that in order to maintain "bodily vigour," men of all ages should only ejaculate about once every seven to ten days, and semen must be even more carefully husbanded with age (23).[13] He notes that "nature has bountifully provided the old man with semen," yet it is "formed slowly, and with effort," and he advises older men "not to spend a great deal out of your small capital" (50).

Acton argues that "the generative function . . . must diminish with a waning frame" and places the onset of male sexual decline at around age fifty (48). Acton enumerates physiological changes occurring at this age that weaken virility: the testes have lessened blood flow, the scrotum becomes "wrinkled and diminished in size, the testicles atrophy," and semen not only becomes less abundant but also "has lost its consistence and its force" (49). As sexual desires "abate," "languish," and then ultimately "cease entirely," a man finds "the wish and the want are no longer one and the same thing" (49). Acton concludes, "The ordinary rule seems to be, that sexual power is not retained by the male to any considerable amount after the age of sixty or sixty-five" (99). He points out the emotional cost of such developments, stating that between fifty and sixty, "man, elevated to the sacred character of paternity, and proud of his virile power, begins to note that power decrease, and does so almost with a feeling of indignation. The first step towards feebleness announces to him, unmistakably, that he is no longer the man he was" (49). Maintaining that all men must come to terms with this diminishment as "the test of manhood, the crowning effort of maturity, and the evidence of decline," he contends that an older man should have only "a paternal, conjugal, patriotic attachment" to his wife and put aside a sexually active relationship (48). As Mike Featherstone and Mike Hepworth argue, Acton believed not only in "diminution of sexual passion" with age but also that "any expression of sexuality in later middle and old age should be seen as an unnatural interruption of the journey towards spiritual perfection" ("History" 253).[14]

Under new pressure to define himself by work and physical fitness, yet facing impending retirement, declining musculature, and waning sexual powers, the man of middle years had much to worry about, a concern that haunts Victorian fiction. Midlife onset becomes an issue of increasing importance, anxious men exploring whether age is a disability to love. As cultural changes challenge masculinity, a midlife man is forced to consider Acton's contention, that "he is no longer the man he was."

II.

Teresa Mangum describes "an outright loss of sexual identity" and "a lapse into a state akin to helpless femininity" for elderly men in Victorian fiction ("Growing Old" 99). Her examples span the century, from Dickens's Scrooge after his rehabilitation (1843), Thackeray's broken and bankrupt Sedley (1848), Gaskell's Job Legh, a single-parent grandfather (1848), Eliot's disheartened yet loving Silas Marner (1861), and the nurturing Tibetan lama so crucial to Kipling's Kim (1901). Feminization of the older male indicates his "fall from one kind of idealized man—the youthful, virile, assertive man of action," a loss that may be offset to some degree by his "moral, spiritual, and domestic fulfillment," though this "maternal masculinity" is in itself feminizing ("Growing Old" 99). Elderly manhood is challenged by emasculation in novels throughout the century.

Age anxiety also is characteristic of fictive nineteenth-century men before they become elderly, and erotic viability becomes an especially significant factor in the male midlife marriage plot that emerges when middle-aged men fall in love with younger women. That the husband should be older than the wife is an axiom not only of Victorian marriage but a cross-cultural norm (Buss 51). Acton recommends that "there should always be an interval of about ten years between a man of mature age, and his wife" (85).[15] In Victorian novels, when spousal age difference exceeds the recommended ten years, the larger the disparity, the greater the chance of failure. In addition, male marriageability is depicted as significantly threatened when a man reaches his forties. Fiction registers a gradual affective and sexual wane as a perceptible crisis of masculinity for the midlife male, especially from the 1850s on, when aging suitors increasingly are concerned about and depreciated by aging.[16]

Before mid-century, male aging causes fictive anxiety, but these plots usually address an age disparity between relatively young men—in their thirties—and younger women, and marriageability ultimately is determined by other issues. In *The Widow Barnaby* (1839), Frances Trollope depicts a man troubled by age, but his concern is qualified by other considerations with equal or greater significance, and he is relatively young by Victorian standards. Colonel Montague Hubert, at age thirty-five, is troubled by his attraction to Agnes Willoughby, not quite seventeen. Though Hubert has a rival for Agnes's affections in his friend Stephenson who is twenty-two, the older man is depicted as the ideal mate, superior to a younger suitor. Stephenson is described only briefly: "the shorter and younger of the two, had by far the more regular set of features, and was indeed remarkably handsome" (133), but Hubert's physical presence is dwelt upon in a much more lingering fashion. He is "bronzed by the effect of various climates" and

> had perhaps no peculiar beauty of feature except his fine teeth, and the noble expression of his forehead, from which, however, the hair had already somewhat retired, though it still clustered in close brown curls round his well-turned head. But his form and stature were magnificent, and his general appearance so completely that of a soldier and a gentleman, that it was impossible, let him appear where he would, that he should pass unnoticed. (133)

Hubert is a man in his prime, his body marked attractively by experience which, along with his manly moderation of "beauty," emasculates the shorter and too obviously handsome Stephenson. The young rival appears callow and romantically foolish when he calls Hubert "crusty old Mars" and Herbert, in return, dubs the younger man "Corydon," an exchange in which the elder is elevated to warrior god while the younger becomes a mere love-sick shepherd (134). Throughout the narrative Stephenson's inexperience contrasts with Hubert's more masculine maturity.

Though dismayed by his attraction to Agnes when he learns her age—young enough, he reflects, to be his daughter (170), Hubert is much more concerned about her social position. Agnes is under the guardian-ship of her Aunt Barnaby who is, according to Hubert, so "utterly vulgar" that he feels "this *aunt* to be a greater spot upon her beauty than any wart or mole that ever disfigured a fair cheek" (142). Hubert is associated with genteel values and embodies the gentlemanly ideal, his reluctance to fall in love with "a little obscure girl, young enough to be his daughter" based first upon her low social position and second on her age (212). A favorite of the Duke of Wellington, Hubert is described by Aunt Barnaby as "proud as Lucifer" (171). He has the loftiness of a Darcy, even though Stephenson is the richer man.

Ever the honorable gentleman, Hubert considers his friend's desire for Agnes an impediment and attempts "crushing with Spartan courage a passion within his own breast" (214). Rather than age giving way to youth, his deferral is an act of honor that proves his superiority. Agnes, however, never considers Hubert's age an obstacle, and she rejects Stephenson outright when he makes a play for her affections. Though her friends suggest that she considers Stephenson, at twenty-two, too old for her seventeen years, she hints that a man "a great deal older" attracts her even more (219).

Eventually Hubert overcomes his scruples and proposes to Agnes, but only after her aunt has been arrested for debt and is removed from Agnes's life, leaving her destitute and in need of a protector. Agnes rejects Hubert's first proposal on the grounds of class incompatibility rather than age. However, though she tells Hubert that she will not allow him to "ally himself to disgrace," he attributes her refusal to his age:

> Had I been a younger man, the offer of my hand, my heart, my life, would not have appeared to you, as it doubtless does now,—the result of sober, staid benevolence, desirous of preserv-ing youthful innocence from unmerited sorrow . . . Such must my love seem . . . So let it seem; . . . but it shall never cost one hour's pain to you . . . even so; let me not be here in vain: listen to me as a friend and father. (301)

However, that Agnes's vulgar family, and not age, is the genuine impedi-ment remains evident from the beginning of the scene. Hubert begins their conversation by telling Agnes he visits her because he has learned that her "foolish aunt" has been arrested for debt, and he then apologizes, "forgive me, Miss Willoughby; but the step I have taken can only be excused by explaining it with the most frank sincerity" (300). Though he desexualizes himself into a paternal mentor, Agnes's distress that he will leave "with the idea that she was too young to love him," makes clear that age merely provides a useful plot complication, delaying their union until Agnes is claimed by more genteel family members, which solves the real problem (301).

Agnes's gentlemanly father finally appears, displacing Hubert's feint at the role, and his presence makes their union possible. Age anxiety then is put to rest easily. When Hubert worries because he is "so much older," Agnes asserts, "if I love you, and you love me, I cannot see how your age or mine either need interfere to prevent it" (392). After the wedding, Hubert's superiority is confirmed as he becomes a general, and he "never again felt any alarm on the score of his age, but had the happiness of knowing that he was beloved with all the devoted tenderness that his heart desired, and his noble character deserved" (400). His midlife virility and gentility further are proven by a reference to their son, Compton Hubert Compton, who inherits a manor house and lands from Agnes's more respectable aunt, property "worthy of the representative of the ancient Compton race" (400). Their story ends by Agnes confessing that her husband is "more like a hero than any other man she had ever seen" (400). A gentleman according to early Victorian mores, Hubert values and protects his gentility. Aging is not a significant handicap to a groom in his late thirties. As a gentleman, he derives masculinity from rank and breeding, and his maturity towers over Stephenson's youthful naïveté. In this novel of the 1830s, a man on the verge of midlife can marry a woman eighteen years younger, because he is in the prime of life.

In *Jane Eyre* (1847), Charlotte Brontë depicts the aging suitor in terms quite similar to those in *The Widow Barnaby*. Though age difference is mentioned as an impediment to Jane and Rochester's union, class is the most salient obstacle, and once the two become more socially leveled, their marriage inevitably occurs. At Rochester's first appearance, the eighteen-year-old Jane (125) assigns him a liminal age status as a man who "was past youth, but had not reached middle age: perhaps he might be thirty-five" (114), and he claims to be an "old bachelor" (130). However, Jane's response, as well readers' cult-like following for the last 150 years, make evident that far from being too old for love, Rochester is the epitome of masculine sexuality.[17] While a younger rival and even younger versions of Rochester himself are deprecated, Rochester triumphs as the seasoned man in the prime of his life, a depiction only partially moderated by his disability in the closing chapters.

The most extensive references to the age difference between Rochester and Jane occur when his housekeeper, Mrs. Fairfax, reacts in surprise at their engagement, but her major concern is class, not age. She declares she is "astonished" and "bewildered" at the prospect of the marriage, and her initial outburst targets Rochester's superior social and economic status: "I could never have thought it. He is a proud man: all the Rochesters were proud: and his father, at least, liked money" (266–67). Only when detailing her objections more fully does she list age, and then it appears second to rank as a possible impediment: "Equality of position and fortune is often advisable in such cases; and there are twenty years of difference in your ages. He might almost be your father" (267). According to Jane's estimation of Rochester's age as thirty-five when she is eighteen, they were born approximately seventeen years apart, but in her consternation Mrs. Fairfax exaggerates the gap. Jane, however, protests that Rochester is not in the least superannuated, evident in her description of being "nettled" by Mrs. Fairfax's comment as well as in her reply, "No, indeed, Mrs. Fairfax! . . . he is nothing like my father! No one, who saw us together, would suppose it for an instant. Mr. Rochester looks as young, and is as young as some men at five-and-twenty" (267). Jane's estimation of Rochester as an age peer is apparent in a telling detail of the gypsy scene, when she recognizes his true identity by his hand, describing it as "no more the withered limb of eld than my own: it was a rounded supple member" (204). Rochester is eminently attractive to Jane, made more desirable because his looks defy the model of the elegant young swain and are, as she says, "not beautiful, according to rule; but they were more than beautiful to me" (177). She responds to him as ruggedly masculine, in no way the superannuated older man.

Rochester outshines younger men because he is an experienced man of the world, the antithesis of a revolting lecher, when he educates Jane by relating his sexual history in stories that feature him as virile and sexually knowledgeable. In the first of these accounts, Rochester tells Jane about Céline Varens, depicting both his younger self and a rival for the "French opera dancer" as foolish and inexperienced lovers. While he is a naïve "spoonie" (141) and Céline's "dupe" (145), his competitor is even more immature, "a young roué of a vicomte—a brainless and vicious youth" whom Rochester shoots "in one of his poor, etiolated arms, feeble as the wing of a chicken in the pip" (145). The younger man is both morally depraved and physically underdeveloped, even sickly, but the young and defeated Rochester retires from Paris a wiser, tougher, and a more experienced lover.

When Bertha Mason's existence is revealed, Rochester relates an even earlier episode from his sexual past that allows him to display both his youthful libido and subsequently improved skills. In this story, he is a young man ruined by naïveté, unable to recognize that his father and brother use him as a pawn, and he is neither a fully responsible adult nor an adept lover: "... I was sent out to Jamaica, to espouse a bride already courted for me" (309). In frankly sexual terms, he divulges that Bertha's beauty aroused his callow virility: "I was dazzled, stimulated: my sense were excited; and being ignorant, raw, and inexperienced, I thought I loved her" (309). He recounts being led by "the prurience, the rashness, the blindness of youth" and seems to marry almost without volition (309). After the wedding, he indulges in excesses with Bertha and subsequently is "dragged ... through all the hideous and degrading agonies" caused by having an "intemperate and unchaste" wife (310). At age twenty-six he is debauched, "hopeless" (311), and by the time he tells his tale to Jane, feels "contempt" for his past behavior as a "gross, grovelling, mole-eyed blockhead" (309–10).

Rochester also portrays these youthful episodes, however, as training for his current hardy masculinity:

> When I was as old as you, I was a feeling fellow enough; par-
> tial to the unfledged, unfostered, and unlucky; but fortune has
> knocked me about since: she has even kneaded me with her
> knuckles, and now I flatter myself I am hard and tough as an
> Indian-rubber ball; pervious, though, through a chink or two
> still, and with one sentient point in the middle of the lump. Yes:
> does that leave hope for me? (133)

Hardened by misadventure, more mature, he retains the hope of true love. As Sandra M. Gilbert and Susan Gubar have pointed out and subsequent critical analysis emphasized, Rochester's revelation of "specific and 'guilty' sexual knowledge ... makes him in some sense her 'superior,'" while simultaneously indicating that Jane is his equal with whom he can be frank (*Madwoman* 354). He declares greater age and experience give him ascendancy over Jane, asserting, "The fact is, once for all, I don't wish to treat you like an inferior. ... I claim only such superiority as must result from twenty years' difference in age and a century's advance in experience" (134). Like Mrs. Fairfax, he rounds up their age difference from seventeen to twenty years, and then hyperbolizes further that his "experience" is equivalent to one hundred years of difficult lessons. Rochester uses his sexual history to impress Jane with his amorous expertise and to display his manly toughness.

I agree with Esther Godfrey's observation that "[t]heir age difference allows for an exaggerated performance of masculine knowledge of sex while preserving, at least theoretically, Jane's angelic and ignorant status" (865), but I would like to stress that even more frightening to Victorian readers would be the suggestion that instead of guarding her virginal status, Rochester tempts it to knowledge, a possibility which both he and Jane suggest by their strenuous objections.[18] He tells her, "Strange that I should choose you for the confidant of all this, young lady: passing strange that you should listen to me quietly, as if it were the most usual thing in the world for a man like me to tell stories of his opera-mistresses to a quaint, inexperienced girl like you!" He comforts himself that Jane possesses "a mind . . . not liable to take infection," so impervious to corruption that even should he wish to entice her, she "would not take harm from me. . . . I cannot blight you" (144). Jane later reflects, ". . . I heard him talk with relish. . . . He liked to open to a mind unacquainted with the world, glimpses of its scenes and ways" and then quickly adds, "I do not mean its corrupt scenes and wicked ways" (147). Their combined protests that she will not and indeed cannot be sullied and seduced by his stories, though seeming to morally sanitize the scene, indicate not only the possibility but also the probability that Jane's imagination has been sexually awakened by Rochester's tales.

Jane's description of lustfully gazing at the unattainable Rochester while he entertains his house guests hints that his forthrightly sexual stories have achieved their purpose and aroused her: "I looked, and had an acute pleasure in looking,—a precious, yet poignant pleasure; pure gold, with a steely point of agony: a pleasure like what the thirst-perishing man might feel who knows the well to which he has crept is poisoned, yet stoops and drinks divine draughts nevertheless" (176). In a description easy to read as explicit sexual longing, Jane genders herself male, a desire-crazed man kneeling before a vaginal well in a metaphor of voracious fulfillment, placing herself in a role akin to Rochester's in the sexual adventures he has narrated. From Rochester she has learned the "acute pleasure" of an excess like his, an addictive yearning in which she revels.

After the fire, Rochester worries that he has become unmarriageable, fear of superannuation suggested by his retirement to the aged, dilapidated Ferndean. However, though Rochester is enfeebled at the novel's end, described by many critics as symbolically castrated (Gilbert and Gubar, *Madwoman* 368), his weakened masculinity is caused by injury, not age. After all, only a year has passed between Jane's flight from Thornfield and her appearance at Ferndean. Rochester suggests to Jane, "I suppose I should now entertain none but fatherly feelings for you . . . you are young—you must marry one day," and she replies, "I don't care about being married" (441). He responds by focusing more on disability than age, as he insists, "You should care, Janet: if I were what I once was, I would try to make you care—but—a sightless block!" and refers to his disfigured arm as "a ghastly sight" (441). Though Jane acknowledges, "It was mournful, indeed, to witness the subjugation of that vigorous spirit to a corporeal infirmity," she is not repelled, describing "lines" on his face due to "habitual sadness," not age (444). Jane sees him as "a lamp quenched" but with a flame "waiting to be relit" (444). Rochester becomes even more attractive to her after the fire as an equal within her reach, and she vows increased love now that she is "useful" to him (451). Her comment that putting salve on his singed eyebrows "should make them grow as broad and black as ever" indicates her belief that his strength and virility will return (443).

After she arrives at Ferndean, Jane compares Rochester to St. John Rivers and again he is proven worthier than a younger suitor, even in his injured state. He queries Jane about her cousin, and she intentionally provokes jealousy to revive Rochester's fighting spirit, never expressing genuine attraction to St. John but merely using him as a tool to interest Rochester, "the means of fretting him out of his melancholy" (444). She describes St. John as "a handsome man: tall, fair, with blue eyes, and a Grecian profile" in order to pique "salutary" jealousy, a "sting" that will provoke her depressed lover to action (446). After teasing him about St. John's attractions, however, she assures Rochester that her cousin is "severe . . . cold as an iceberg," that neither felt passion for the other, and that she still loves her former master (449). Rochester continues to protest he is unsuitable for Jane, both disabled and aged, akin to "the old, lightning-struck Chestnut tree" at Thornfield while she is "a budding woodbine" whose "freshness" will be joined to his "decay" (449), but he lists disability before years as he worries she will not be happy with a "crippled man, twenty years older" (450). Jane responds, "You are no ruin, sir—no lightning-struck tree: you are green and vigorous. Plants will grow about your roots, whether you ask them or not, because they take delight in your bountiful shadow; and as they grow they will lean towards you, and wind round you, because your strength offers them so safe a prop" (450), a metaphor stressing both new growth and mature strength.

Jane's words prove prophetic. As the book closes, Rochester not only gains partial sight, but also becomes the father of a son, establishing his continued virility; age is never again mentioned as an issue. Instead, Jane describes a companionate marriage: "I hold myself supremely blest—blest beyond what language can express; because I am my husband's life as fully as he is mine" (456). Godfrey contends that Rochester is "increasingly feminized in his role as older husband" (863), but though he is diminished by the vestiges of injury, he is not made obsolete by age. As Gilbert and Gubar stress in their landmark reading, all significant impediments are class-based, and in the end neither Rochester nor Jane has an advantage; they are "equals" (*Madwoman* 369). Aging remains a factor, however, as Gilbert and Gubar note in their citation of Robert Bernard Martin's descriptor "autumnal" for the Ferndean section (*Madwoman* 369), but they conclude the house "is green as Jane tells Rochester he will be, green and ferny and fertilized by soft rains," associating Rochester with an image of new, hardy growth rather than age (Gilbert and Gubar, *Madwoman* 370). Of course, both Hubert and Rochester are men in their thirties, which makes questions of age easy to dismiss in their narratives. In the next decade, however, age anxiety becomes a more stubborn problem in novels that feature older men who face more intractable age-based challenges to their masculinity.

III.

In the 1850s, Charles Dickens was in his forties, increasingly disenchanted with his wife, Kate—from whom he eventually separated in 1858—and writing fiction about older men who attempt to find love with younger women. Aging characters, as well as satire and commentary on age, feature prominently in Dickens's novels from Samuel Pickwick on, but he especially was concerned with love plots involving older men during what has become known as his "dark period" in his forties. Such liaisons would develop special significance for Dickens in 1857, when he met the eighteen-year-old Ellen Ternan, with whom he would remain romantically involved until his death. Dickens's novels written in the years just preceding her advent into his life make plain that during that time he was haunted by the question of a midlife man's affective viability.

Dickens's sensitive portrayals of aging men contrast sharply with his harsh versions of female midlife that I discuss in chapter 3. *David Copperfield*, which Dickens wrote and published in monthly installments during 1849–1850, includes a subplot about the May-December marriage between sixty-two-year-old Dr. Strong and his young wife Annie that expresses deep anxiety about an elderly man's competence as a husband. Then, from 1852 to 1855, Dickens produced three novels in succession that move the age theme back to midlife, *Bleak House* (1852–53), *Hard Times* (1854), and *Little Dorrit* (1855–57) featuring middle-aged men who pursue a twenty-year-old. While the suitor becomes successively younger in each book—late fifties, late forties, and early forties—the novels question whether a man of a certain age is too old for love. In the first two books, the aging lover serves as a foil to a successful younger rival, and only in *Little Dorrit* does a forty-ish suitor, after many misgivings, win his quest. In contrast to Hubert's easy self-confidence and Rochester's dark Byronic experience, the successful Dickensian groom in middle age possesses a capacity for self-doubt that ensures his emotional, and therefore sexual, viability. When considered together, these novels reveal Dickens's increasing preoccupation with aging.

On its surface, the story of Doctor Strong and his young wife Annie presents an ideal marriage that demonstrates true love triumphing over age. As Kelly Hager and Alexander Welsh both note, the standard reading of this plot has been that Annie's faithful love for her elderly husband sets the moral tone for the entire novel (Hager 1011; Welsh 136). Welsh identifies the "flattering sexual interpretation of a Cordelia-like loyalty to a husband" that purports to be "proof that an attractive young woman—at least in a novel—can pair successfully with a man old enough to be her grandfather" (Welsh 136–37); however, the qualifier, "at least in a novel," shows Welsh's reluctance to accept this premise, and, I would argue, that of most readers as well as the characters in the book.

A chorus of suspicious voices rises against Annie Strong in *David Copperfield*, conjecturing that at age twenty she could not possibly prefer her sixty-two-year-old husband to a younger man. Doubts begin with Mr. Wickfield and are furthered by Uriah Heep, who convinces a reluctant David. Of course, the young rival, Jack Maldon, believes that he has enough of a chance with Annie to pursue his suit. Even Annie's mother, Mrs. Markleham, unwittingly furthers suspicion by constant references to her daughter's close relationship with Maldon. I agree with Gerhard Joseph that each of these characters as well as the reader approaches the marriage with a "prejudice . . . [that] arises out of his or her own . . . generic expectations concerning January-May marriages, which then color the interpretation of this particular marriage" (685). We know this match is doomed to fail.

The narrative purposely misleads readers into what Joseph terms "Heep's *sub*textual or 'shadow' hermeneutics of suspicion" followed by the revelation of "Copperfield's textual hermeneutics of exoneration," a shift that is supposed to provide a welcome and convincing resolution (685). The Heepian (mis)interpretation accretes by consistent evidence: first, Mr. Wickfield's belief that Dr. Strong wants to get rid of Jack, and though it is soon made clear that Strong has no such wish, suspicions in the reliable Wickfield are not easy to dismiss (221). Maldon furthers doubt when he insinuates to David, Wickfield, and Heep that Annie wishes him to remain in England while her husband has sufficient reason to send him away. Annie's habit of "running gaily across the Cathedral yard" with David, where they often encounter Maldon, "who was always surprised to see us," intimates that Copperfield is the dupe who covers their arranged meetings (233). Repeated descriptions by Annie's mother of Jack "making baby love to Annie behind the gooseberry bushes in the back-garden," as well as Annie's immediate shushing of her mother, seem portentous (234). Annie's care to avoid the suspicious Wickfield and his desire to prevent her from friendship or close contact with his daughter appear further to confirm guilt. On the day Maldon leaves for India, Annie's "complexion was not so blooming and flower-like as usual," a sure sign of her stricken heart (233). As Kelly Hager points out, "there is something striking about the way in which the purported adultery plot spreads so quickly and gains so many believers" (1012). Dickens contrives these misunderstandings to pack drama into the reversal when Annie's innocence is revealed, but despite this seeming resolution, the conclusion drawn by so many continues to ring true—that a marriage between sixty-two and twenty is incompatible by virtue of age. The Strong's marriage is not a union of equality and happiness, despite taglines about love that later haunt David and provide insight about his relationship with Dora.

Abundant commentary within the narrative questions the suitability of "that sort of marriage," as Jack describes it (225), and characters seem to hold the opinion later stated by Acton in the sixth edition of *Functions and Disorders*, ". . . I must not be supposed to set my face against even elderly men marrying if they will, but let them select a suitable companion. What I object to is December allying itself with May" (252). Hager points out, "All these characters seem to believe that there must have been an ulterior motive behind Annie's marriage to Dr. Strong since a marriage based on love and sexual attraction seems out of the question" (1013). Mr. Wickfield confesses to Dr. Strong that he has wondered whether Annie was in it for the money: ". . . I thought . . . that, in a case where there was so much disparity in point of years— . . . a lady of such youth, and such attractions, however real her respect for you, might have been influenced in marrying, by worldly considerations only" (600). Jack Maldon bases his manipulations on the assumption that a wife so much younger is owed some sort of recompense, arguing that "Annie's a charming young girl, and the old Doctor—Doctor Strong, I mean—is not quite a charming young boy," and she should be able to induce Strong to provide him with a job nearby, because ". . . I suppose some compensation is fair and reasonable, in that sort of marriage" (225).

The history of their engagement related by Mrs. Markleham also raises doubt. She comments to Strong about his proposal: ". . . you first overpowered me with surprise . . . because, you having known her poor father, and having known her for a baby six months old, I hadn't thought of you in such a light at all" (235), her words emphasizing a generation of age disparity. Markleham reveals that Annie accepted Strong from obligation not love, repeating her daughter's tearful account of the proposal, including her comment, "I am extremely young" (235), to which Markleham replies that Strong "will not only be your husband, but he will represent your late father" (235), which raises the specter of incest. This disturbing dimension of the marriage is evoked in addition by Wickfield's suspicions about Annie that seem to arise from his own incestuous desires for his daughter (Joseph 687).

Despite its pretensions, this is not a love match that spells a happy ending but an unsuitable, even improper, union between age and youth. There is no basis for compatibility between Annie and Dr. Strong. His obsession with composing the never-ending dictionary amuses Mr. Dick but is never of interest to Annie. Strong has only reached the letter D by the end of the account, and as Joseph notes, is a precursor to Casaubon and his unfinished "Key To All Mythologies" that George Eliot will later create to depict aged futility (685). Annie may respect her husband, but she is not in love with him. He is consistently presented as elderly, a father figure, not a lover or even a peer. Strong's virility remains a question; in Joseph's words, we "may wonder but cannot know" whether or not their marriage was consummated (687), but no births are reported—often a sign of an unhappy or ill-suited marriage in a Dickens novel. Hager points out that the marriages Dickens presents as happy "are ones in which the wife has been disciplined or subdued to her husband's liking" (1014). In the case of the Strongs, it is difficult to read Annie's profession that her love is "founded on a rock, and it endures" as anything other than an heroic surrender (646). Just before these words, her final utterance in the novel, she reiterates that Strong's face is "revered as a father's" before she adds "loved as a husband's" (645). Though Dickens tries to convince his readers that this May-December marriage is worthy of emulation, instead we are left with the impression that, as Welsh describes it, Annie Strong finally functions as "an unfallen fallen woman" (136). Though chaste by rule, she seems to have prostituted herself from a false sense of duty, making an inappropriate, even incestuous, marriage, and Dr. Strong, far from lingering on the threshold of marriageability, has entered old age.

The theme of older man and younger woman contained in a subplot of *David Copperfield* resurfaces in the central plot of each of Dickens's next three novels, but as he tells the story over and over again, Dickens continually decreases the age disparity until he represents men solidly in midlife. *Bleak House* is the tale of a would-be husband who must face the fact that he has aged out of affect, a point driven home even more clearly when he proves his virtue by ungrudgingly assisting his young rival to supersede him and marry the girl. In his late fifties, John Jarndyce is moving out of middle age, and from the first Esther views him in a paternal role, not as a lover. When she arrives at Jarndyce's house, he kisses her in what she records as "a fatherly way" (60), and she describes him as "nearer sixty than fifty" (60). Though she adds that he is "handsome" and "lively," her words "quick," "hearty," and "robust" imply that at twenty, she finds him surprisingly active considering his age (60). Esther, Ada, and Richard look with affectionate amusement on Jarndyce's habit of attributing depression to "the east wind" and retreating to his "growlery," and Esther's mention of these idiosyncrasies as "eccentric gentleness" consigns them to aging quirkiness (75).

As we later learn, early in his guardianship, Jarndyce begins to hope he can marry Esther, and he sets out to refashion her identity in accord with that dream. He initiates a custom, soon taken up by Ada and Richard, of calling her elderly women's names—Dame Durden, Mrs. Shipton, and Mother Hubbard, and the most common of her nicknames—"Old Woman," a ploy that makes Esther seem much older than her age peers. Referring to Ada as "my rosebud" and Esther as "little woman" (211), Jarndyce consistently treats Ada as a "blooming" girl just coming out into the world and Esther as much older, though only three years divide them. In addition, he often places Esther with himself in a parental position, supervising his other wards, at which point she always records in her narrative, "O my goodness, the idea of asking my advice on such a point!" (91). Though apparently professing unfitness for such an honor, she covertly protests being placed in this position. Ada tells Jardynce he has taken her father's place and she transfers all "love and duty" to him, which he accepts without deferral (162), but when Esther expresses a similar feeling he is taken aback (214). Ada and Richard adopt Jarndyce's fiction and treat her as a guardian when they enlist Esther to ask Jarndyce's permission to become engaged (161), a matronly helper role that is the hallmark of postmenopausal women, as I discuss in chapter 3.

However, despite Jarndyce's maneuvering, Esther continues to view him as her guardian rather than a potential suitor. Sometimes catching Jarndyce mulling over some "trouble" in his mind, obviously moments when he is considering whether he should propose, she always views him in terms of age. For example, interrupting him during one of these contemplations, she describes Jarndyce "sitting looking at the ashes . . . lost in thought . . . his silvered iron-grey hair . . . scattered confusedly upon his forehead as though his hand had been wandering among it while his thoughts were elsewhere, and his face looked worn" (212). When she learns her history, she is grateful for his care and thanks him for being "the Guardian who is a Father" (214), though the idea upsets him: "At the word Father, I saw his former trouble come into his face" (214). Immediately after relating this scene, Esther records that Allan Woodcourt has visited and specifically points out, "He was seven years older than I," which she follows with the demur, "Not that I need mention it, for it hardly seems to belong to anything" (214). Esther's disclaimers always signal significance, and her juxtaposition of Jarndyce's anxiety against Woodcourt's age reveals that she sees the younger man as a much more fitting suitor.

Jarndyce is aware that age places him at risk as a lover. Though he has long been in love with Esther, he cannot bring himself to propose marriage until her face has been scarred by smallpox and her illegitimacy has been established. Only when her marital value is discounted and she is no longer a young, "blooming" beauty with acceptable origins, can he contend for her hand. Though Esther, in her usual self-denying way, describes this as "generosity" that "rose above my disfigurement" (538), Jarndyce's proposal is not an act of pity toward a cut-rate fiancée, but an opportune moment he exploits to further his long-held hope. Jarndyce has all the requisites of a good match except one—he has money, position, an estate, a genial, loving temperament—but not youth. His proposal is fraught with age anxiety and conducted obliquely by letter, revealing fear that he will not cut a fine figure in a love scene. She writes that the note "dwelt on my being young, and he past the prime of life; on his having attained a ripe age, while I was a child; on his writing to me with a silvered head, and knowing all this so well as to set it in full before me for mature deliberation" (537). Jarndyce never directly asks Esther to be his wife, but the mistress of Bleak House and his "dear companion" (537), a request for allegiance to the house instead of the man that allows her eventually to fulfill her promise by becoming Woodcourt's wife, the mistress of *his* Bleak House. The letter's tone, "impartially representing the proposal of a friend" as Esther describes it, suggests Jarndyce may be willing to accept a nonsexual, non-romantic love if that is all she is willing to give (538). The letter emphasizes Jarndyce's anxiety about his liminal position between father and lover that hints at incest and child abuse, when he writes that if she chooses to forego his offer, he will return to "his old manner, in the old name" as guardian (538).

Because of her facial scarring, illegitimate birth, and Woodcourt's possibly permanent absence, Esther agrees but cries at the idea of the engagement, not only because she is in love with Allan, but also because, as she confesses, of "the strangeness of the prospect" of becoming Jarndyce's wife (538). Though Esther appears content, her hesitation is evident. She accepts him not merely bashfully but so indirectly that her emotional virginity is saved for her later marriage to Woodcourt. By continuing to call Jarndyce "guardian" and refraining from telling Ada about the engagement for some time, suspecting she will disapprove, Esther reveals her aversion to the marriage (540). Dickens depicts their betrothal as unnatural, the unrealistic dream of an aging man with inappropriate romantic impulses, the sadly misplaced hopes of a genial father figure who finally learns his true role.

Jarndyce clearly is outclassed as a suitor by Allan Woodcourt, the personification of mid-century manliness. Though Jarndyce is propertied while Woodcourt struggles to establish himself as a surgeon, even leaving England as a ship's physician in order to raise money, *Bleak House* demonstrates that the largest fortune and highest social class do not ensure a man is the best suitor. The shipwreck incident proves Woodcourt to be the more manly, possessing qualities that Jarndyce, with his gentle sensitivity, lacks. "Calm and brave" while he valiantly attends the injured, Woodcourt becomes famous as "a hero" who provides leadership and is "all but worshipped" by the other survivors for his skill, courage, and authority (442). With his physical strength, work ethic, and sacrificial courage, Woodcourt exemplifies a manliness which makes him desirable to Esther. She responds to the news of his thrilling deeds by finally admitting "the little secret I have thus far tried to keep," that Woodcourt has shown signs of love for her, even speculating that his lack of money prevented a previous proposal, but professing herself now too ugly for love (443). Her face has been scarred for some time, however, and she only admits her hope when his manly heroism inspires her.

That Woodcourt's attractions supersede older notions of masculinity is emphasized by satire on his mother's outmoded ideas. Pompously reciting Welsh verse that is indecipherable to her audience at the dinner table, she loftily informs Esther that because her son bears the blood of Morgan ap-Kerrig, his choice of a wife is constrained much as "the matrimonial choice of the Royal family is limited" (365). Her son shares none of these affectations, however, and his choice at the end of the novel, "an appointment to a great amount of work and a small amount of pay" as a physician of the Yorkshire poor, further enhances his attractiveness, because he is ennobled by work rather than inherited wealth. In contrast, Mrs. Woodcourt's faith in blood and rank are lampooned as pretensions of greatness that make her ridiculous.

When Jarndyce realizes Esther's love for Allan, he succumbs to age by making himself a paternal figure and helping the younger man supplant him. Despite her protestations to the contrary, Esther has stayed true to Woodcourt, but when he finally makes his profession, her immediate thought—"too late"—is followed by shame because of her promise to Jarndyce. She tells him that she has accepted her guardian's proposal out of "attachment, gratitude, love," but her tears after Woodcourt leaves make evident that her love is more that of a daughter than a wife (733). Jarndyce senses this, telling Esther later, "... I began to doubt whether what I had done would really make you happy" (752). When Woodcourt returns to England, the guardian becomes a Prospero figure, the "beneficent old fairy" that Roger Carbury will despair of becoming in Trollope's *The Way We Live Now* (1.74). Jarndyce tells Esther, "I am your guardian and your father now" (752) and arranges her future, bestowing her upon Woodcourt as his property: "take from me, a willing gift, the best wife that ever a man had" (753). He not only arranges Allan's job in Yorkshire, but also gives the young couple a new Bleak House as Esther's dowry, asking only, "Let me share its felicity sometimes, and what do I sacrifice? Nothing, nothing" (753).

Bleak House is not merely the story of a man too old for his fiancée who should seek a more age-appropriate bride, but one whose marginal marriageability proves to have expired. Jarndyce never considers finding another woman and is written into a completely asexual elderhood as he resolves, ". . . I am going to revert to my bachelor habits" (753) and then assumes a desexualized role. He acts as a father and grandfather to the widowed Ada and her child, and, in his frequent visits, Esther treats him as an elderly paternal figure, recreating his growlery in her house (though, she adds, the wind is never "in the east" again). Jarndyce enters a happy decline as the serviceable grandfather, a depiction of aging men that Teresa Mangum describes as common in Victorian fiction ("Growing Old" 99). In John Jarndyce, Dickens portrays men in their late fifties as sexually and maritally obsolete, completely disqualified from courtship due to age, appropriately supplanted by younger, more manly candidates.

While *Bleak House* asks whether a man in his late fifties is too old for love, *Hard Times* (1854) poses the same question about a suitor in his late forties. Though Bounderby marries Louisa Gradgrind, the novel stresses from the start that he is far too old to be a suitable husband. Dickens focuses on their age disparity as the novel opens: she is "a child now, of fifteen or sixteen" (14) while Bounderby is her father's age peer, and, though "a year or two younger" than Gradgrind, he "looked older; his seven or eight and forty might have had the seven or eight added to it again, without surprising anybody" (15). Their chronological difference becomes part of Gradgrind's manipulations as he distorts population statistics so that the thirty year age gap "almost ceases to be disparity, and (virtually) all but disappears" (77). Dickens allies their mismatched union with other bitter repercussions of "Fact, fact, fact" (9) that ruin so many lives in the novel.

The marriage is presented as the barbaric sacrifice of an emotionally deprived young woman to a pompous, self-deluded man incapable of love, his insensitivity a major impediment to their happiness. He entirely lacks feeling—about every social problem the novel raises and about aging as well—proving himself far too inwardly bankrupt to be a commendable husband. Bounderby's name says it all—he is a hard-hearted bounder, dishonest and cruel, and a large part of his incompatibility with Louisa in his denial of his own age inappropriateness. Mrs. Sparsit, Bounderby's housekeeper, in an attempt to turn his amorous attentions toward herself, constantly peppers him with hints that he is much more suitable as a father figure than a lover for Louisa. He stubbornly ignores her suggestions, refusing to acknowledge that Louisa is young enough to be his daughter, and his disputations with Sparsit become occasions for more satire about age and romance that further denigrate him as a desirable partner. *Hard Times* indicates that at a certain point, a true gentleman must age himself out of romantic affect and sexuality, and to remain stubbornly ignorant of this metamorphosis is not only foolish but brutal. Though Bounderby embodies the masculine ideal as a hard worker, his industry is excessive and disqualifies him from being a companionable mate, because he lacks the earnest sincerity also necessary in the manly man.

Bounderby's insensitivity is apparent in his physical relationship with Louisa. From the first time he touches her, Louisa is repelled: he kisses her cheek, and she tells her brother, "You may cut the piece out with your penknife" (20). After their wedding, she clings to her brother while leaving the church, "a little shaken in her reserved composure for the first time," suggesting her apprehension about their wedding night (85). Their courtship has been flavored by his occupation—"Love . . . on all occasions during the period of betrothal, took a manufacturing aspect" (83)—and their honeymoon in Lyons, arranged "in order that Mr. Bounderby might take the opportunity of seeing how the Hands got on in those parts" (85), hints that their physical union is distasteful and disgusting to Louisa. Helena Michie explores ways in which Victorian honeymoon accounts bear "a profoundly sexualized relationship to landscape" (*Honeymoons* 77). Dickens chose a town for their wedding journey that he had experienced as filthy and ugly on a visit there in 1844. He describes features of Lyons in *Pictures From Italy* that he would later incorporate into Coketown—houses "dirty to excess, rotten as old cheeses," a town over-populated by inhabitants who are "living, or rather not dying till their time should come," a place ". . . I would go miles out of my way to avoid encountering again" (270–71). Lyons is a location perfectly suited for Bounderby and Louisa's honeymoon, the groom more focused on business than romance, their deteriorating surroundings associating him with the proverbial "dirty old man," and the fact that Louisa bears no children hints that the marriage may have remained unconsummated. The union is a failure, ending in separation after Louisa is tempted by the scheming, dishonest Harthouse, and Bounderby remains a self-centered buffoon until the end, even after his death as a succession of paupers inherit his name and his money. In Bounderby, Dickens valorizes age anxiety as the appropriate response to budding romance for the man who pursues a younger woman. By acknowledging the possible limits of marriageability, a midlife man displays his honest, feeling heart, but when he refuses to do so, he is portrayed as deluded, impotent in personality and virtue as well as, the text hints, in his physical body.

In *Little Dorrit* (1855–57), Arthur Clennam becomes a successful midlife suitor and father in his early forties who fulfills expectations of the hardworking and sensitive mid-century man, but only after he grapples with issues Bounderby ignores. Describing himself as "in middle life" (59), Arthur struggles with age anxiety from the beginning of the book, reflecting that at forty he has already "lived the half of a long term of life" (86). His family is characterized by "age and decay" (95), from the near failure of their business in China, where Arthur spent twenty years "exiled . . . grinding in the mill" until his father's recent death (59), to the dilapidated state of their house that has become "out of date and out of purpose" (85). Arthur is in the habit of associating himself with decline, so it is only natural that when he falls in love, he fears age may disqualify him as a suitor.

When he returns to England, Clennam is attracted to Minnie "Pet" Meagles who is "about twenty" (54), but he asks himself whether he should "allow himself to fall in love" considering he is twice her age (239). Arthur seems to overcome age anxiety at this point, comforting himself, "He was young in appearance, young in health and strength, young in heart. A man was certainly not old at forty; and many men were not in circumstances to marry, or did not marry, until they had attained that time of life" (239). Despite this outward show of confidence, however, he imagines he is "deficient" and disqualified as a worthy contender—his loveless upbringing and his decades-long absence from England make him an alien—and he uses these excuses to avoid romance, deciding "it might be better to flow away monotonously, like the river," immune to both happiness and pain (244). Despite his protestations to the contrary, however, he merely is repressing rather than resolving age anxiety.

Arthur's rival for Pet's affections, the thirty-year-old Gowan, serves as a foil against which Clennam's manly attributes shine. Arthur displays the earnest respectability and self-discipline admired in the mid-century male, refusing to work for his miserly and corrupt mother, taking a modest inheritance to seek his own fortune, and though his business ventures fail due to the incompetent Merdle, he is valorized as honest and hardworking. Gowan, on the other hand, is satirized for his profligate character. He also has received a small inheritance, but "his genius, during his earlier manhood, was of that exclusively agricultural character which applies itself to the cultivation of wild oats" (250). He pursues painting as a career, but only in a desultory fashion. Sullen, cruel, and dissipated, Gowan is the antithesis of industrious, upright, mid-century masculinity.

A friend of the family, Arthur must watch Gowan court Minnie, and as her affections turn toward the younger man, Clennam's superiority is made even more evident. He tries to think well of Gowan, acknowledging to his friend Doyce that he is "young and handsome, easy and quick, has talent," and when Doyce is skeptical, he warns they must "resolve . . . not to depreciate him" just because he is successful with Minnie (355–57). Doyce

insists Clennam is the better man, "upright ... much to be respected" and
that Gowan will be unable to make her happy (356). Clennam continues to
school himself in a "high principle of honour and generosity," ungrudgingly
attributing Minnie's growing preference for Gowan to "greater attractions
of his person and manner" as well as his youth (357). He remains humbly
unaware of his own "wealth of ... matured character," an asset Gowan
lacks (254).

From his first appearance in the novel, Gowan is characterized by
sadistic behavior, maliciously teasing his dog, and as the older man struggles
to accept Minnie's choice, his "modest truthfulness" and "quiet strength
of character" (357) contrast with Gowan's insensitivity as he cruelly baits
Arthur about his disappointed affections. At one point, Clennam wonders
as Gowan kicks stones, "Does he jerk me out of the path in the same careless, cruel way?" (366). However, his immediate "rush of shame" at even
having such suspicions only further evinces his modest virtue (367).

Minnie's betrothal to Gowan sets off a new storm of age anxiety. After
the engagement, he considers himself a different kind of person: "from that
time he became in his own eyes, as to any similar hope or prospect, a very
much older man who had done with that part of life" (383). He begins to
refer to himself as her father's friend, placing himself in the next generation
as a paternal figure (384). Minnie's ultimate unhappiness, however, suggests
that the midlife man can be more manly and worthy as a suitor than a
younger and lesser rival.

All this time, Clennam has been a friend to Amy Dorrit, to whom he
initially responds as a "little creature," almost a "child" (135–36) and then
maintains the stance of unmarriageable bachelor. He adopts a paternal role,
assisting Amy and her family, looking upon her as his "adopted daughter"
while he pines for Pet Meagles (231). He tells Little Dorrit that age has
made him unfit for love:

> forgetting how grave I was, and how old I was, and how the
> time for such things had gone by me ... I fancied I loved some
> one. . . . I found out my mistake ... and got wiser. Being wiser, I
> counted up my years and ... found that I should soon be grey.
> I found that I had climbed the hill, and passed the level ground
> upon the top, and was descending quickly. . . . I found that the
> day when any such thing would have been graceful in me, or
> good in me, or hopeful or happy for me or any one in connec-
> tion with me, was gone, and would never shine again. (432)

At age forty, Arthur believes he has passed life's prime, and his words are
a confession that makes a midlife man's attraction to a younger woman

tantamount to sin. The final sentence especially equates his desire with immorality—while lack of "grace" can be read as a breach of manners, lack of "goodness" is a moral failing. Arthur tells Amy heartache has made him "far removed, so different, and so much older" that he must be her "friend and advisor" (433), a "father" or "uncle," and instructs her, "Always think of me as quite an old man" (434), casting his marital and sexual future into decline.

Little Dorrit, however, harbors feelings for Clennam that are far from daughterly, made more evident when she encounters another of his former sweethearts, Flora Casby. In her chaotically loquacious yet candid manner, Flora recounts her history with Clennam in a gush of unpunctuated effusiveness: "we were all in all to one another it was the morning of life it was bliss it was frenzy it was everything else of that sort in the highest degree" (331). Though her parents disapproved and she married another, Flora hints she and Clennam are still in love. At this, Amy becomes unwell, avoids Arthur, frequently cries in her room, and tells her charge Maggy a tale about a young "tiny woman" that metaphorically reveals her resolve to die an old maid now that Clennam has chosen Flora (342).

Clennam further resolves that he is too old and therefore unworthy of love, and unaware of Amy's feelings, he languishes in debtors' prison and sickens. Helena Michie argues that illness serves in Victorian fiction to mark the advent of sexual arousal in young women, as they often become ill in the critical period between their realization of love for a suitor and his reciprocal declaration in a marriage proposal, thereby "punishing . . . her body for its desires" (*Flesh* 25). Age anxiety functions in a similar way for the middle-aged suitor in *Little Dorrit*. Only after disciplining desire through sickness does Clennam finally reach a consummation that proves him emotionally worthy and sexually potent.

When another younger rival, the buffoonish John Chivery, reveals Amy's love, Clennam is transformed. Sedulously maintaining his paternal attitude, Arthur continues to consider Amy "his innocent friend, his delicate child" and regards himself "as a much older man than his years really made him" (573), until Chivery's disclosure. Though "stunned" and "bewildered," he comes to terms with the conflict between father figure and lover, first telling himself, "Consider the improbability. He had been accustomed to call her his child, and his dear child, and to invite her confidence by dwelling upon the difference in their respective ages, and to speak of himself as one who was turning old" (798). He then reexamines their relationship: "Yet she might not have thought him old. Something reminded him that [once] he had not thought himself so. . . ." (798). Thus enlightened, Clennam rereads her letters, finding in them "new meaning" (798–99). He realizes his fatherliness has been a feint, that there has been a "suppressed something on his own side that had hushed as it arose" (799). He sees that he had continually "whispered to himself . . . that he must be steady in saying to himself that the time had gone by him, and he was too saddened and old" (799); he understands that he has aged himself out of love by choice, not necessity.

Arthur symbolically recoups the roses of romance he had put in his breast when Pet announced her engagement: he awakes in debtor's prison to "a blooming nosegay" Amy has left for him, and he "opened his parched hands to them, as cold hands are opened to receive the cheering of a fire" (824), reclaiming the "bloom" and "fire" of youth. When he reunites with Amy, her manner has "a new meaning . . . in his perception" (826), but he still feels "so much older, so much rougher, and so much less worthy" (829). Though he recovers emotional and sexual libido, he still refuses to marry her, because he is a financially "ruined" man (829). However, when Amy's money is lost, he joyfully agrees to share her "fortune" (885).

Clennam ultimately finds a "healthy autumn" with Little Dorrit, their union described by a metaphor of second harvest that depicts midlife romance as better than young love (883). They have reached the season when "the golden fields had been reaped" and "the summer fruits had ripened and waned," but a second crop has matured and produced the new fruits of fall, apples and berries (883). Denuded of foliage, the trees offer a clearer view than during "drowsy summer weather," and the sea, no longer flat from summer heat, has "its thousand sparkling eyes . . . open," leaping with "joyful animation" (883). Poised between summer and winter, the mature lover also finds an autumnal bloom with a clear vision won by experience. His health regained, Arthur can hear "all that . . . Nature was doing" and remembers the "hopeful promises" of youth (883–84). Clennam is transformed from a shrinking, self-deprecating case of age anxiety to a confident husband. As they leave the church after their wedding, Arthur and Amy look out of the door "at the fresh perspective of the street in the autumn morning sun's bright rays" (894–95). A reference to his children in the final paragraph emphasizes that Arthur was mistaken to believe "the time for love had gone by," and he has journeyed back from the borders of affective decline. A combination of manly work and midlife crisis enable the middle-aged suitor to learn he can still find romantic and sexual consummation.

After telling the aging suitor's tale again and again, Dickens finally writes a story that claims an autumnal triumph in middle age. Hardworking and honorable, Arthur is able to find romance because he exhibits the traits of manliness requisite at mid-century to make a good husband, but in addition, he shows himself to be sensitive and self-deprecating about age, recognizing and resolving the perilous contest between father and lover that the midlife suitor must negotiate in order to prove himself an eligible husband. Clennam demonstrates the possibilities of midlife in the liminal space between youth and old age, a theme that haunts Dickens's works as he crosses his own midlife threshold.

IV.

I turn next to two midlife marriage plots from the 1860s and 1870s, one almost entirely forgotten and the other considered by many the quintessential Victorian novel. Both of these books critique the aging male, though Caroline Norton sets out to prove him a superior mate, while George Eliot uses age disparity as a source of marital incompatibility and instability. In *Old Sir Douglas* (1868), Caroline Norton champions the midlife male from the first sentence of the novel, professing, "There is no example of human beauty more perfectly picturesque than a very handsome man of middle age" (1.1), but she calls this claim into question by her immediate anticipation of contradiction—"No, smiling reader, not even a very handsome young man: not even that same man in his youth" (1.1). Simultaneously defending and challenging romance for men of a certain age, Norton's novel unsettles the male midlife marriageability she sets out to advance.

When twenty-two-year-old Gertrude Skifton is pursued by her age peer, Kenneth Ross, as well as by his middle-age uncle, nicknamed "Old Sir Douglas," she chooses the older man. Sir Douglas is a Scottish baronet, and though some characters speculate this is the chief reason for his marriageability, other qualities make him superior. His mature and noble character, evident in his irreproachable behavior, self-restraint, and genuine goodwill, contrast with unprincipled selfishness in the younger man. However, though "Old Sir Douglas" eventually triumphs, the novel is rife with suspicions that Gertrude prefers the younger man even after she marries Sir Douglas, concerns that reveal a growing nervousness about male aging.

Gertrude is the epitome of the desirable Victorian woman—young, beautiful, accomplished, sweet-tempered, admired by every eligible man in the novel—and her preference for the older suitor establishes his marriageability. The contrast between his nickname, "Old Sir Douglas," and Gertrude's surprise at his youthfulness when they first meet accentuates his marginal status between youth and age. She interprets his maturity as an asset, describing him as a man of experience with many options as she tells her mother, "I think him perfect! My wonder is that he could choose *me:* he must have seen so many far worthier than I am to be his wife" (1.204). Her mother agrees, finding her son-in-law not only financially but also physically superior to Kenneth, assuring Gertrude he "is a great deal handsomer than any young man I see going about . . . handsomer even than his saucy nephew" (1.303).[19] Gertrude rejects Kenneth not in spite of, but because of, his age, declining his proposal with the declaration "you are very young; I think you are very little, if at all, older than myself" (1.156). The chapter title, "Nominal Love," echoes her belief that age parity makes them incompatible and unable to find the deeper affect made possible by Douglas's maturity.

Though Gertrude and her mother embrace the midlife suitor as ideal, others are not so sure. Their neighbor Lady Clochnaben firmly believes Gertrude "married Douglas from the basest motives of self-interest" (2.182–83). Kenneth finds Gertrude's choice not only difficult to accept but also to understand. Initially, he is scornful and incredulous, seeing her rejection as an attempt to reform his intemperance "by ridicule" (1.154); he then accuses her of "coquetting and flattering" Douglas into proposing due to his wealth and title (1.157). When Kenneth eventually becomes convinced of their love, his resultant suicide attempt and its enfeebling effects feminize him, while Douglas appears even more manly as he attempts to rescue his drowning nephew and then nurtures him back to health, displaying his skills as an ideal husband and father.

Douglas also entertains doubts of his own, however, creating marital problems with his age anxiety. Douglas has been his nephew's guardian since childhood, and he is horrified to vie for a woman with his surrogate son: "He was Kenneth's rival. KENNETH! his petted, idolised, spoilt boy,—his more than child" (1.184). He begins to wonder whether it was "more natural that these young companions should love each other, than that Gertrude should lean across the gap of years that sundered her from himself" (1.201) and feels "ashamed" that as "a man in mature life" he has made such a proposal (1.202).

Gertrude remains true to Sir Douglas even when his age insecurity causes trouble, and their love seems threatened. A description of their son running his "strong little rosy fingers" through the "silver" in Douglas's hair and over his forehead that was growing "higher and barer" emphasizes that at midlife he is a sexual and fertile husband (2.113). The couple is beset by intrigues against them, however, perpetrated by Douglas's half-sister, and even more damagingly by Kenneth, who continues to pursue Gertrude after casting off his flirtatious Spanish wife. Through their machinations, Douglas becomes convinced that his wife is in love with Kenneth and he goes to the Crimean War, but two years later he realizes his mistake and returns to be forgiven. The book ends with "the glowing light of reconciled love, and the glorious autumn sunshine" of their reunion (3.306). Though Norton initially sets out to adulate the "perfectly picturesque" midlife lover, this formulation is challenged by a plot beset with doubts about his suitability, and age anxiety is reinforced as much as it is resolved in *Old Sir Douglas*.

George Eliot makes no such attempt to shore up the fortunes of the late midlife husband in *Middlemarch* (1871–72). Edward Casaubon is a poor match for his young wife, made more so by his obliviousness to the significance of their twenty-seven year age difference, the fact that he is a generation older than his bride. The prospect of their marriage is met with mixed reactions—her would-be suitor, Sir James Chettam, perceives Casaubon to be a "dried up bookworm towards fifty" (13), exclaiming when he hears of the engagement, "Good God! It is horrible! He is no better than a mummy" (38); however, her uncle and guardian supports the match. Though Brooke may hint at impotency in Casaubon when he cautions his niece, "he is not young, and I must not conceal from you, my dear, that I think his health is not over-strong" (26), he also acknowledges qualities that make Casaubon desirable: he is learned, has a good income, and owns "a handsome property" (26), attributes which, he believes, make Casaubon a suitable match for any young girl despite his waning vigor.

Their honeymoon foreshadows the marriage's eventual failure with details that emphasize Casaubon's unsuitability due to age. We are first introduced to the married Dorothea alone in a Roman museum, her youth highlighted when Will Ladislaw and his friend Adoff Naumann perceive her as a "breathing blooming girl" standing next to a statue of Ariadne (131). Though Naumann is unaware of her May-December marriage, when he calls this sight "a fine bit of antithesis" between "antique beauty" and "breathing life," he unwittingly evokes the age disparity between Dorothea and her "antique" spouse (131).

Casaubon's failures as a honeymooner and a husband become especially apparent in frequent contrasts with Ladislaw that presage his role as Dorothea's second husband. Casaubon is described in terms of dimness and antiquity, while Ladislaw is represented with metaphors of light, imagery stressing the younger man's compatibility. Even before the wedding, Casaubon's house, aptly called "Lowick," has been pictured with "an air of autumnal decline," filled with "old maps," "old vases," and other relics of the past (49), an appropriate setting for a man who has "no bloom that could be thrown into relief by that background" (49). On the honeymoon, he dedicates himself to study, "lost among small closets and winding stairs, and in an agitated dimness" (137). When Will seeks out Dorothea, even Casaubon's anger is lackluster, a jealousy of "very little fire: it is hardly a passion, but a blight bred in the cloudy, damp despondency of uneasy egoism" (146). In contrast, Will's smile is "a gush of inward light illuminating the transparent skin as well as the eyes" (142). When the two men appear side by side, Causabon is "all the dimmer and more faded" and stands "rayless," while Ladislaw beams with "sunny brightness" and "his hair seemed to shake out light" (145). When Will and Dorothea are together, their shared youthfulness is enhanced. Her tears make "her open face look more youthful and appealing than usual" to Ladislaw, and, attempting to act the matron, she looks even younger still (142). As for Ladislaw, "he looked much the younger, for his transparent complexion flushed suddenly" when he saw her (142). When he discovers Dorothea crying while Casaubon pursues his Vatican research, Will is aghast, filled with "comic disgust" at "the idea of this dried-up pedant . . . having first got this adorable young creature to marry him, and then passing his honeymoon away from her, groping after his mouldy futilities" (142). In contrast to Causabon's "mouldy futilities," Will illuminates Dorothea's vision with his version of "history as a whole" (147).

Dorothea's descriptions of Roman art reveal her sexual antipathy toward her new husband. She is surprised and distressed by Casaubon's lack of affection, while he, in turn, finds her desire for kisses and caresses "rather crude and startling" (138), a response that leads Dorothea to renew her wifely efforts, "repressing everything in herself except the desire to enter into . . . her husband's chief interests" (140). She sedulously attends to his disquisitions, but her descriptions of Roman art—"a consecration of ugliness rather than beauty. . . . low and brutal, and sometimes even ridiculous"—hint that though Casaubon has attempted to perform his conjugal duty, she has found his sexual advances repulsive, sentiments echoed in her words to Will, "I have often felt since I have been in Rome that most of our lives would look much uglier and more bungling than the pictures, if they could be put on the wall" (153). Helena Michie argues that Dorothea's descriptions of her honeymoon "sound very much like the horrifying and repetitive dreams of rape survivors" while "the visual violations of St. Peter's and of a spectacularly carnal imperial city suggest the more overtly sexual violations of marital rape" (*Honeymoons* 86). Dorothea's references to "ugly" and "bungling" suggest that the elderly Casaubon is a failure as a lover, and is perhaps impotent (Morse 53), further evinced by their childless union.

Casaubon "had no idea of being anything else than an irreproachable husband, who would make a charming young woman as happy as she deserved to be" (138), any understanding of his limited romantic viability sorely lacking. As Amy M. King argues, "Casaubon's decision to marry a 'blooming young lady' . . . is criticized through its devastating failure" and his "principle" that high social position will win any man a "blooming" bride "is not validated, first by Dorothea's refusal of Chettam and more powerfully by Eliot's refusal to endow that narrative with success" (157). Like Bounderby, he proves to be insufficient as a husband, the sagacity which had attracted Dorothea revealed as empty pedantry, his age exacerbating the querulous, narrowness of his disposition, and their short union ends in his death. Casaubon's failure to consider the possibility of his own impotence—whether emotional or sexual—reveals his deficiencies, and the romance plot is satisfied only when Dorothea unites with her age peer, Ladislaw. Eliot shows that a husband "towards fifty" who is unwilling to consider the affective danger of marrying a younger woman will fail, replaced by a younger and more suitable lover.

V.

Anthony Trollope often depicted midlife in his novels, but two parallel tales of male midlife reveal his heightened sense of aging masculinity at risk in the last decades of the nineteenth century. Trollope's final novel, *An Old Man's Love* (1882), written in the months before his death and published two years later, is in many ways a retelling of Roger Carbury's plot in *The Way We Live Now* (1874–75).[20] While Roger's narrative is interwoven with several other plots, in *An Old Man's Love*, as its title announces, the relationship between marriageability and aging is the main focus, intensifying the age anxiety that haunts both texts.

Trollope wrote in his autobiography that he was "instigated" to write *The Way We Live Now* after returning home from eighteen months in Australia, appalled to find that deceitfulness in business, society, the church, and marriage "has become at the same time so rampant and so splendid . . . there seems to be reason for fearing that men and women will be taught to feel that dishonesty, if it can become splendid, will cease to be abominable" (224–25). The novel records his concern that society was deteriorating in late-century England, an idle aristocracy declining in the wake of the Reform Acts, while newly rich industrialists-turned-gentlemen possessed far more money and far less gentility than the weakened traditional upper class (Glendinning 432–33). Though the book focuses on money grabbing that replaces older values, this dynamic does not dominate the marriage plot. Instead, young love trumps avarice when Hetta Carbury chooses an age peer with precarious finances over the older, more propertied Roger. In his autobiography Trollope calls the love triangle between Roger, Hetta, and Paul "uninteresting" (225), but their tale reveals his growing anxiety about the older man superseded by younger rivals, a problem he found sufficiently interesting to repeat and expand a decade later in *An Old Man's Love*.[21] Roger indicates the fate of the old-fashioned gentleman in "a newer and worse sort of world" as he describes it (1.71), where masculinity is defined by new paradigms, and he has become an anachronism.

Roger proposes to his cousin Henrietta for the first time when he is thirty-six and she is twenty, a sixteen year age difference, but his age is presented as liminal, considered appropriate for marriage by most of the characters, but, unfortunately for his plans, not by Hetta. He is described by her brother Felix as "not what you'd call a young man," but he then adds, "He isn't very old" (1.221). In the neighborhood of his estate, he still is regarded "as a young man" and spoken of as "the young squire" (1.130). Hetta's mother sees him as an eminently eligible suitor for her daughter and age is not an issue: "to her thinking . . . a man of thirty-six was young enough for any girl" (1.52).

In Henrietta's opinion, though, Roger is too old to be a suitable partner. Despite repeated refusals, Roger continues to pursue her, making his third proposal at just over age forty, and she specifies their age difference as a major impediment. Though overtly declaring she is too young to consider marriage to anyone, "[s]he had meant to imply that the difference in their ages was too great, but had not known how to say it" (1.57). She reiterates this point again, when she later asserts that even if she had accepted, he would soon find her "too young for your tastes" (1.73). She does see him as marriageable to someone older, telling her mother: "When we were joking, I said he was old. You know I did not mean that he was too old to get married. Men a great deal older get married every day" (1.146). Later, Paul Montague, Roger's rival for Hetta, makes the same judgment, and flinches at the idea that Hetta "would be forced into a marriage with a man almost old enough to be her father" (2.248). Roger is not unmarriageable but merely unsuitable for such a young woman.

Roger is a bad match for the young Hetta not only due to their age difference, however, but also because he embodies genteel values that are passing away. Roger calls himself "old-fashioned" (1.71) and confesses that he has "old-fashioned notions" (1.131). His love of the landed gentry is evinced by his enjoyment of what he terms the "old English habits" maintained in Suffolk, where the poor touch their hats to the rich and the rich help the poor, preserving clear class distinctions (1.153). He considers it a "disgrace" for a gentleman to consider entering Melmotte's house, a man with money but no breeding (1.69), and when county families receive the Melmotte family, he comments: "Things aren't as they were, of course, and never will be again" (1.136). His lament "People live now in a way I don't comprehend" (1.437–38) registers his feeling of obsolescence. It is not that Roger is one of the idle rich—he diligently tends to the affairs of his estate, including "the care of the farm which he kept in his own hands" (2.349), but he is a squire who lives off the proceeds of his estate according to tradition, a gentleman who privileges propriety and noblesse oblige, values that are becoming passé. Lady Carbury sums up the situation when she comments "dear Roger was old-fashioned, and knew nothing of people as they are now. He lived in a world which, though slow, had been good in its way; but which, whether bad or good, had now passed away" (1.283).

The sixteen years of age that divide Hetta and Roger are more significant at mid-century than they would have been a few decades earlier, because according to the new masculinity, Carbury is a relic of the past.

When Roger is contrasted with two younger men, Felix Carbury and Paul Montague, he is aligned with outmoded standards that emphasize his superannuation, a family patriarch rather than an appropriate suitor for a young woman. Trollope records in his autobiography that one of the "vices" he attacks in this novel is the "the luxury of young men who prefer to remain single" (225), a problem epitomized by Felix Carbury, an indolent habitué of "Clubland," the haunt of rich and idle young men in a new "age of bachelors" (Showalter 11).[22] The members of the Beargarden act out satirical versions of capital investment with worthless IOUs that parody the novel's more serious plot, regularly rescued from ruin by their elders. Replete with male camaraderie, they are in no hurry to take on the responsibilities of a wife and children. Felix immures himself in debt, pursues the heiress Marie Melmotte in a desultory fashion, and dismisses Roger's charge that her father is an acknowledged "adventurer and a swindler" (1.138). Roger proves his outmoded gentlemanliness by objecting to Felix's behavior, referring to his courtship of Marie as "stealing a girl's money" (1.137). The antithesis of Roger, Felix's slothful avarice evokes the squire's respectable yet obsolete gentlemanliness.

Even more significant is Roger's contrast with Paul Montague, a rival suitor and ultimately Hetta's husband. Youthful and inexperienced, Montague is a version of "the way we live now," the victim of schemers who take advantage of him. Paul becomes involved in Melmotte's railway scam, unaware of its fraudulence, and though he ultimately confronts the speculator, he is shown to be financially tenuous, lacking foresight and matured business expertise. Before the book's opening, Paul has been involved with Winifred Hurtle, who not only has shot a man in the American West but also pursues Paul while allowing him to believe she is either divorced or a widow when actually she is married. Roger calls Paul "a city adventurer" who oscillates between wealth and poverty (1.133) and believes his behavior with Hurtle makes him "unworthy of Hetta" (2.353), an "unsafe husband, a fickle husband" (2.347). Paul's relationship with Winifred shows him to be a weak but a highly desirable young man. Her description of Paul rings true—he is "a tame, sleek household animal," a "soft over-civilised man" (2.379), and she accuses him of being caught between "youthful ardor" and "cautious . . . old age" (2.387). However, her final vision of Paul accentuates his youth. Even though he has been "false as hell" to her, Winfred silently confesses that she still loves him "with all her heart," reflecting that, while she has been tainted by their broken engagement, "because he was a man. . . . [H]e could change his love as often as he pleased, and be as good a lover at the end as ever. . . . He could look about for a fresh flower and boldly seek its honey" (2.439). Hurtle's metaphor attributes Paul's romantic triumph both to gender and youth, the younger suitor able to move from one blooming girl to the next with impunity while women, and by inference older men, do not possess the same privilege.

Paul is a young gentleman of the new era beside whom Roger appears stodgily conventional, unyielding, and insecure. Roger and Paul have long been friends, and when they discover that both have hopes of marrying the same woman, after some "hot words," Roger's farewell brings tears to Paul's eyes (1.54–55). Roger, however, is more severe, insisting that the younger man should abandon his courtship, because he has no income and should defer to the squire's previous claim in gratitude for past patronage (1.75). Roger vilifies Paul, accusing him of being "false and ungrateful," one who "undermined my treasure, and stole it away" (2.152). He tells Hetta he feels "hatred" for the man and cannot forgive (2.206). While Roger's wrath grows, Paul remains a calmly loyal friend, extremely magnanimous. Initially he agrees to forego declaring his love for a time so that Roger can try to win Hetta (1.58), and even after his open pursuit begins, Paul tells Hetta that he loves Roger, praising him as "a gentleman all round and every inch," and offers to withdraw his suit (1.362). Paul's characterization of Roger as the "beau ideal of an English gentleman" points to the problem with the older suitor: Roger is old-fashioned, grumpy, and stuffy, while Paul remains flexible and open, the product of a new era (1.440). Roger is insecure about emasculation, and he resolves never to forgive Paul because that would be "weak, womanly, and foolish" (1.75).

Finally, Roger begins to "school" himself to a new duty (2.468), his admission that she "loves the younger man" revealing his conviction that her preference is based on age, and he commits to disengaging from affect as a man who is too old (2.468). Earlier, he despaired of playing this role, quizzing himself bitterly, "what should he do? Annihilate himself as far as all personal happiness in the world was concerned, and look solely to their happiness, their prosperity, and their joys? Be as it were a beneficent old fairy to them, though the agony of his own disappointment should never depart from him?" (1.74). When he acquiesces to age, his disgust over the role of "beneficent old fairy" gradually gives way to a more passive acceptance. He tells himself that Hetta "looked upon him as an old man to be regarded in a fashion altogether different from that in which she regarded Paul Montague. He had let his time for love–making go by, and now it behoved him, as a man, to take the world as he found it, and not to lose himself in regrets for a kind of happiness which he could never attain" (2.353). Confessing "he felt himself at times to be eighty years old" (2.354), though he is around forty, Roger ages himself out of marriageability and then promotes Hetta's marriage to Paul.

Roger takes on the role of fatherly guardian who provides solutions to problems and enables the marriage, much in the style of John Jarndyce. Lady Carbury objects to Paul's financial instability, dealings with Melmotte, and past with women, but Roger immediately responds that "his income . . . may be managed" and his dealings with Melmotte were "unfortunate" but "no fault of his" (2.409). Roger loans Paul money to travel to California and recover investments his uncle has been neglecting, settling his financial woes. As Hetta has assured Paul, Roger "is always right," he is a "rock of strength," and Paul agrees with ample reason (1.361).

Roger uses age to sanitize his sexuality into benevolent affection, shielding him from desire as he disqualifies himself from affect. Selfless service becomes his compensation for giving up reproductivity, as he takes on the role of father and grandfather. His declaration to Hetta, "I will hurry to grow old that I may feel for you as the old feel for the young" (2.407), emphasizes the liminality of his position, that he chooses to make himself "old." He resolves to act the grandfather, that their "future infant" will be a comfort "in his old age" (2.405), and he tells Paul, "You may now count on any assistance you could have from me were I a father giving you a daughter in marriage" (2.411). After the engagement is settled, he struggles to see their happiness as his duty while he works to "conquer" and "crush" his own heart (2.468). He tells himself, "He must learn to regard himself as an old man,—as one who had let his life pass him too far for the purposes of his own home, and who must therefore devote himself to make happy the homes of others" (2.469).

Roger's borderline age status remains, however, and his neighbor, the Bishop, urges Roger not to relinquish his property to Hetta and Paul's children, arguing that he may yet be a father himself. When Roger baldly claims, "I shall never marry," the Bishop counters, "How is a man of your age to speak with certainty of what he will do or what he will not do in that respect?" (2.469). The Bishop claims that for a man to give away "the power, which properly belongs to him" is to "ignore the ordinary rules of life" (2.470). The concerned neighbor is able to convince Roger to give up his plan to make Hetta's children his heirs, but Roger remains "not . . . the less resolute in his determination to make himself and his own interest subordinate to those of his cousin" (2.470). As he gives away the bride, the guests comment on how happy Roger looks, and the narrative suggests that Roger will succeed in his attempt to channel desire into the paternal, an option his liminal status allows.

In his final novel, *An Old Man's Love*, completed at sixty-seven a few months before his death, Trollope suggests that at a certain age male sexuality becomes inappropriate and should go dormant. He takes up the aging suitor again but does not confine the story to a subplot, centering the book around whether a fifty-year-old man is suitable for a woman half his age. In many ways, William Whittlestaff's story is a hyperbolic version of Roger's, but issues of aging and affect are settled by a distinction drawn between outmoded gentlemanliness and the new manliness tested and proven by empire.[23] His name suggests what the plot will prove, that at fifty Whittlestaff is a diminishing phallus, a theme the book explores in terms of physical strength, virility, authority, and general cultural capital.

Just as in *The Way We Live Now*, the older man vies with a younger suitor, but in *An Old Man's Love*, the age difference is widened. At fifty, Whittlestaff pursues the twenty-five-year-old Mary Lawrie, and his contrast with the thirty-year-old John Gordon provides a decisive answer to the question of which would make the best husband. Mary moves into her guardian Whittlestaff's house when her stepmother dies and she is homeless, but she is in love with John Gordon. Three years earlier her stepmother had forced Mary to refuse Gordon's proposal, deeming him too poor. As a result, Gordon has gone to the South African diamond mines seeking a fortune upon which to marry. Because John did not propose before his departure, when Whittlestaff offers marriage, Mary accepts out of obligation, in gratitude for his guardianship, unaware when or even if her former lover will come home. Gordon returns that very afternoon, a rich man, and the dilemma is born—will Mary honor her promise to marry William while in love with another, and, if she does, should he give her up to the younger man? The choice between Mary's or William's happiness is not the true struggle in the novel, however. Mary easily resolves to honor the engagement, and, disturbingly passive, is willing to take on a loveless marriage out of duty to her benefactor. The question then becomes who will make the better husband, fifty-year-old Whittlestaff or thirty-year-old John Gordon.

The novel sets up a rivalry between Whittlestaff and Gordon that is decided in terms of late-Victorian masculinity, and the young man becomes the standard against which the older's masculinity is measured. Gordon is, as Mary describes him, "the personification of manliness" who exemplifies physical vigor and masterful authority—he is "somewhat full of sport of the roughest kind" and "[t]hat which he resolved to do, he did with an iron will" (1.73). He is "six feet high, with dark hair cut very short" (1.73), and Mary is attracted to him for his rough exterior: "She could not boast that he was handsome. 'What does it signify?' she had once said to her stepmother, who had declared him to be stiff, upsetting, and ugly. 'A man is not like a poor girl, who has nothing but the softness of her skin to depend on' " (1.73–74). In addition, Gordon is industrious and independent, having earned a fortune in a South African diamond mine and proven his masculinity by contributing to the national imperial project.

While Gordon is wealthy through his own hard work, Whittlestaff has inherited his income and been unsuccessful in business. As a young man, he rebelled against his father's plans to train him as a solicitor, and he tried to get a literature fellowship but failed, spending his money on an unsuccessful attempt to publish his poetry. At fifty, he is served by a house-keeper, groom, gardener, and other assorted domestics, occasionally stealing away to read poetry. Whittlestaff is the antithesis of the new masculinity embodied by the public school ethos with its suspicion of intellectuals and adulation of the athlete (Mangan 149).

Whittlestaff is described in terms of liminal aging at midlife. Though the title claims that the protagonist is "old," the opening contends with that description, representing Whittlestaff in a border space of late midlife. As his housekeeper, Mrs. Baggett, tells him, "You ain't a young man—nor you ain't an old un" (1.9). Initially Whittlestaff accepts this version of his age, thinking, "He was not a young man, because he was fifty; but he was not quite an old man, because he was only fifty" (1.25–26). He has not deteriorated physically: "He was now fifty, and as fit, bodily and mentally, for hard work as ever he had been" (1.20), and though he sees some gray hairs on his head, these are "signs indeed of age, but signs which were very becoming to him. At fifty he was a much better-looking man than he had been at thirty" (1.34). However, his foppish neighbor, the Reverend Mon-tagu Blake, initially assumes that Whittlestaff has "made . . . [Mary] . . . his own daughter" (1.163), and after due consideration announces, "Fifty is old. I don't mean that he is a cripple or bedridden. . . . He has got a very nice girl there with him; and if he isn't too old to think of such things, he may marry her" (1.164).

Though he may appear a confirmed bachelor, Whittlestaff is ambivalent about whether or not to give up on love. Even before Gordon's reappear-ance, Whittlestaff is caught in a quandary, undecided about pursuing Mary. Sustaining this ambiguous position until the denouement, Whittlestaff bal-ances at the periphery of marriageability through most of the narrative. He likes to read classic love stories, and "as years had gone by, he had told himself that for him there was to be nothing better than reading. But yet his mind had been full, and he had still thought to himself that . . . there was still room for a strong passion" (2.142). At the same time, however, Whittlestaff is insecure about his suitability as a lover. He tells himself, "I am an old man, and an old man shouldn't ask a young girl to sacrifice herself. . . . Love, I fear, is out of the question" (1.31).

His resolve to wed Mary may seem a declaration of romantic viability, but when he eventually proposes, he does so not in confident tones of love, but as a suitor devalued by age: "Mary . . . can you endure the thought of becoming my wife? . . . Of course I am an old man. . . . But I think that I can love you as honestly and as firmly as a younger one. I think that if you could bring yourself to be my wife, you would find that you would not be treated badly" (1.58). Gordon's reappearance provokes an even greater indecisiveness and age crisis. Though Whittlestaff considers himself "the safer staff of the two on which a young lady might lean" (2.21–22), he also is aware that "still there was a pang in his bosom—a silent secret—which kept whispering to him that he was not the best beloved" (2.22).

His liminal position that allows him to be either lover or father also associates him with incest. In the beginning of the novel, he sees Mary as "almost a daughter" (1.5), but soon he is asking himself whether it "would it not be better for her that he should stand to her in the place of a father than a lover" (1.26). Twenty-five years her elder, he literally could be her father. When Whittlestaff tells Gordon about the engagement, the younger man's face and voice show he is thinking, "What! an old man like you to become the husband of such a girl as Mary Lawrie! Is this the purpose for which you have taken her into your house, and given her those good things of which you have boasted?" (1.127). Hints of coercion and impropriety sully Whittlestaff's love for Mary, because the boundary between husband and father is unclear for a man of fifty.

Whittlestaff's vacillation and insecurity contrast with Gordon's resolution about making Mary his wife. Though Gordon's intentions waiver when he learns Mary is engaged, after he ascertains that she secretly loves him still, he is courteous to Whittlestaff, but insistent upon his superior claim. He attempts to convince Whittlestaff that the engagement is based on obligation and will dishonor Whittlestaff if he presses Mary to fulfill her pledge. In the face of Gordon's tenacity, Whittlestaff becomes more and more hesitant, fearing that if he gives up Mary, he will be "subject to the remarks of men" who will say he "has maundered away his mind in softnesses" (1.200). His qualms about marrying and insecurity about his masculinity only increase.

Mary sees Whittlestaff as an admirable but older man in much the same way that Hetta reveres Roger Carbury. Initially, her attitude toward Whittlestaff is one of "respect, and almost veneration" (1.29); she agrees to marry him in spite of her conviction that it is "impossible" for her to ever love him (1.70). After the betrothal, however, she feels trapped with an incompatible partner, and he seems even older to her, with "no look about him as that of a thriving lover" (1.81). Even though she believes that her kisses are "his by all the rights of contract" (1.71), she draws away yet feels "in his power" (1.69), a "possession" who must obey (1.92–93). Mary tries to endure her engagement, but thinking of Gordon as her "natural" mate, suitable as an age peer, she asks herself, "Was it not in human nature that she should bind herself to the younger man, and with him go through the world, whether safely or in danger?" (2.37).

Whittlestaff's housekeeper, Mrs. Baggett, serves as an advocate for the aging suitor, but her henpecking only emasculates him further. As John Tosh explains, one of the fundamental "measures of manliness" for Victorians was "the degree of mastery exercised over others within or outside the home" (200), and Whittlestaff's deferral to his domestic's hectoring indicates unmanliness. Baggett's ideas are predicated upon outmoded concepts of masculinity, and when she urges Whittlestaff to behave as the superior because of his seniority, her strategy backfires. She takes it upon herself to teach her master that an older man can and should defeat a younger rival: "What has he to say? Only that he is twenty years younger than you. Love! Rot it!" (1.195). She adjures Whittlestaff to exert his mature authority by rallying a show of force: "A man has to be master; and when he's come to be a little old-like, he has to see that he will be master" (2.68). According to Mrs. Baggett, giving in to Gordon would cause Whittlestaff to lose respect, conclusively proving lack of manliness:

> When you've said that you'll do a thing, you ought not to go back for any other man, let him be who it may,—especially not in respect of a female. It's weak, and nobody wouldn't think a straw of you for doing it. It's some idea of being generous that you have got into your head. There ain't no real generosity about it. I say it ain't manly, and that's what a man ought to be. (2.128–29)

Whittlestaff decides to heed Mrs. Baggett's advice, telling himself that it is "not yet too late," and he resolves to adopt a "stern and unbending" attitude toward Gordon and Mary (1.201). He has to struggle to muster firmness, however, urging himself, "Surely a man could bring himself to sternness and cruelty for once in his life, when so much depended on it" (1.202). He warns himself against becoming "maunderingly soft" (1.201).

The older lover's attempt at power lapses into satire when Baggett's advice rebounds upon her, and Whittlestaff decides to practice mastery first over her. Again steeling himself against "maundering softness," he decides that "it behooved him to learn to become cruel and stern" toward Baggett and locks up the housekeeper's trunk so she cannot leave as she has vowed to do in deference to his fiancée (1.206). Their conversation about who should control her "box" becomes farcical, and though Whittlestaff does prevent her departure, Baggett's attacks on his lack of masculinity become even more vehement, making him appear weak, ordered about by his domestic.[24] By allowing Mrs. Baggett to advise and bully him, Whittlestaff calls both the strength of his love and his masculinity into question. As Mary watches him allow Baggett to interfere with their romantic affairs, she reflects that were she marrying Gordon, "[t]heir love, their happy love, would be a thing too sacred to admit of any question from any servant, almost from any parent" (1.85). Badgered by Baggett to prove his authority as the elder, instead he only reveals his weakness, and his masculinity is undermined thoroughly.

Trollope wrote *An Old Man's Love* during the 1880s as Britain was involved in the scramble for Africa, and the novel's contest for most suitable husband is predicated upon concepts of masculinity determined by empire. Many nineteenth-century bachelors viewed the colonies as sites of preparation for marriage made possible by a colonial fortune, Gordon's purpose in going to South Africa (Tosh 208). In the process of earning his fortune, Gordon also becomes the epitome of manliness. Late in the century, empire came to be seen as a way of "making men" (Tosh 209), a view expressed by the Hall sisters, neighbors to Whittlestaff, when they fawningly admire his colonial wealth, asking to see his diamonds. Blake requests an appraisal of his fiancée from Gordon, seeking "the true candid opinion of a man who has travelled about the world, and has been at the diamond-fields," because he believes that an African adventurer is sophisticated and "must have a different idea about women to what we have" (2.12). According to Blake and the Hall sisters, Gordon's travels make him a man of the world, displaying his courageousness and capacity for adventure in dangerous and exotic locales, while also establishing his prosperity.

Colonial manliness is problematic, however, for characters who interpret Gordon as unstable, uncivilized, and corrupted by Africa, in comparison to Whittlestaff's solid Britishness. Though his imperial exploits make Gordon even more manly in the eyes of society, Mrs. Baggett says he is tainted, "a savage . . . as has just come home from South Africa" (1.191). His fortune, so quickly gotten, can be as quickly lost and is not to be compared with the capital of her master, which, though lesser, is thoroughly English: "When them diamonds is gone, what's to come next? I ain't no trust in diamonds, not to live out of, but only in the funds, which is reg'lar" (1.193). To Baggett, African diamonds are "all a flash in the pan, and moonshine and dirtiness" (2.65), an attitude Whittlestaff soon takes up as well. He begins to see diamonds as "volatile, — not trustworthy" (1.199), fragile objects that "melt and come to nothing" (2.21), while his smaller income is "fixed and sure as the polar star, in the consolidated British three per cents" (1.200). Whittlestaff also accuses Gordon of being sullied by diamonds: "These things stick to the very soul of a man. They are a poison of which he cannot rid himself. They are like gambling. They make everything cheap that should be dear, and everything dear that should be cheap. I trust them not at all, — and I do not trust you, because you deal in them" (2.165–66). He worries that after Gordon has "run through" his imperial fortune "there would be nothing but poverty and distress" for Mary (1.199), and by emphasizing his thorough Britishness, Whittlestaff claims himself the superior husband.

The narratological voice furthers the perspective that South Africa has tainted Gordon. Kimberley, where Gordon has obtained his fortune, is described in racist terms that figure the British as vulnerable in and corrupted by Africa:

> I know no spot more odious in every way to a man who has learned to love the ordinary modes of English life. It is foul with dust and flies; it reeks with bad brandy; it is fed upon potted meats; it has not a tree near it. It is inhabited in part by tribes of South African niggers, who have lost all the picturesqueness of niggerdom in working for the white man's wages. The white man himself is insolent, ill-dressed, and ugly. The weather is very hot, and from morning till night there is no occupation other that [stet] that of looking for diamonds, and the works attending to it. (1.113)

Though this passage recognizes European exploitation, its assumptions of white superiority are evident in expectations of African simplicity and "picturesqueness," "savageness," lack of "civilization," and demeaning epithets for people of color, a view reiterated in Gordon's descriptions of mining. When the Hall sisters eagerly ask for a description of his diggings, he tells them, "The diamond is generally washed out of the mud by some nigger, and we have to look very sharp after him to see that he doesn't hide it under his toe-nails. It's not a very romantic kind of business from first to last" (2.40). Accusing Africans of stealing from their own soil as they work to enrich him, Gordon is astonishingly callous, but he voices the Victorian assumption of Britain's right to dominate, ignoring European looting of natural resources from indigenous peoples.

Gordon's brutal attitude toward Africa and Africans does not undermine his valorization, however, but makes him more attractive according to new standards of masculinity.[25] While early nineteenth-century anti-slavery campaigns had stimulated British sympathy for Africans, by the 1880s the "manly citizen" exchanged abolitionist goodwill for imperialist fervor, and displays of British power shored up flagging confidence in the face of imperial loses at the fin de siècle (C. Hall 538). In an 1888 essay, Meredith Townsend warns of a crisis in colonial control due to waning masculinity, that "a great change is passing over Englishmen" who fear taking authority: "They have become uncertain of themselves, afraid of their old opinions, doubtful of the true teachings of their consciences. They doubt if they have any longer any moral right to rule anyone, themselves almost included" (811).[26] Empire became "a test of the nation's virility" (Tosh 193), and "honest brutality" was expected of the "true man" in the colonies (Tosh 201). A "stiffening of masculine resolve" was considered necessary for continued rule of the empire, including a willingness to take forceful action when necessary (Tosh 201). Colonial men filled the need at home for masculine heroes as exemplars of independence, courage, and self-reliance (Tosh 193–94).

Gordon's dominance over African men and African resources is not considered callous by other characters but proves his manliness according to the standards of empire. His behavior confirms his superior Britishness and preeminence over other European men who have not ventured to the colonies, allaying anxiety about weakened masculinity and proving him to be the manliest of men. That Whittlestaff agrees with this assessment is evident when he first surrenders Mary and then attempts to shore up his faltering manhood by emulating Gordon's African feats. Gordon mentions he is selling his share in the mines, and Whittlestaff asks, "Why should not I go in your place?" (2.175). Gordon objects to the scheme, and Whittlestaff's first question is, "I am too old? I'm not a cripple, if you mean that. I don't see why I shouldn't go to the diamond-fields as well as a younger man" (2.175–76). Though Gordon answers, "It is not your age," Whittlestaff's immediate assumptions ring true—he is beyond the recuperative powers of empire, because imperialism is a young man's game played according to the dictates of the new masculinity. Gordon tells Whittlestaff, "You are a gentleman, Mr. Whittlestaff.... And of that kind that you would have your eyes picked out of your head before you had been there a week. Don't go. Take my word for it, that life will be pleasanter to you here than there, and that for you the venture would be altogether dangerous" (2.176). Whittlestaff cannot become another John Gordon, because he is a gentleman cut according to an outmoded pattern. A life centered around reading poetry, its greatest worry when the post will arrive, contrasts sharply with the younger man's imperial endeavors. Gordon's assertion that Whittlestaff is too much the soft gentleman to survive the challenges of empire proves him the more manly man, while Whittlestaff finishes in second place as a gentleman fitted only for a "pleasant" life.

Whittlestaff finally is pushed past the boundary of marriageability, surrenders his suit, and acquiesces to a paternal role. In a plot detail recycled from *The Way We Live Now*, Whittlestaff decides to "abolish himself as far as abolition might be possible" (2.31–32). After informing Gordon he relinquishes Mary, Whittlestaff goes to his room and "sobbed, alas! like a child" (2.172), the interpolated narratorial "alas" as well as the tears speaking volumes about the distance Whittlestaff's masculinity has fallen. He lapses into gentlemanly old age with visions of living in Italy with his books. He assumes the language of paternity, calling Mary "my dear" and his daughter (2.207–08) and considers giving his house and money to the younger couple (2.201). Described as "moody and silent" at her wedding, he never recovers good humor but remains mildly embittered (2.218). His assertion to Mary that "You will find me better when you come back, though I shall never cease to regret all that I have lost" (2.218) stresses failure rather than a comfortable and thriving paternity like that of John Jarndyce or Roger Carbury. The last paragraph leaves him under Mrs. Baggett's "supreme domination over all womenkind at Croker's Hall," implying that Whittlestaff has abandoned his Italian plans and accepted emasculation under her rule (2.218).

Robert M. Polhemus has asserted that "clearly Trollope's own psychology was wrapped up" in this novel (*Changing* 219), and though it is, of course, not possible to know to what extent Trollope depicted his own feelings about aging in a tale written when he was in his sixties and within months of death, his exacerbation of age's consequences between *The Way We Live Now* and *An Old Man's Love* suggests his conviction that men increasingly lost cultural capital as they aged. Perhaps more important than increased marital age disparity is the effect of a decade's difference between Whittlestaff in his fifties and Carbury in his forties. Both older suitors feel they have a strong prior claim to the younger woman, and both surrender that claim based on unsuitability due to age, but Roger is able to regain a genuine friendship with his rival and enter a prosperous paternity over the younger couple and their children while Whittlestaff is shut out. In *The Way We Live Now*, the young rival is tainted by the degenerative nature of his era, on the borders of a dishonesty that haunts the novel and concerns Trollope, though his youth ultimately makes him suitable for Hetta despite that stain. They are both part of "the way we live now" and not, like Roger, part of a past that has become obsolete. In *An Old Man's Love,* the only suggestion of Gordon's unfitness, his association with Africa, actually serves to make him a stronger candidate for Mary's affection and esteem from others in the community. While it is suggested Roger may still wed, William is beyond that possibility (Morse 138). In these novels, Trollope depicts midlife liminality stretched too thin, but *An Old Man's Love* suggests that times have become even more difficult for a middle-aged man, and fifty is too old for love. By telling two versions of the same story, Trollope demonstrates the increased devaluation of midlife men.

VI.

Though the novels I've considered are a small sampling of Victorian fiction, they suggest a pattern of increasing liability for midlife males, that somewhere in his forties, a man crosses a threshold when his marriageability is called into question, a decline ideology that increased through the century. While Frances Trollope and Charlotte Brontë champion male characters in their thirties, their maturity an asset to courting, recurring stories of age anxiety appear repeatedly from the 1850s on that depict increasing age apprehension for men in their forties and fifties. Of the suitors I've considered, the only one purported to found a successful marriage past his forties is Dickens's Dr. Strong, but that union is a sacrificial duty for Annie rather than true compatibility. These midlife suitors go far beyond William Acton's ideal marital age disparity of ten years, but they demonstrate its limits, and especially past twenty years, older suitors who seek the prime Victorian bride, a woman in youthful "bloom," are shown up by younger candidates. Dickens and Trollope wrote particularly troubled midlife plots, and their novels clearly reveal a conviction that Victorian men were challenged by aging as they reached the middle years. In Jarndyce and Clennam, Carbury and Whittlestaff, we see the emergence of Tatcho's consumer, a man who must worry about the effect of midlife aging on his "chances in life."

Chapter 3

"The Neutral Man-Woman"

Female Desexualization at Midlife

When Eliza Lynn Linton's essay "The Girl of the Period" appeared in the July 11, 1868 issue of *The Saturday Review*, her invective against "fast" young women of the upper class created a sensation, and soon the acronym "G.O.P." became a catchword. In a follow-up article published several months later, however, Linton set out to expose a yet more terrible example of modern womanhood, claiming, "Bad as the girl of the period often is, the horrible travesty of her vices in the modern matron is even worse" (50). Linton uses graphic terms to describe a middle-aged woman "engaged in her frantic struggle against time . . . obstinately refusing to grow old in spite of all that nature may say or do" (50). She continues:

> Dressed in the extreme of youthful fashion, her thinning hair dyed and crimped . . . her flaccid cheeks ruddled, her throat whitened . . . there she stands, the wretched creature who will not consent to grow old, and who will still affect to be like a fresh coquettish girl when she is nothing but *la femme passée—la femme passée et ridicule* into the bargain. (50)

Linton is horrified by this spectacle of "artificial youth" who attempts "to simulate the attractiveness of a girl" so that she can "dazzle some very young and lowborn man who is weak as well as ambitious"—a man who could be, Linton stresses, her son (50). In contrast to *la femme passée* is "the ideal middle-aged woman" who submits to aging without demur, letting the world see that her hair is "streaked with white," her skin now lacks "firmness," her body is no longer "slender," and she is unsullied by makeup. This model of midlife is attractive, according to Linton, because she acts "in harmony with her age" (50).

Linton's disgust at the middle-aged seductress is based on her conviction that the most essential female quality is maternity manifested in acts of sacrificial nurture. Every woman, whether she has given birth or not, is "essentially a mother—that is, a woman who can forget herself, who can give without asking to receive, and who ... can yet live for and in the lives of others, and find her best joy in the well-being of those about her" (50). Selfless service is "the fulfillment of woman's highest duty—the expression of that grand maternal instinct which need not necessarily include the fact of personal maternity" (50). Though abnegation was seen as an essential trait for all Victorian women, Linton makes it clear that she considers such behavior especially necessary in "women of a certain age" who must accept that their time for romance is over and leave sexual conquest behind forever.

This theory of proper matronly conduct is based on a generational exchange that was required of midlife women as they made the passage from reproductive to nonreproductive life. The average age of Victorian menopause was considered to be in the mid-forties, a point at which many women were mothers of young adults either looking for spouses or newly married.[1] Linton espouses her belief that all middle-aged women must promote the next generation by assisting their courtships, relinquishing their own marital aspirations for a desexualized matronliness. She recoils at the prospect of a middle-aged woman acting as if she has romantic possibilities akin to the next generation's: "Wife and mother as she may be, she flirts and makes love as if an honourable issue was as open to her as to her daughter" (50). There can be no "honorable issue" from midlife flirtations, because matrons are to be superseded by the amorous aspirations of the young.

Linton's essays in this series became famous, and her descriptions of women were notoriously labeled as stereotypes. Even she admitted that they were sometimes "excessive," but she also defended them as genuine and necessary attempts to teach women their weaknesses (N. Anderson 125). Linton voices a view of female midlife that was, in many ways, a majority opinion, the sexless and socially serviceable matron endorsed by medical theories of menopause in the emerging field of gynecology and represented repeatedly in Victorian fiction.[2]

While the observation by Victorian physician William Acton that most women "are not very much troubled with sexual feeling of any kind" has been shown to distort Victorian sexual attitudes (Mason 195), medical texts do suggest that after "the change of life," to be in accord with "nature" (a word that Linton repeatedly invokes), women were to age out of sexuality. In this chapter, I explore ways in which sexless service was posited as the matron's norm. The story of the single midlife woman, often a widow, who was expected to surrender her own matrimonial chances and cede the field to the younger generation is told over and over again throughout the century by medical theorists and novelists.

Of course, menopause is not discussed overtly in Victorian fiction, but intergenerational dynamics reveal a menopausal trope of sexless service as the standard for women's lives, with valorization for those who comport themselves accordingly and censure for those who do not.[3] In contrast to his sensitive treatments of male age anxiety, Charles Dickens's novels repeatedly satirize older women as inappropriate love objects who thwart the marriage plots of the young. At mid-century, Charlotte Brontë's *Shirley* (1849) upholds service as the model for midlife mothers, representing Mrs. Pryor as the maternal ideal who subsumes her future into her daughter's marital fortunes, though she questions imposing a factotum function on "old maids." Elizabeth Gaskell, however, applies the menopausal model to spinsters in *Cranford* (1851) when the Jenkyns sisters, who easily fulfill the first tenant of sexless service, become even more valorized as they struggle to satisfy the second as well, learning to assist younger women's romance plots. Margaret Oliphant demonstrates the extent to which the selfless service stereotype has become entrenched in *Miss Marjoribanks* (1865–86). When a marriageable young woman assumes a maternal guise, maneuvering a reluctant midlife widow into a love plot, Oliphant reverses and satirizes the stereotype of the ideal matron, questioning the rigidity of its parameters. Finally, H. Rider Haggard's adventure fantasy *She* (1886–87) reveals a fin-de-siècle terror of "mutton dressed as lamb" that, free from the limits of realist fiction, imagines a female age defiance of hyperbolic proportions. Though sexless service is not the only version of middle-aged women in Victorian novels, as I will explain in chapter 4, it is an extremely common convention, the sexually extinct matronly guardian a version of female midlife presented repeatedly throughout the century in tales about women "of a certain age."

I.

Thomas Laqueur argues that at the end of the eighteenth century, an epistemological shift away from the "one-sex model" reversed the belief that women existed below men in the great chain of being as a lesser type of the same created entity, their organs of generation merely an inversion of the male's. In the new "two-sex model," women were the sexual opposites of men, more reproductively complicated, as well as diseased and hysterical (149–50). As a result of defining women's bodies in terms of difference, menopause became a paramount factor in female aging, putting women at risk for physical and mental debility, though with a possibility of delivering them into a postmenopausal healthy and libido-less androgyny.[4] This view contrasts markedly with stereotypes of the early modern postmenopausal woman who, freed from reproduction, becomes sexually insatiable, a stock figure of Restoration comedy (Thane, "The Age of Old Age" 21).

Some age theorists have argued that because average female life expectancy in the nineteenth century was about forty-seven or forty-eight, women rarely lived past middle age and most of them did not even experience menopause (Lock 52). According to this theory, postmenopausal women are a twentieth-century phenomenon and were not a significant factor in the past. Margaret Lock points out, however, that this misrepresents the concept of mean life expectancy. If women lived past the dangerous years of infancy and survived into young adulthood, at twenty their life expectancy was raised into the sixties (Wilbush, "Climacteric" 2; "La Menespausie" 145). Nineteenth-century medical texts make clear that menopause was well-known in nineteenth-century England, a common and significant event of the female life cycle, and postmenopausal women were an established feature of British populations (Lock 52).

Gynecology became a distinct branch of medicine during the nineteenth century,[5] and a burgeoning medical discourse included the first British book on menopause, Edward John Tilt's *The Change of Life in Woman, in Health and Disease*, which appeared in 1857 and was republished in four editions, the final version appearing in 1883. This discourse represented women as much more vulnerable than men to the reproductive events of their bodies, female organs of generation understood to determine conduct of every area of their lives.[6] As Linton's essay makes clear, reproduction came to be seen as the most important element in women's lives, their only possible roles as "potential mothers, actual mothers, or retired mothers" (Jalland and Hooper 5). Pat Jalland and John Hooper explain that "If the primary meaning of female life was achieved through maternity, then the woman's world after reproduction was necessarily characterized by the loss of meaning" (281). In the nineteenth century, menopause took on major significance, because it ended the highly fraught reproductive stage of life and initiated a new era wherein a woman's value shifted.

Victorians considered menopause to be a fraught period that intensified the irritations and internal turmoil that had already been experienced during menstruation (Stolberg 426).[7] Physical symptoms discussed by physicians include digestive disorders, headaches, tingling, numbness, giddiness, fainting, sinking feelings, drowsiness, cold chills, and hot "flushings" (Tilt 29, 36; Webster 44; Barnes 291; Galabin 297). It is important for the purposes of this study to understand that though menopause is a biological fact, it is, in addition, culturally constructed, and the question is not as simple as whether symptoms Victorians associated with "the change" were real or imagined.[8] As Dona Davis points out, the physical signs of menopause are produced within a complex cultural matrix that can render them either "(*a*) biologically experienced but not recognized or culturally elaborated; (*b*) not recognized and therefore not experienced, or (*c*) simply not physically present in the population" (73). Anthropological studies of menopause report a surprising variation in symptoms between cultures and classes. For example, Margaret Lock reports that in Japan, the most typical symptoms of menopause or *kônenki* are shoulder stiffness, headaches, and dizziness, and the most common complaints of Western menopause—hot flashes and night sweats—are hardly reported at all (63). Nineteenth-century understanding of menopause was shaped by the idea that women's deviant reproductive organs made them subject to all sorts of disturbances, both physical and mental. The uterus was thought to have dominion over female behavior, because it directly communicated to the brain through nerves and blood vessels (Formanek 19). This "sympathy" between uterus and mind led to mental disturbances during both menstruation and menopause (Wilbush, "La Menespausie" 147). Physicians list emotional effects of menopause ranging from minor depression to fully developed hysteria and insanity (Formanek 14).[9] Accordingly, a character such as Bertha Mason could have been easily understood in terms of menopausal dementia.

Victorian women in their forties and into their fifties were judged according to a menopausal paradigm; they were considered subject to erratic behavior and health problems associated with the change of life. Adrienne Munich points out that Victorians witnessed their Queen displaying behaviors that physicians associated with menopause.[10] Especially after Albert died when she was forty-two, Victoria manifested multiple symptoms described by Tilt and other physicians as characteristically menopausal. Her excessive weight gain would have been considered typical, because unshed menstrual blood was believed to be saved in the body as fat (Munich 107). Victoria preferred unheated rooms during the coldest weather and even was known to use an open carriage on snowy days, a symptom of excessive menopausal body heat associated with the change of life (Munich 107). After the death of both Albert and John Brown, a trusted servant rumored to be her lover, her legs were paralyzed temporarily, a condition often attributed to hysteria and considered a common danger of the change of life and postmenopausal years (Munich 108). The behavior of all midlife women, however, from the Queen to the lowliest pauper, was suspect, tainted by the menopausal paradigm.

Though women were considered to be at risk for physical and mental debility during the cessation of menstruation, physicians theorized that postmenopausal women were rewarded with new vitality (Stolberg 417), an experience Margaret Mead would later term "postmenopausal zest" (Bateson 28).[11] These physicians argued that when the depression, headaches, and irritability abate, menopause is "followed by a fresh renewal of good health and strength" (Weatherly 295). Even if a woman has been weak throughout much of adult life, she can experience "a settling of the constitution" after menopause which brings about better health than she has ever enjoyed (Ashwell 149). Tilt writes that the "object" of menopause is "to endow a healthy woman with a greater degree of strength than she had previously enjoyed" (8), asserting that female longevity, which exceeds that of men, proves postmenopausal women can achieve a stronger constitution than at any other period of life (9).

However, whether or not Victorian women were rejuvenated by the end of menstruation, menopause robbed them of sexuality. Some physicians write of a mild change—at this time women become "more masculine in appearance," claims J. C. Webster (39), but others describe postmenopausal women stripped entirely of gender:

> All the characteristics of puberty and the peculiarities of women cease, the breasts collapse ... the skin shrivels ... and loses its colour and softness, and many diseases develop ... in the womb, ovaries, and breasts, which had lain dormant for years. The cheeks and neck wither, the eyes recede in their sockets, and the countenance often becomes yellow ... women become corpulent, and lose the mild peculiarities of their sex. (Ryan 287–88)

Tilt describes menopausal masculinization of both body and mind, claiming that after women finish going through "the change," "their mental faculties" take on "a more masculine character" (44). They can look on the past "safely anchored in a sure haven" of age, a vantage point from which they "understand what Madame du Deffand meant by saying, '*Autrefois, quant j'étais femme,*'" the French grand dame's reference to her premenopausal years as "in the past, when I was a woman" (Tilt 44).

The expectation that most women became sexless after menopause appears repeatedly in Victorian medical texts. Perhaps the most concise description is J. Braxton Hicks's 1877 pronouncement that at menopause women often "revert to the neutral man-woman state" and "losing sexuality and its various impulses," they become free from "sexual activity and its many demands" (475).[12] In the second (1857) and third (1871) editions of *The Change of Life*, Tilt writes that after "the great change," women "should be reminded that many intimate sources of pleasure are attached to every age, but that it would be unfair to ask of one period the pleasures allotted to another" (130).[13] In the fourth edition, Tilt becomes more technical, eliding this sentence and writing instead that with "the change" female sex organs "have a tendency to become atrophied," and there can be no "clearer indication that their hitherto appropriate stimulus is [now] likely to interfere" with the "natural process" of menopause (40). J. C. Webster argues for "variations" in "sexual appetite" at menopause: "In many women it disappears more or less completely; in some it remains unaltered, while in others it may increase in intensity." He concludes, however, "There can be very little doubt that the first of these variations is to be considered as the most common" and that increase in libido is a sign of disease that can manifest in ailments such as genital tumors (47). Tilt also links heightened sexual desire at menopause to "uterine disorders," concluding: "My experience teaches me that a marked increase of sexual impulse at the change of life is a morbid impulse" (40).[14] The idea that at "the change" women should become nonsexual was a widely held view.[15]

These theories of sexlessness had repercussions for midlife women's function in society. It was traditionally held that at menopause women entered the early stages of old age (Mangum, "Growing Old" 99; Smith Rosenberg 192), and in this new era their roles changed as well, even though many would have been only in their forties. Tilt takes issue with this position, calling it "a prejudice" to be "guarded against" (34), but the fact that he feels he must make this statement indicates that many envisioned women undergoing a major shift in age category at "the change." The idea that women began to draw near old age with menopause made them no longer sexually viable, and the middle-aged woman was to become a sexless matron and grandmother. Roe Sybylla argues that while a reproductive woman's body was constructed as diseased, fragile, and therefore in need of control, after menopause these particular rules no longer held; however, she still was kept from power by simply ceasing to be a reproductive "player" and instead, in her role as grandmother, she "invested her life in the family institution and had an interest in its maintenance" as a prop to the system (208).

This new calling of serviceable grandmother and charitable matron often was depicted as a reward for midlife women. Braxton Hicks argues that when a postmenopausal woman enters "the neutral man-woman state. . . . she becomes more capable of rendering herself useful" (475). Tilt concurs, writing at length about the "autumnal majesty . . . blended with amiability" that postmenopausal women acquire when they "find their influence fading with their charms" and decide to turn to "a less perishable empire" than mere fleshly beauty (44). He describes a point in the female life cycle wherein postmenopausal women "find an energy of self-sacrifice" and focus their efforts on others rather than themselves: "This brings me to the noblest motive to be offered to the laudable ambition of women—that of doing the greatest amount of good to the greatest number of their fellow-creatures" (44). He suggests several pastimes that are appropriate for this time of life, but the most significant are those in which matronly women heal "the discordant elements of society" through their hospitality and by "guiding many young women in the difficult paths of life" (44). He describes not only mothers in this role but also middle-aged spinsters who minister to the suffering in "country cottages" or "hovels" in the city (44). Carolyn Dever notes that by either refusing or failing to marry, the spinster "poses a challenge to the sex/gender system of 'patriarchal' power" (168), but single women compensate for their interruptions of the norm when they assist in the next generation's marriage and reproduction, thus reinforcing the status quo.

The special task of midlife women is guiding the next generation's mating, a job that requires them to put aside their own attractions. Trollope's *The Small House at Allington* (1862–64) describes this mind-set in the Widow Dale: "she had been a beauty; according to my taste, was still very lovely; but certainly at this time of life, she, a widow of fifteen years' standing, with two grown-up daughters, took no pride in her beauty" (22). Instead, as the worthy menopausal mother, she took as the "theory of her life . . . that she should bury herself in order that her daughters might live well above ground" (23). In this metaphorical "burial," the midlife mother becomes sacrificial compost, providing nutriment to the next generation while she quietly deteriorates. Though the narrator also asserts that at age forty, Mrs. Dale can and should be "young in spirit" (24), her primary duty is to her daughters, as she tells Bell in regard to her own and Lily's future, "What else have I to look for but that she and you should both be happy?" (200).

As Amy M. King points out, the sexual reproduction of plants through flowers, discovered by Carolus Linnaeus in the eighteenth century, appears in Victorian novels as a botanical vernacular of bloom used to describe youthful female sexuality (8). The ambiguous language of botany made sexual descriptions possible in realist fiction while upholding standards of decorum (King 7); bloom became such an effective rhetorical device, it was used to the point of cliché by mid-century (King 133). I would like to add that the language of bloom also was used to describe the sexuality of older women, the words "fading" and "withered" frequently employed to indicate aging out of erotic viability, because sexuality was considered inappropriate and unlovely in women "of a certain age."

Eliza Lynn Linton's condemnation of flirtatious matrons, medical prescriptions of sexlessness, ubiquitous metaphors of withering: all reveal and contribute to entrenched menopausal expectations in Victorian culture and its fictions. Middle-aged women in novels who fail to live up to its dictates are denigrated, chastised, ridiculed, or even feared for daring to defy the precepts of sexless service. However, those who comport themselves as sexually neutered menopausal matrons, fulfilling their duty to serve others, are celebrated as good mothers and esteemed spinsters, exemplars of exceptional womanhood, beloved by the entire community.

II.

The novels of Charles Dickens provide excellent examples of the midlife woman who is satirized for failing the menopausal standard. Dickens does not always vilify amorous midlife women, as evinced by the risible yet pleasingly companionate marriage of Wemmick and Miss Skiffins in *Great Expectations*. For the most part, however, when Dickensian matrons seek their own matrimonial fortunes, they are vilified as comedic antagonists to younger women's marriage plots, often those of their daughters, and judged in accordance with the model of sexless service that medical literature suggests for the postmenopausal woman. Mrs. Nickleby in *Nicholas Nickleby* (1839), Mrs. Skewton in *Dombey and Son* (1848), Miss Sparsit in *Hard Times* (1854), and Miss Havisham in *Great Expectations* (1861) are depicted as absolutely outside any possibility for credible romance and abusive to younger women for even trying, because they neglect their responsibility to foster youthful marriage plots.

The well-meaning but foolish mother of Nicholas and Kate Nickleby fails both parts of the postmenopausal ideal, neither effectively serviceable nor willingly sexless. Blind to the fact that she has ruined her husband's career and shortened his life, her vanity and deficient judgment also imperil her daughter's future (Slater 21). Instead of assisting her daughter's chances on the marriage market she instead places her in danger, advancing a disastrous match with an unworthy man. Dickens shows us again and again that Kate is threatened not only by the plans of her avaricious and emotionally conflicted uncle but also by her foolish and insensitive mother. Because Mrs. Nickleby lacks sense, prudence, and wisdom, she cannot be of service, but places her daughter in harm's way.

Mrs. Nickleby's constant misjudgments frequently endanger Kate. When she first meets the villainous Ralph Nickleby, she decides he has an "honest face," and, following his advice, puts her children in abusive work environments (301). Approving Kate's job at the Mantalini's shop, she is unruffled by the necessity for her daughter to work outside the domestic sphere. There, Kate not only is exposed to the vulgar and foolish ostentation of her employers, comedic to the reader while appalling to Kate, but also is forced into what would have been considered unladylike situations, as she models hats, is ogled by men, made the subject of gossip, and treated with condescension. Mrs. Nickleby dreams that Kate will be taken into partnership, and when the establishment fails, pushes her into working with the vain and silly Mrs. Wititterly, where she is again thrust into compromising situations.

Mrs. Nickleby fantasizes about matches for her daughter that are clearly not in Kate's best interest. First, she calculates probable deaths for the hypochondriac Julia Wititterly, envisioning Kate as the widower's bride. Then, the proverbial hen leading a predator to her coop, she furnishes the scheming and ungentlemanly Sir Mulberry Hawk with directions to her house. Her worst errors in judgment are evident in daydreams about the conniving Sir Mulberry and dissipated Lord Frederick Verisopht as delightful matches for Kate, and, predictably, she chooses the consummate scoundrel Hawk as the better husband. Her aspirations are not only misguided but self-serving, apparent when she envisions Kate as Lady Mulberry Hawk with her own picture featured in the annuals, mother of a celebrated lady (419).

Mrs. Nickleby most clearly falls short of the sexless service ideal, however, in her mock love affair. Though she seems to resist modestly when "the gentleman in the small-clothes" makes advances, her constant misreading of the situation is ridiculous and vain, revealing how gravely she lacks the qualities of the good menopausal mother. She makes too much of her current charms as well as her past conquests, telling the shocked Kate she has had a dozen suitors (619). She clearly thinks herself worthy of her neighbor's attentions, not considering herself to have aged out of desirability.

Her neighbor's courting techniques—tossing cucumbers over her fence and stuffing himself down her chimney—are phallic advances of comedic insanity, but Mrs. Nickleby misreads them as professions of true love. The narrator satirizes her response in terms of postmenopausal expectations: amidst her protests that she can never remarry while she has an unmarried daughter (568), Mrs. Nickleby adds "juvenile ornaments" to her mourning that transform respect for the dead "into signals of very slaughterous and killing designs upon the living" (615). Though Nicholas cautions that their neighbor's overtures are "unworthy of a serious thought" to "one of your age and condition," Mrs. Nickleby thinks that his attentions are "flattering . . . at this time of day" (570). She admits her suitor's lunacy only when he rejects her and then turns his favor on a spinster, Miss LaCreevy, and even then she interprets his new quest as a breakdown caused by her rebuff (745). Conflating her midlife romance with psychosis, Dickens indicates that courting a woman with marriageable children is not merely amusing behavior, but outright insanity.

Mrs. Nickleby also falls short of the menopausal ideal by thinking she appears too young for motherhood, considering herself as nubile as Kate. After receiving her neighbor's ardent vegetable missiles, she preens and strolls in front of a mirror, reminded of someone's comment when Nicholas was a child that at "one-and-twenty he would have more the appearance of her brother than her son" (570). Mrs. Nickleby also protests disingenuously that when acquaintances have mistaken her for Kate "no doubt the people were very foolish and perhaps ought to have known better, but still they did take me for her, and of course that was no fault of mine and it would be very hard indeed if I was to be made responsible for it" (744). Her defensive response reveals her certain knowledge that a mother should not pose as her daughter's sister, but gracefully retire to the sidelines when her child reaches marriageability. As Mrs. Nickleby glories in her purported youthfulness and entertains a satirical courtship, she reveals her unwillingness to acquiesce.

As Robert L. Patten points out, this is a story about parental lack, children suffering because their parents do not provide the requisite guidance and support necessary to achieve healthy adulthood. This is especially true in the case of Mrs. Nickleby, who "has the right plot (marriage and confirmed middle-class status for her children and herself) constantly on her lips and in what passes for her mind" but is "only at the end willing to exchange the marriage plot with the madman next door for a parenting plot on behalf of Nicholas and Kate" (28). Her belief that she retains romantic viability makes her a joke in Dickens, who castigates Mrs. Nickleby for not being the proper nonsexual and serviceable mother, creating not only a buffoon, but a negligent, hazardous parent.

Dickens intensifies his spoof on midlife women who fail to surrender their sexuality and serve the next generation in *Dombey and Son* with Mrs. Skewton, an aging and grotesque femme fatale. At age seventy, she is well past menopause and should have been behaving postmenopausally for years, but her nickname, "Cleopatra," one of Dickens's many satirical jabs at her role as coquette, makes evident that she has not retired from the field. As she vends her daughter on the marriage market, her postmenopausal infractions are even greater than Mrs. Nickleby's, because she is no longer in middle age but elderly. Skewton attempts to marry off her daughter, the young widow Edith Granger, to a rich man, egregiously transgressing the selfless service paradigm both by overtly striving to be treated as marriageable and in her attempts to gain wealth for herself by arranging a lucrative match for Edith. Trying to seduce men and parley her daughter on the marriage market, Skewton is presented not merely as a buffoon but a monstrous, unnatural woman and unworthy mother, her advanced age affording Dickens an opportunity to hyperbolize her violations.

Mrs. Skewton's breaches of age-appropriate manner and dress are a constant source of humor: "The discrepancy between Mrs. Skewton's fresh enthusiasm of words, and forlornly faded manner, was hardly less observable than that between her age, which was about seventy, and her dress, which would have been youthful for twenty-seven" (306). Dickens contrasts her "juvenile" air with her wheeled chair pushed by a "butting page," appropriately named Withers (305–06). The narrator highlights her affected and unnatural appearance by her protests against artifice—"We are so dreadfully artificial. . . . I want Nature everywhere" (307)—and by reiteration, as she goes about "slightly settling her false curls and false eyebrows . . . and showing her false teeth, set off by her false complexion" (306). Dickens's focus on "falseness"—her cosmetics, dentures, and wigs—emphasizes that her attempts to hide age actually have the opposite effect.

Skewton especially violates standards for aging women when she flirts in a parodic version of courting. The object of her attentions is Major Joe Bagstock, himself presented as comedically aging, having "arrived at what is called in polite literature, the grand meridian of life, and was proceeding on his journey downhill with hardly any throat" (91). Skewton is coy with Bagstock, calling him names such as "shocking bear" (310), "false creature" (305), and "perfidious goblin" (306). He returns the flirtation by introducing her as one who "makes havoc in the heart of old Josh" (306). Though he feigns attraction, Bagstock does not consider her either authentically attractive or a serious matrimonial prospect, however, telling Dombey that she is too old and directing his attention toward Edith. Placing herself in a position where she is compared to her daughter, Skewton demonstrates her failure as a worthy matron.

Skewton is false not just in her makeup and wigs, not only in her coquettish attentions to the Major, but also in her selfish actions and avaricious motives. Beneath a thin facade of delicacy, she schemes with Bagstock to marry Edith to Dombey, flirting all the while: ". . . I can hardly approach a topic so excessively momentous to my dearest Edith without a feeling of faintness. Nevertheless, bad man, as you have boldly remarked upon it, and as it has occasioned me great anguish . . . I will not shrink from my duty" (389). When the Major comments that Dombey is "a great catch," she shrieks, "Oh, mercenary wretch! . . . I am shocked," but when he persists that Dombey is "in earnest" she is all attention, asking, "You really think so, my dear Major?" (392).

Though the emotionally frozen Edith is indifferent to any match, her outrage at her mother registers how far Skewton misses the maternal mark. Edith protests angrily that she has been denied a childhood, "taught to scheme and plot when children play." She describes Skewton's mothering as inhumane and mercantile: "There is no slave in a market; there is no horse in a fair: so shown and offered and examined and paraded, Mother, as I have been for ten shameful years" (417). Since coming out in society, she has felt "hawked and vended here and there until the last grain of self-respect is dead within me" (418).

A grasping gold digger who induces Edith to sell herself in marriage, Skewton serves her own ends instead of acting for her daughter's happiness.

Her outrageous claims of self-sacrifice—for example, "My whole existence is bound up in my sweetest Edith" (390)—satirize her self-involvement. She uses her daughter's attractions in an attempt to bolster her own, claiming, "Edith...who is the perfect Pearl of my life, is said to resemble me. I believe we *are* alike" (391). She sets up a similar but even more hyperbolic comparison between herself and fourteen-year-old Florence, ordering a copy of the girl's dress for Edith's wedding, to which the sycophantic dressmaker responds that "all the world will take her for the young lady's sister" (456). Instead of being the sexless, serviceable dowager, advising and assisting younger women through the vicissitudes of the marriage market, Mrs. Skewton is an exaggerated picture of grasping self-service and ridiculous attempts at sexuality.

When Skewton has a stroke that affects her coordination and speech, her coquettish theatrics are pushed to the height of grotesquerie. She has her hair curled and "a little artificial bloom dropped in the hollow caverns of her cheeks," and the descriptions become macabre: "It was a tremendous sight to see this old woman in her finery leering and mincing at Death" (559). She seems to be even "more cunning and false than before," insisting that her daughter's marriage is "proof of her being an incomparable mother" (560), while Edith is living in luxurious degradation. Twisting the matronly maternal into villainy, Skewton ruins the life of the daughter she is supposed to serve.

Another Dickensian version of the aberrant matron appears in *Hard Times,* when Mrs. Sparsit, a childless widow, becomes the jealous and comedic rival of a young woman's romance. We are not told Sparsit's age (though we do know that she has been a widow since she was thirty-nine)—she is introduced merely as "an elderly lady," but she is presented as a contemporary of Josiah Bounderby who "presides over his establishment" as a paid housekeeper and hostess (35). Sparsit's attempts to win Bounderby for herself, despite his intention to marry Louisa, are satirized from her first appearance in the novel, as she and Josiah sit at breakfast. When Bounderby brings up the younger woman, Sparsit comments that he is "quite another father to Louisa," and her agitation is clear "as she bent her again contracted eyebrows over her steaming cup, [and] rather looked as if her classical countenance were invoking the infernal gods" (38). Bounderby then begins to expound upon his past sufferings, and she responds, "I hope I have learnt how to accommodate myself to the changes of life" (39). Though her words overtly refer to reversals of fortune, she also invokes the Victorian term "change of life," a perhaps unconscious acknowledgement that her value has been lessened as a postmenopausal woman. After this conversation ends, "...Mrs. Sparsit got behind her eyebrows and meditated in the gloom of that retreat, all the morning" (41), lampooned as ridiculous and futile in her scheming as a desexualized and unmarriageable old woman.

Sparsit's machinations are a running gag throughout the book, both
before and after Bounderby's wedding, the basis for satire on age and
romance. Attempting to transcend the gendered double standard that would
make Bounderby marriageable while she is not, Sparsit sets out to prove
that, as his age peer, she would be the better wife, a campaign for which she
is ridiculed and castigated. Visiting the Bounderbys at home, she persists in
calling Louisa "Miss Gradgrind" because "to persuade herself that the young
lady whom she had had the happiness of knowing from a child could be
really and truly Mrs. Bounderby, she found almost impossible . . . the more
she thought about it, the more impossible it appeared; 'the differences,' she
observed, 'being such' " (142). The narrator implies that Bounderby secretly
may suspect the same—when Stephen Blackpool describes his alcoholic wife,
she comments, "I inferred, from its being so miserable a marriage, that it
was probably an unequal one in point of years," and Bounderby "looked
very hard at the good lady in a sidelong way that had an odd sheepishness
about it" (59). Her malicious ill-intent fuels Tom's sarcasm, who parodies
the maternal standard she fails to meet: "Mother Sparsit's feeling for Loo
is more than admiration. . . . Say affection and devotion. Mother Sparsit
never set her cap at Bounderby when he was a bachelor. Oh no!" (105).
Sparsit continues to insinuate herself into Bounderby's good graces as a
sympathetic figure while Louisa shows only indifference.

The opposite of the nurturing matron, she delights in and advances
Louisa's ruin. Represented in metaphorical terms as "Mrs. Sparsit's Staircase," the title of chapter 2.10, Louisa's fall is depicted as a product of
Sparsit's mental powers: "She erected in her mind a mighty Staircase, with
a dark pit of shame and ruin at the bottom; and down those stairs, from
day to day and hour to hour, she saw Louisa coming" (153). Tracking
Louisa to her forest assignation with Harthouse, she stands in the rain
as a hag-like figure of malevolence: her "white stockings were of many
colors, green predominating; prickly things were in her shoes; caterpillars
slung themselves, in hammocks of their own making, from various parts
of her dress; rills ran from her bonnet, and her roman nose" (161), insects,
damp, and mold characterizing her decay. As ever, she makes an excellent
target for ridicule of age: "Regarded as a classical ruin, Mrs. Sparsit was
an interesting spectacle at her journey's end" (177). Sparsit hastens to tell
Bounderby her discoveries, and, having "exploded the combustibles with
which she was charged," she "blew up" by swooning onto Bounderby's
shoulder (177), her enmity toward Louisa proving volatile enough to cause
her own descent that parallels Louisia's. After leading Bounderby errone-
ously to believe that Louisa has run away with Harthouse when she has,
in actuality, returned to her father's house, Sparsit receives her just reward.
Utterly despised by Bounderby, she is dispatched weeping from the scene,
unemployed and homeless (179).

Great Expectations is even more severe on the aging spinster who ruins matrimonial prospects for the younger generation. Miss Havisham is the epitome of the aging female grotesque. An heiress jilted by her fiancé twenty-five years before the book opens, when Pip first meets her she is, according to Dickens's notes, in her mid-fifties but is presented as a disturbing blend of "residual youth and moribund old age," associated with decay and the grave (Walsh 73). Her derelict wedding finery becomes a metonymic representation for the elderly body near death, as Pip reports, "the bride within the bridal dress had withered like the dress. . . . the dress had been put upon the rounded figure of a young woman, and . . . the figure upon which it now hung loose, had shrunk to skin and bone" until it had become a "wax-work and skeleton" (57). In Pip's eyes, her "withered bridal dress" resembles "grave-clothes" and "the long veil . . . a shroud" (59). This decay is extended in her surroundings, perhaps the most memorable detail moldering remains of the bridal feast with spiders crawling in and out of the wedding cake's dried husk. By obstinately clinging to a decomposed wedding-that-never-was, Havisham "keeps the idea of a sexual self always before her, gleefully watching the gap widen between bridal promise and atrophied reality" (Walsh 91). Aged far in excess of actual years, she portrays midlife decline hyperbolically, as a monstrous living death.

Havisham performs an exact reversal of both tenants of sexless service. Persistently wearing her wedding garb as it disintegrates on her body, she is the blooming bride deteriorated by age into a freakish aberration of womanhood. While her parodic moldering sexlessness may cause her acquaintances a psychic shock, Havisham's perversion of the second component of the menopausal paradigm has more lasting effects—for Pip, who imagines she fulfills her matronly duty as his secret patroness (Walsh 74), but even more for her adopted daughter, Estella. From the first time he meets the duo, Pip is subjected to Havisham's revenge scheme, luring men to adore her irresistibly beautiful yet frigid daughter. Though she later tells Pip, "when she first came to me, I meant to save her from misery like my own," she confesses that lust for vengeance soon overcame these intentions: "as she grew, and promised to be very beautiful, I gradually did worse . . . I stole her heart away and put ice in its place" (395).

Havisham's emotional voyeurism thrives, from Pip's first visit when she urges Estella, "break his heart" and "beggar him" (59), to her increasingly "ravenous intensity" as she goads and queries Pip, "Love her, love her, love her! How does she use you?" (237). She is depicted as "devouring the beautiful creature she had reared," both through her "dreadful" devotion for and use of Estella to "attract and torment and do mischief" to all men (298). Havisham's frigidity training is successful, and Estella informs Pip, ". . . I have no heart. . . . I have no softness there, no—sympathy—sentiment—nonsense" (235). When Pip finally confesses his love, she is "perfectly unmoved" (358). He objects, "You fling yourself away upon a brute," as she prepares to marry the dull and cruel Bentley Drummle, but her deadened affect allows her to do so without a qualm (359). Estella parallels Edith Dombey, their frigid and contemptuous demeanor a direct result of maternal influence, mothered by women who do not nurture and promote their welfare but use the younger generation for their own ends. While Mrs. Skewton is audaciously ridiculous, Miss Havisham develops "the intensity of a mind mortally hurt and diseased" (298), an insanity that results from perverting the maternal to an extreme.

Dickens reinforces sexless service as the norm when Havisham ultimately repents for having transgressed its final tenant so thoroughly. She accuses Estella of being a "stock and stone," a "cold, cold heart" toward her, and the daughter replies, "I am what you have made me" (300). Havisham repents when she realizes that, in extinguishing all her daughter's affections, she has prevented Estella from loving even her own adoptive mother. Havisham watches the scene with a "ghastly look" as Estella announces to Pip her loveless marriage (359). After that point, she begins to have a fearful "new expression on her face" when she looks at Pip and tells him she is "not all stone" (391). When Pip forgives her, she begins crying and repeating, "What have I done!"—her refrain until death (394). She also begins to make amends with the help of Pip, secretly financing Herbert Pocket's career and bequeathing his father Matthew thousands of pounds, rewarding the only relatives who have not been avaricious. The fire of resentment is not so easily assuaged, however. Havisham continues to wear the tattered remains of her wedding dress, indicating either that her repentance is partial or that her anger is too strong and has left too entrenched a mark to be completely reversed. The withered gown becomes her doom, catching fire and burning her to death.

Havisham's attempt to pervert motherly service is assuaged to a certain extent by a suggestion at the novel's end that Estella may heal. Abused by Drummle and then widowed, she meets Pip on the razed remains of Satis House and no longer claims she cannot love. Instead, her eyes have a "saddened and softened light" and her "once insensible hand" has a "friendly touch" (477). She has learned to value what she once "had thrown away," and concedes that now ". . . I have given it a place in my heart" (478). In the original ending of the novel, Dickens marries Estella to "a Shropshire doctor" who, before Drummle's death, intervened to stop the abuse (Cardwell 481). In the conclusion that Dickens ultimately chose, however, Estella states that she and Pip will "continue friends apart," but he undermines this claim in the last sentence, as they leave the ruins in a "broad expanse of tranquil light" and Pip sees "the shadow of no parting from her" (479). In both endings, Estella allows herself to be loved by a caring man, suggesting that her icy center has been replaced by a warm human heart. Though Havisham has been a parasite rather than a resource, her adopted daughter does overcome the ruin her mother caused, at least to a certain extent.

In the cases of Nickleby, Skewton, and Havisham the older woman must either serve a daughter or become a monstrosity. These postmenopausal mothers expose a troubling commodification of reproductive sex, as they vend younger females like bordello madams in mercantile images of the marriage market that permeate Dickens's caricatures of aging women. Dickens poses little possibility of a healthy or socially valorized romantic love for women nearing or past the age of menopause. His harsh female depictions continued throughout his career, while he showed a ready sympathy for male midlife struggles, as I have discussed in chapter 2.[16] In contrast to Dickens's satires on the matron gone wrong, Brontë and Gaskell are far kinder to women "of a certain age."

III.

Charlotte Brontë endorses sexless service for mothers in *Shirley* (1849), describing the ideal matron whose life centers around her daughter's marital success, but she protests its tyranny over single women. At the outset of Brontë's novel, the separated and then widowed mother of Caroline Helstone is a failure, because while she was married to the "man-tiger" James Helstone, his cruel treatment caused her to abandon her daughter and become an "unnatural parent," as she describes herself (452, 437). When she first appears in *Shirley*, Agnes Grey Helstone is using a name from her mother's family, Mrs. Pryor, to hide her true identity, and even though she has been widowed ten years, and was estranged from her husband for several years before he died, she still wears mourning (234). By the time she reaches menopausal age, she has long been settled into a protracted widowhood, consigning herself to decline. Though she possesses "naturally young-looking features," she appears "matronly," "obsolete" and "eccentric," with "no youthful aspect, nor apparently the wish to assume it" (195). She sees herself as old, confessing "my complexion—my very features are changed; my hair, my style of dress—everything is altered" (438). She has become taciturn and cold, consigning herself to decline because she believes, as she says, that "it is late to begin" to find a happy life (381).

After revealing herself as Caroline's mother, Agnes becomes a youthful and active woman, but her transformation always is conducted in terms of serving her daughter. When Caroline complains that she dresses like a grandmother but could be young and pretty, Mrs. Pryor wants to buy a dress for her daughter instead of herself (447). Caroline insists on sewing dresses for her mother, saying, "I will not let her be old-fashioned," and, induced to wear the new finery to please her daughter, Agnes appears charming and attractive (599). When Robert Moore calls Agnes "the old lady," Caroline objects, "She is not old" but then adds, "She does not pretend to be young," presenting her mother in an appropriately middling state (599). Caroline describes her as the ideal matron: "she is charming to talk to: full of wisdom; ripe in judgment; rich in information; exhaustless in stores her observant faculties have quietly amassed" (599). Agnes has value due to her experience, and she becomes the ideal postmenopausal mother when she uses that experience to mentor her daughter.

Agnes reaches her height as maternal paragon when she becomes instrumental in Caroline's love plot, assisting with the romance and therefore the reproductivity of her daughter. Mrs. Pryor is the first one Robert Moore asks when he is ready to propose to Caroline, and she and Robert work out the details of the marriage before her daughter even knows of his intentions. As the quintessential good mother, Mrs. Pryor obtains true happiness by moving into Robert and Caroline's house, retaining a private room and her own servant, giving them privacy yet always on-call to the newly wedded couple. In the role of helpful, selfless elder, she will be a suitable grandmother, because her desire is not for her own love plot but the happiness of the next generation. Agnes's existence is ancillary to Caroline's plot, the post-reproductive woman who lives for her children.

Brontë contrasts this embodiment of the ideal midlife woman with the plight of spinsters, a group she depicts as grossly abused by Victorian society, because they are held to the same standard as matrons, yet maligned instead of praised. Specifically equating the maternal widow and childless spinster, Brontë seats Mrs. Pryor on a sofa between Miss Mann and Miss Ainley, presenting all three in terms of sexless service: "They formed a trio which the gay and thoughtless would have scorned, indeed, as quite worthless and unattractive—a middle-aged widow and two plain spectacled old maids—yet which had its own quiet value, as many a suffering and friendless human being knew" (271). Brontë describes these spinsters in precisely the same terms as Braxton Hicks uses to delineate the menopausal model—the "neutral man-woman" who assist others, a conflation that suggests all women eventually will take on the spinster's role, desexualized servants to their families and community.[17]

Brontë objects to such an alignment, however, stressing that spinsters are not valorized like mothers but unfairly denigrated. Several men in the novel function as mouthpieces for cultural insensitivity toward aging women. Robert tells Hiram Yorke, that he would "rather break stones on the road" than "take an old woman," a sentiment to which York responds, "So would

I" (164). Roslyn Belkin points out a correlation that Robert Moore makes between obsolete workers and spinsters: "Like the labourers he no longer needs, they have no market value and are, therefore, to be treated as though they, too, were 'machines,' rather than human beings. Indeed, when an elderly spinster crosses his path, however innocently, Moore appears at his most inhumane, his behaviour ranging from childish pettiness to outright aversion and scorn" (53). Belkin argues that men in *Shirley* such as Moore, Helstone, and Yorke evaluate older women according to a "tradesman mentality" that assesses them for their usefulness, demonstrating that though they are "men of principle" they also "have been morally eroded by . . . selfishness" in their attitudes toward aging, unmarried women (56).

Brontë configures Victorian stereotypes about old maids differently depending on whether they are held by males or females—unattractive looks commented upon by men and ceaseless acts of service noticed and praised by women. The bitter and cantankerous Miss Mann serves as a prime example of the desexualized "old maid." Her name itself identifies her androgynous state—though she is a woman, she is also "Mann," not entirely female. Moore cruelly compares her to his youthful love interest, Caroline Helstone: "he had amused himself with comparing fair youth—delicate and attractive—with shrivelled eld, livid and loveless, and in jestingly repeating to a smiling girl the vinegar discourse of a cankered old maid" (177). Miss Mann is made repulsive by Moore's words, her (non)sexuality a spreading sore and sour acid, and he uses his easy assumption of sexlessness to amuse himself while thinking of Caroline's younger body. Caroline realizes however: "she had passed alone through protracted scenes of suffering, exercised rigid self-denial, made large sacrifices of time, money, health for those who had repaid her only by ingratitude" (179). For Caroline, Miss Mann is an exemplar, a model of selflessness who deserves praise.

In Miss Ainley, stereotypical spinsterish qualities are even more extreme. Age has increased her already-evident unattractiveness: "In her first youth she must have been ugly; now, at the age of fifty, she was *very* ugly" (181)—an outer repulsiveness that coexists with great inner virtues of selflessness: "She talked never of herself—always of others. Their faults she passed over; her theme was their wants, which she sought to supply; their sufferings, which she longed to alleviate" (182). Caroline is inspired to "reverence" by her (183), and Brontë goes so far as deifying her when Cyril Hall, the vicar of Nunnely, says that "her life came nearer the life of Christ, than that of any other human being he had ever met with" (183).

These passages echo an admiring defense of middle-aged spinsters Brontë wrote three years before *Shirley* was published. She mentions that the subject had been much on her mind, due in part, no doubt, to her thirtieth birthday which was looming in April, an event of portent to her as an unmarried woman.[13] In this letter, Brontë describes middle-aged spinsters not only as examples to women but also as the persons most worthy of admiration by all Victorians:

> it seems that even "a lone woman" can be happy, as well as cher-
> ished wives and proud mothers—I am glad of that—I speculate
> much on the existence of unmarried and never-to-be married
> women nowadays, and I have already got to the point of con-
> sidering that there is no more respectable character on this earth
> than an unmarried woman who makes her own way through life
> quietly, perseveringly—without support of husband or brother,
> and who, having attained the age of 45 or upwards—retains in
> her possession a well-regulated mind—a disposition to enjoy
> simple pleasures—fortitude to support inevitable pains, sympathy
> with the sufferings of others, and willingness to relieve want as
> far as her means extend. (Brontë, "Wooler" 77)

Brontë dismisses the idea that the highest calling of all women is mother-
hood, endorsing a single woman's right to be admired as a worthy member of society whose autonomy provides an existence perhaps more sane and fulfilling than that of a married sister. Brontë returns to this theme in *Shirley*, defending single women's right to independence and self possession that contrasts with the maternal selflessness necessary in Mrs. Pryor. She has Caroline vindicate spinsters as she considers whether she will remain unmarried:

> What is my place in the world?.... that is the question which
> most old maids are puzzled to solve: other people solve it for
> them by saying, "Your place is to do good to others, to be
> helpful whenever help is wanted." That is right in some mea-
> sure, and a very convenient doctrine.... I perceive that certain
> sets of human beings are very apt to maintain that other sets
> should give up their lives to them and their service, and then
> they requite them by praise.... Is this enough? Is it to live? Is
> there not a terrible hollowness, mockery, want, craving, in that
> existence which is given away to others, for want of something
> of your own to bestow it on?... Does virtue lie in abnegation
> of self? I do not believe it. (174)

Brontë suggests that single women need a larger scope of existence, should be able to consider their own needs and desires rather than constantly serving their families and community. Instead of consigning all women at menopause to the service model, Brontë protests the paradigm, her strenuous objections testimony to its pervasive power. While she portrays Agnes Helstone's sacrifice as natural and appropriate in a midlife mother whose life is configured around reproduction and assisting her offspring, Brontë champions a different standard for unmarried women, arguing they should be free from reproductive paradigms that were so dominant in Victorian Britain, possessing instead an independent existence, valued as worthy in their own right.

IV.

In contrast to Brontë, Elizabeth Gaskell upholds sexless service as a standard not only for mothers, but also for all women, when she requires spinsters to fulfill both of its tenets in Cranford (1851–53). Critics such as Nina Auerbach and Lisa Niles view Cranford's spinsters as empowered women in a supportive community, but Laura Fasick points out ways in which they are caught in a culture of devaluation both for their marital status and their age.[19] Gaskell describes Miss Deborah Jenkyns and her sister Miss Mattie with affectionate humor as postmenopausal old maids who are, for the most part, content as single women, but in order to assure continued validation by village society and their reign as Cranford's queens, the sisters must conform to the postmenopausal paradigm. Though their virginal sexlessness is assumed, they also must overcome matrimonial aversion sufficiently to foster a love plot in the younger generation. Cranford society further reinforces the menopausal model by resisting a midlife marriage in their midst as improper, admiring instead a sexless sibling household.

The Jenkyns sisters easily fulfill expectations that, as postmenopausal women, they are sexless. Aging is a recurrent theme in this novel set in an early-century village where the past is venerated and, though time has not exactly stopped, proceeds at a leisurely crawl. When Mary Smith visits one summer, she finds, "There had been neither births, deaths, nor marriages since I was there last. Everybody lived in the same house, and wore pretty nearly the same well-preserved, old-fashioned clothes. The greatest event was, that Miss Jenkynses had purchased a new carpet for the drawing-room" (13). In accord with their environment, the sisters are associated with old ways and old things. Deborah insistently champions the works of Johnson as superior to those of Dickens,[20] and her piano, which "had been a spinet in its youth" and is now "an old cracked" instrument, serves as a metaphor for her body (7). Miss Mattie is only fifty-one as the book opens, but her maid Martha guesses her age at close to sixty (36). Both sisters are perceived as elderly women.

The demands of the menopausal model are not satisfied merely by sexless spinsterhood, however.[21] The sisters live in a female-dominated, anti-male country town where "[a] man . . . is *so* in the way" (1), and, while the assertive elder sister Deborah often is critical of men, and the gentle Miss Mattie finds them intimidating, each must undergo a change of heart in order to assist younger women in finding proper mates. Each sister is converted to a marital mentor by the death of a man she might have married, and she assumes the role of patron to a reproductive union which she has not been able to accomplish for herself. Gaskell, who valued motherhood as the apotheosis of womanhood (Fenwick 415), put each sister in a substitute maternal role, bringing about the marriage of a younger woman who then herself becomes a mother, so that the Jenkyns comply by proxy with societal norms that figure all women as mothers.

Deborah serves as a surrogate parent of sorts to Jessie Brown after her father dies, a man who has been the object of Deborah's particular attention. Though there has been no suggestion of a romance between the two, Brown is the closest that she comes to having a male partner. She sees in him a worthy adversary, her spirited attacks on his literary taste a feisty flirtation of which he genially remains unaware. He serves as the sisters' "tame man about the house," allowed into their inner sanctum outside the usual hours of social calls to adjust their smoking chimney flue (4).

As she assists her young protégée, Deborah becomes a "neutral man-woman" and is described in androgynous terms (Braxton Hicks 475).[22] As Jessie's self-appointed guardian, she proclaims, "It is not fit for you to go alone. It would be against both propriety and humanity were I to allow it" (18). She dons her characteristic hat, a "hybrid bonnet, half–helmet, half–jockey cap" (18), both feminine covering and warrior's protection, an accessory that represents her postmenopausal lack of femininity. Deborah supports the grief-stricken young woman at the funeral "with a tender, indulgent firmness which was invaluable, allowing her to weep her passionate fill before they left" (18).

Next, Jessie's sister dies, and "equipped in her helmet bonnet" of androgynous service (18), Deborah both assists at the deathbed and installs Jessie in the Jenkyns house after a second funeral (20). At thirty, the impoverished Jessie is nearing spinsterhood. As she sits in the Jenkyns living room pondering her prospects, Deborah countermands her plans for nursing, housekeeping or sales, and stands over the young woman "like a dragoon" as she eats—martial yet nurturing, a patriarchal matriarch (20). Deborah facilitates Jessie's reunion with her former lover, Major Gordon, who had known her as "a sweet-looking, blooming girl of eighteen" and been rebuffed because of Jessie's devotion to her ailing sister (21). The deus ex machina, who conveniently solves Jessie's problems, is summoned by

Deborah, her stumbling announcement of his arrival revealing the extent to which matchmaking challenges her staid dignity and even incites the magisterial Jenkyns to nervous prevarication: "I have been so much startled—no, I've not been at all startled—don't mind me, my dear Miss Jessie—I've been very much surprised—in fact, I've had a caller, whom you knew once, my dear Miss Jessie—" (20). As matriarch, Deborah might have steered Jessie into a confirmed spinsterhood like that of the Cranfordian Amazons, but she fulfills her responsibility to promote what she has not sought for herself. Her matrimonial encouragement is so uncharacteristic Mattie is startled, reporting in astonished tones, "Oh, goodness me! . . . Deborah, there's a gentleman sitting in the drawing room with his arm round Miss Jessie's waist!" Mattie then receives a "double shock" because Deborah proceeds to "snub[] her down in an instant" proclaiming, "The most proper place in the world for his arm to be in" (22). After their wedding, Deborah continues her patronage, and when she is "old and feeble" their daughter Flora becomes her companion (22).

When Elizabeth Gaskell wrote the first two installments of *Cranford* for *Household Words,* she intended to end at Deborah's death, but the sketches met with such success she returned to the story (Croskery 201). In the new material, Miss Matty undergoes a change that parallels her sister's experience as she takes on matchmaking duties. Matty never assumes her sister's androgynous air, though her attempts to acquire a "sea-green turban," an accessory akin to Signor Brunoni's, suggests a timid attempt to emulate the authority of her sister's hybrid bonnet, but she meekly acquiesces when Mary Smith overrules her and provides instead "a pretty, neat, middle-aged cap" more suited to Matty's aging femininity (81).

Her conversion to matronly patron is a struggle, because, not only is she childlike, similar to her own mother (Fenwick 416), but also her matchmaking for her maid Martha is inspired by stirring the cold ashes of her own expired marital hopes. Cranfordian ladies commonly forbid romantic fraternizing between servants, and Miss Matty has been opposed to any man courting Martha. However, Matty's former beau, Mr. Holbrook, reappears and renews their acquaintance, who "[w]ith his honesty appetite, loud voice, and love of books . . . seems a resurrection of the hearty Captain Brown" (Auerbach 83), a parallel to her sister's not-quite lover. Even though worrying about disloyalty to her now-dead sister, she sadly remembers how their failed romance was prevented by her snobbish father and sister, and her demeanor shows "how faithful her poor heart had been in its sorrow and its silence" about Holbrook (36). When Holbrook unexpectedly dies, Matty becomes amenable to Martha's love affair with Jem Hearn, remembering her lost hopes and thinking, "God forbid . . . that I should grieve any young hearts" (40). Though she later worries that her need to live with

Martha and Jem hurries their marriage, her residual aversion to matrimony only stresses the sacrificial nature of her support.

Later, Matty becomes a substitute mother for Martha's baby, who is not only her namesake but also "as much at home in her arms as in its mother's" (155). Because all Victorian women were defined as mothers whether or not they actually give birth (Jalland and Hooper 5), even the childless woman, whether single or married, proves her true womanhood by promoting reproduction in others. Matty is ennobled by serving the marital and reproductive fortunes of the next generation, fulfilling her cultural role, which is necessary for her to be lauded as the most loved elder in Cranford, a position she fills by the novel's end.[23]

In *Cranford,* midlife sexuality, especially for women, is censured as proof of personal failure and the cause of societal discord, while a sexless sibling relationship is held up as the epitome of happiness and source of unity in the village. Lady Glenmire, an aristocratic widow who disappoints the Cranford ladies by acting like a commoner, transgresses against the Amazons' expectations not only in her lack of proper aristocratic behavior, but also by failing to adhere to the postmenopausal paradigm. Lady Glenmire arrives in Cranford "a bright little woman of middle age, who had been very pretty in the days of her youth, and who was even yet very pleasant-looking" (76). As I discuss in the next chapter, though Victorian widowers were encouraged and expected to remarry, widowhood was seen as "a final destiny" (Jalland 231). This standard is staunchly upheld in Cranford, and Lady Glenmire is expected to remain single and sexless due to her age and widowhood.

When Lady Glenmire has the audacity to become engaged, the arrangement is frowned upon by village society. Miss Pole calls the planned nuptials "madness" and prophesies, "What a fool my lady is going to make of herself!" (144). Miss Matty finds it hard to believe that a titled lady would wed Mr. Hoggins, because, even though he "is rich, and very pleasant-looking, . . . and very good-tempered and kind-hearted," he is also a mere doctor with no pretensions to gentility, and she hopes to find it is all inaccurate gossip (115). The collected ladies agree that Lady Glenmire is "degraded" by the engagement (115), the formidable Mrs. Forrester even asserting that she has "brought stains on the aristocracy" (116). Miss Pole disapprovingly asserts, "there was a kind of attraction about Lady Glenmire that I, for one, should be ashamed to have" (114), hinting at a distasteful midlife sexuality. In Cranford, such "attractions" are inappropriate, a disgrace for midlife women who should be comporting themselves in accordance with standards of sexlessness.

The engaged couple is characterized by a near-youthfulness that emphasizes their age. Lady Glemire has "almost something of the flush of youth," and Mr. Hoggins, looking "broad and radiant" wears "bran-new" boots that are an exact copy of his old ones that had been "new-pieced, high and low, top and bottom, heel and sole, black leather and brown leather, more times than any one could tell" (117). These "new-pieced" boots gently lampoon a midlife marriage that, even though new, is a patchwork union that combines fragmentary freshness with well-worn age. The ladies of Cranford also display a patchwork "almost" youthfulness, indulging in a flurry of shopping after the engagement, but their pretensions to bloom become just an occasion for more gentle satire on their age. The shopping scene is akin to Miss Matty and Mrs. Forrester's earlier entrance into the Cranford assembly rooms to attend Signor Brunoni's performance. Reminded of their youth, they "bridle up . . . and walk mincingly up the room" in a space that, like themselves, is "old . . . dingy . . . faded" while "a mouldy odour of aristocracy lingered about the place" (85–86). The "bridling up" of bloom at the Hoggins's marriage gives occasion for smiles at their expense as they indulge in a fantasy about what they are not and no longer can be.[24]

The marriage consistently is presented as rather indecent, considered "in the same light as the Queen of Spain's legs—facts which certainly existed, but the less said about the better" (117). Only Miss Matty contemplates "almost coming round to think it a good thing" (126). Hoping the best for her friend, she reflects that "it is pleasant to have . . . [a man] at hand," that after her nuptials Lady Glenmire can have a more settled life, and that her betrothed is "a very personable man," "good" and "clever," even though "not what some people reckoned refined" (127). Miss Mattie does not speak up in support of the marriage to others, though, and never tries to break the social censure against the Hogginses. After the wedding, when Lady Glemire drops her title and becomes Mrs. Hoggins, Mrs. Jamieson triumphantly announces she has proven herself a "creature" of "low taste" (143), and all the village continues to view the union as aberrant and mistaken.

The later-life partnership that receives Cranford's collective approval is the sibling household Miss Matty and Peter set up when he returns from India. The narrator stresses the suitability of their arrangement in terms of age. Now in her late fifties, Matty is surprised at how old her brother looks and emphasizes her elderliness in solidarity with his, refusing the pearl necklace he brings her with the claim, "I'm afraid I'm too old; but it was very kind of you to think of it. They are just what I should have liked years ago—when I was young" (151). Matty and her brother settle down into an elderly, asexual sibling partnership, enriched by his career in the colonies, a union esteemed by all.[25]

This sibling alliance then becomes the basis for returning harmony to the village that has been disrupted by the Hoggins's midlife match. Peter takes on this project for the love of his sister, saying, "I want everybody to be friends, for it harasses Matty so much to hear of these quarrels" (160). He sets up a luncheon at which he hopes to restore the peace, flirting with the august Mrs. Jamieson in order to achieve his plan. Because she has been the most vociferous opponent of the Hoggins's union, he tells tall tales of India to "propitiate" and amuse her, attempting to prevent her having "time enough to get up her rancour against the Hogginses" (159–60). Miss Pole objects to Jamieson entertaining this flirtation, commenting that "It was so wanting in delicacy in a widow to think of such a thing" (158), which stirs up continued censure against Mrs. Hoggins who has been indelicate enough not only to contemplate "such a thing" but also actually to do it. Peter, however, displaces the problems of midlife romance onto empire by telling stories of savages and sacrilege in India that inspire the Cranfordians to unite as the civilized British against heathen foreigners. When the newlyweds finally appear, their marriage looks far less abominable against the backdrop of Peter's frightening exotic tales, and the disturbing midlife union, which has been "the only subject for regret" that remains in Cranford, is no longer condemned (156). Peter restores their "old friendly sociability," his sexless sibling arrangement with Matty valorized as it overcomes the chaos caused by a midlife marriage (160).

The novel's ending focuses on Miss Matty as a matriarchal figure universally admired and loved for her gentle, sacrificial qualities. Nina Auerbach argues, "the natives of Cranford have achieved beatitude under her aegis without the usual novelistic sacrament of marriage" (88), a blessing made possible by her asexual union with her brother. As "an old lady of fifty-eight" (132), the sexless, nurturing, postmenopausal woman is now "past middle age" (130). The narrator enjoins the "rising generation" to use "her patience, her humility, her sweetness, her quiet contentment" as their model (132). The last sentence of the book eulogizes her as Cranford's most esteemed citizen: "We all love Miss Matty, and I somehow think we are all of us better when she is near us" (160). In this closing portrait of Matty Jenkyns as the ideal older woman, an inspiration to all for her self-effacing support of generations that follow, Gaskell specifies that not only mothers, but also spinsters too, must conform to the sexless service paradigm.

V.

Critical analysis of Margaret Oliphant's *Miss Marjoribanks* (1865–66) has been dominated by arguments about her challenges to and revisions of stereotypes for nineteenth-century women, but the novel's extensive scrutiny of the relationship between aging and marriageability has not been explored.[26] In *Miss Marjoribanks*, Oliphant satirizes sexless service, reversing the customary roles of matron and ingénue, the younger woman mentoring the older, postponing her own romantic possibilities while she acts as the magnanimous benefactor to a reluctant middle-aged widow. In *Miss Marjoribanks*, Oliphant lampoons the paradigm of sexless service as an established stereotype.

When nineteen-year-old Lucilla Marjoribanks returns from school to her widowed father, she announces her "programme" to "be a comfort to dear papa" for the next ten years (6), at which point she will be in danger of "going off" and must marry or remain single for life (48). This seemingly self-sacrificial act establishes a ten-year reign for Lucilla not only over her father but also the entire village of Carlingford. She dispatches her father from his role as head-of-household on the first morning, simply by seating herself at the head of the table, and she performs a similar feat in Carlingford society, inaugurating musical evenings that set a new standard and directing the lives of those around her, dictating their marital plans and political careers. Among her many projects is a middle-aged widow, and in this subplot, Oliphant questions the rigid boundaries of aging which the novel seems on its surface to advance, as Lucilla undermines the prescriptions for marriageability which she espouses for herself.

The novel contains a highly developed awareness of aging that calibrates marriageability and indicates when one has become middle-aged and therefore undesirable, a change designated by a special term: "going off." To "go off' in *Miss Marjoribanks* is to suffer a physical change that marks one as past youth and lessened in value, a debility for both genders but especially for women. This phenomenon is easily recognizable and much discussed by characters who constantly scrutinize themselves and others for its signs. "To go off" not only means to leave behind a younger, ideal self, but also connotes physical decay, suggesting spoiled food or soured milk. Dr. Marjoribanks even associates "going off" with death, telling Lucilla when Mrs. Chiley recovers from a serious illness: "People at our time of life don't go off in that accidental kind of way. When a woman has been so long used to living, it takes her a time to get into the way of dying" (393–94). In Lucilla's judgments about whether she and others have "gone off," Oliphant acknowledges conventions of midlife aging which often are not overtly represented in Victorian novels but nevertheless operate within them.

Lucilla's announcements that she will "go off" at thirty are so repetitive and dramatic that they call themselves into question, exposing the constructed nature of the theory behind them. She presents as undisputed "fact" that women undergo a fundamental change in desirability, sexuality, and marriageability at thirty, an assessment shared by others. When Mrs. Chiley, a family friend, hears Lucilla's plan to stay single for a decade, she responds, "Oh yes; I have heard girls say that before . . . but they always changed their minds. You would not like to be an old maid, Lucilla; and in ten years—" (61). Clearly, both women believe that in a decade, the nineteen-year-old Lucilla's chances will have expired.

Though Lucilla and Mrs. Chiley seem to be certain about the age of spinsterhood for women, chronological markers of unmarriagability for men, though they exist, are less clear. Several men are evaluated in terms of going off, but we are never told their ages, in stark contrast to Lucilla's emphasis on thirty for women. When Mrs. Chiley presents the middle-aged Archdeacon Beverley to Lucilla as a possible suitor, she describes his age in protean terms: "they say he is a very nice man; and young—enough" and, she goes on, "My dear, he is a clergyman . . . and you know a nice clergyman is always nice, and you need not think of him as a young man unless you like" (127). Not only is his age indeterminate and open to interpretation, but qualities other than age are equally or more important to his romantic viability, the repeated commendatory "nice" comedically underscoring that profession and disposition are perhaps more significant than years for males. The narrator later describes Beverley as in "the prime of life," a descriptor never used for women (138).

Though Lucilla states that women go off at thirty, the novel also espouses a theory that "going off" is caused in both genders by individual conduct and is therefore preventable, at least up to a certain point, the responsibility of each individual, a theory Oliphant derives from conduct books of which she makes Lucilla a big fan. As Alex Ross argues in *Hints on Dress and the Arrangement of the Hair* (1861), a beauty manual contemporaneous with *Miss Marjoribanks*, it is "the duty as well as the privilege of all persons to make their exterior as prepossessing as possible," and he further asserts that "we cannot doubt the obligation of this duty when we consider that to attempt to produce pleasing feelings in the minds of others is a principle all philanthropic individuals entertain" (3).

While Lucilla fulfills her duty to society by not aging, others fall short, providing evidence of what does and does not cause "going off" as the novel details its etiology in several characters. Weight gain is a significant signal: when Harry Cavendish returns to Carlingford after a ten-year absence, he is "stout and red in the face," having lost his "figure" and "elasticity," qualities much remarked upon by other characters as evidence that he has gone off (384). Mr. Centum, for example, cries, "Good Lord! Cavendish, is this you? I never expected to see you like that! . . . You're stouter than I am, old fellow; and such an Adonis as you used to be!" (384). However, appearing too thin also makes one look older, faded and withered, and Helen Mortimer looks ten years younger due to the "filling-up of her worn frame" (196). Aging can be caused by bad behavior, such as Cavendish's habit of "living fast" that has cost him "ease of mind" (384). Lucilla, on the other hand, retains youthfulness because of her knack for moderation in all things. Cavendish reflects that she has the "feminine incapacity for going too far" while, in contrast, "he *had* gone too far . . . [and] not been as careful in his life as he might have been" (386). Excessive emotional displays also accelerate aging, and Lucilla warns the nervous Helen Mortimer against crying because "one never knows what harm one might do oneself" (250). The signs of "going off" in Barbara Lake, who eventually marries Cavendish, are caused by hardships that have made her become "worn, and like a creature much buffeted by the wind and waves" (442).

The careful detailing of these aging symptoms indicates Oliphant's familiarity with standard conduct book advice on the subject. Regular health regimens involving diet, exercise, fresh air, and early rising as well as moderate temper and behavior were considered essential to retain youthfulness. *The Ladies' Handbook of the Toilet* (1843) instructs that the only way to "preserve . . . bloom and freshness" is "the maintenance of good health, regular habits, an even and cheerful temper, a due attention to diet, with bathing . . . and, above all, early rising" (2). *The Elixir of Beauty* (1848) argues that "[f]resh air, pure simple food and exercise, mental and bodily" are important, enabling those of sixty to look and feel forty (47). One's state of mind, however, is the most significant factor in staying young: "Whenever you see in an old person a smooth unwrinkled forehead, a clear eye, and a pleasing cheerful expression, be sure her life has been passed in that comparative tranquility of mind, which depends less upon outward vicissitudes than internal peace of mind. A good conscience is the greatest preservative of beauty" (47). *Beauty's Mirror* (1830) asserts that "gluttony, intemperance, late hours and immoderate drugging" cause wrinkles (55), while Lola Montez warns in *The Arts of Beauty* (1858) that "perpetual care, great anxiety, or prolonged grief, will hasten white hairs" (79). *The Etiquette of the Toilette-Table* (1859) cautions against personal practices such as "abuse of ardent liquors," "immoderate use of tobacco," "late hours," and "irregular practices," all of which can cause baldness (An Officer's Widow 37). Cavendish's habit of "going too far" and being "careless"—smoking, drinking, keeping late hours—makes him a prime candidate for premature aging, according to the best advice of conduct books.

Though Lucilla insists upon the parameters of "going off" as a fact of life for women at thirty, she soundly contradicts this theory in her patronage of the widow, Helen Mortimer. When the Rector Bury brings Mortimer to Dr. Marjoribanks's house as a possible chaperone for his daughter, Lucilla suspects a threat to her authority. She thwarts his overtures by willfully misinterpreting their visit as the widow's attempt to court her fifty-year-old father, embarrassing Bury and humiliating Mrs. Mortimer to the extent that she nearly faints. While Lucilla feels "the full importance of her victory" over Bury—he leaves indignantly—she also takes pity on Mrs. Mortimer as a necessary victim and decides to be "kind" to her (68). When next we see Helen Mortimer, Lucilla has taken her in hand, establishing a small school in the widow's home, using her own gardener to beautify the grounds, and even has decorated Helen's parlor.

This new interest has a startling effect on Mrs. Mortimer's aging. When first introduced to Lucilla she is a "deprecating woman, with a faint sort of pleading smile on her face," weak and subject to swooning (64). Suddenly, the marks of "going off" reverse, indicated by "the bloom on her cheeks, and the filling-up of her worn frame" (196), and the "poor faded widow . . . found her youth again and her good looks" (197)—developments that are "all Miss Marjoribanks's doing" (196–97). Lucilla's tutelage has had such an effect, in fact, that "[s]he had grown younger by ten years during the period of comparative comfort and tranquility which Lucilla's active help and championship had procured for her" (196).

The matron role reversal is made complete when the Archdeacon Beverley, who had been regarding Lucilla with such "marked regard" that "it was impossible for her not to recognise that a crisis might be approaching," transfers his attention to the widow (196). Lucilla tells Beverley she wants him to meet her friend, and he objects to "those dreadful women that have seen better days" whose "faded existences" he finds "a great social difficulty," but when he actually encounters her, he is stunned to discover that Helen is his former sweetheart, and he is immediately smitten (195). Helen confesses to Lucilla that she had known Beverley "long, long ago—when we were both quite young" (209). By reactivating the widow's youthfulness, Lucilla returns Helen's marital viability, reversing her own precept about thirty as the expiration date for female romance.

At first, Helen attempts to reinstate the proper age order and do her matronly duty, believing Lucilla's interests have precedence because she is the younger woman. She has heard rumors that the Archdeacon and Lucilla may be a match, and she wrings her hands wondering whether "her miserable presence here" will "dispel perhaps the youthful hopes of her benefactress" (204). She is not able to sustain this behavior, however, quickly relapsing into dependent status, and turns to Lucilla as "her sustainer and guardian" (205). Initially, Lucilla is a bit miffed that her putative suitor has thus realigned himself, but, no ordinary woman, she soon "took matters into her own hand with the confidence of a superior nature" (201–02). Realizing that she is not in love with Beverley, she champions his courtship with Helen. Because she enjoys being "appealed to and called upon for active service," delights "to take the management of incapable people, and arrange all their affairs for them, and solve all their difficulties," she welcomes Helen's request for guidance (207). The middle-aged widow's fortunes continue to be fostered by her nineteen-year-old guardian.

Mortimer still must overcome her qualms about a return to romance as a widow and woman of age. She tells Lucilla, ". . . I have had my life . . . and done with it" (208), and protests, ". . . I have a—a horror . . . in general—of second marriages" (212). Helen finally warms to the idea, however, and when she attempts subtly to elicit more information about Beverley, Lucilla sees through her casual ruse, which mortifies Helen: "The idea that she, a mature woman, a married woman and widow, who ought to have done with all these vanities, should have been found out by a young girl to be thinking about a *gentleman*, struck poor Mrs. Mortimer with as sharp a sense of shame as if her wistful preoccupation had been a crime" (250). Lucilla refuses to be cast in the role of "young girl," however, behaving more like Helen's mother, warning her, "Spoiling your eyes with crying, and making everybody uncomfortable never does the least good" and again provides a sustaining cup of tea (250).

Oliphant takes Lucilla's matronly guise to new heights of humor when, as she soothes the widow, Dr. Marjoribanks notices her regained good looks and is charmed by Mrs. Mortimer. Lucilla suddenly sees "a new and altogether unsuspected danger" in what she considers her father's "ridiculous exhibition of interest" (251). She has thought of him as a man "who certainly was old enough to know better," but now, as he lingers over Mrs. Mortimer with "a warmth which was quite uncalled–for," she reflects, "If he were still accessible to such influences, nobody could answer for anything that might happen" (251). Even in the face of this new danger, however, "Her faith in herself did not fail her for an instant" (252). Instead, Lucilla casts herself as a saint, feeling a "sense of pain at the unbelief of her followers . . . mingled with that pity for their weakness which involves pardon" (252). Those whose lives she is trying to manage are, she feels, simply deluded when they fail "to believe in the simple force of genius," but she will continue her campaign to save them despite this shortsighted-ness, and as she retires to bed "with a smile upon her magnanimous lips," it is, the narrator assures us, "a sublime moment" (252–53).

This comedic horror at her father's romantic possibilities is an example of the gap between Lucilla's awareness of her own motivations and actions and that of the narrator.[27] Melissa Schaub points out that though Lucilla is a "conscious calculator," she also "is never self-conscious in her plotting . . . she has no sense of humor and cannot understand irony," a fact which she freely admits about herself (210). Lucilla constantly maneuvers others into doing what she thinks they should, "inventing potential future plots that she can exploit" (Schaub 204). Oliphant produces ironic humor with Lucilla's mock heroic tone as well as by creating a fissure between the narrator's story and the plots Lucilla conjures up for herself and others (Schaub 204). Thus, Lucilla remains unaware that in her patronage of Mortimer she is contradicting the age ideology which she has so confidently espoused, and humor is created by the rift between her actions and her blithe ignorance of their repercussions.

When Helen Mortimer and Beverley part over a disagreement, Lucilla untangles this difficulty, putting the couple together again, and soon Beverley is proposing to the widow in the window recess of Lucilla's parlor. Though Carlingford society believes Helen is "not like a *real* bride after all; a difference which was only proper under the circumstances," and she is married in lavender "as was to be expected" of a widow, Lucilla continues to perform the role of matriarch sponsoring an ingénue (313). Not only had she "made all the arrangements for Mrs. Mortimer's marriage, and took charge of everything," but she "presided over the ceremony as if she had been Mrs. Mortimer's mother" (313). While she acts the part of matron at twenty, disregarding her own matrimonial chances in favor of the midlife women, eventually the decade designated for her singleness is completed, and she marries her cousin Tom as her most fit mate.

Oliphant's satirical presentation of the young matron Lucilla and timid midlife bride Helen suggests that the menopausal model had become a bit hackneyed in the 1860s. That Oliphant lampoons the convention suggests both its pervasiveness and its enduring power. The final novel I discuss in this chapter goes further, evincing a fin-de-siècle anxiety about menopausal women overthrowing the restrictions of sexless service, a fearsome possibility with the potential to change the nature of relationships between the sexes as well as the entire British nation.

VI.

While Oliphant feels free to invert the stereotype in order to parody it, H. Rider Haggard performs another kind of reversal, co-opting the woman of age as a perfect subject for adventure fiction. Why should the "imperial gothic," as Nancy Armstrong terms it in *How Novels Think* (23), be considered alongside the novels of Dickens, Brontë, Gaskell, and Oliphant? Victorians encountered these texts together, reading *She* serially in *The Graphic* as a fantasy adventure published beside more realist works by Trollope, Eliot, and Hardy. The simultaneously seductive and grotesque aging female that appears in Haggard's fantasy is a hyperbolic presentation of age anxiety that more subtly haunts mainstream novels.

She has been highly popular since its appearance—seven editions were necessary to meet demand in its first year, and it has not been out of print since (Etherington xv, xxii). Sandra M. Gilbert and Susan Gubar attribute its success among Victorian readers to three interconnected fin-de-siècle preoccupations—empire, spiritualism, and the New Woman—which are "explored and exploited" by the narrative (*No Man's* 26). *She* also is absorbed by another issue that disturbed Victorians, however, in its depiction of the eternally youthful Ayesha, white queen of a lost African tribe, a sensationalized version of Eliza Lynn Linton's greatly feared *femme passée*, "mutton dressed as lamb" who can and will seduce men. At 2,000-years-old, *She-who-must-be-obeyed* is by no means in midlife, but even though her chronological age reaches far beyond normal human existence, her body appears to be only about thirty. Haggard's narrative continually raises anxiety about age, especially female senescence. The question of whether Ayesha is young or old not only exposes the need of Victorians to place women within a matrix of age-determined value but also evokes the liminal quality of midlife aging and its implications for women. Many critics have followed Gilbert and Gubar in linking the novel with fear of the New Woman (*No Man's* 34–36). It also is important to consider that this independent free spirit usually is envisioned as young, and *She* registers apprehension about mature female power, the femme fatale whose experience gives her incredible dominion over men.[28] Ayesha, the virgin queen, is a spinster in the strictest sense of the word, but in her very essence, she contravenes not only expectations of old maids but also the paradigm of sexless service expected of all postmenopausal woman, and her overthrow reveals anxiety about and denigration of female sexuality caught between youth and old age.

A fantasy about an all-male society of three that journeys into a matriarchal land, *She* consistently presents women as dangerous and to be feared. The moment Horace Holly takes charge of his foster son Leo Vincey, he seeks out a "suitable male attendant" for the boy, because "I would have no woman to lord it over me about the child, and steal his affections from me" (15). Holly and the childtender, Job, both are self-identified misogynists. Leo's father also evinces antiwoman tendencies before his death, bequeathing his son a letter and map that will lead him to "the greatest mystery in the world," but he adds that Leo may wish to ignore the entire story as "an idle fable, originating in the first place in a woman's disordered brain" (21). The chaotic brain to which he refers belongs to their ancestor Amenartes, whose instructions outlining a "revenge quest" against Ayesha, her husband's seducer, have been passed down from generation to generation of Vincey men (Stott 120). Female treachery and inferiority are made clear not only by Ayesha's seduction attempt but also because she has obtained unending youth not through her own wisdom but by stealing nature's deep knowledge from a male priest who discovered it "by purity and abstinence, and the contemplations of his innocent mind," qualities which

Ayesha, as a scheming woman, does not possess (85). Though the priest has wisely refused to make use of the secret, Ayesha selfishly appropriates the ancient power for herself. "The secret of life" is now controlled by another "woman's disordered brain," the ancient-yet-powerful matriarch who must be vanquished by questing male explorers.

While *She* expresses alarm about women in general, the narrative also anxiously is obsessed with the idea of aging, and these two fears combine into the book's paramount concern—an overpowering ancient woman. According to Norman Etherington, Haggard was "haunted" by the idea of death, and his liberal use of mummies embalmed in perfectly preserved youthfulness reveals a fascinated horror with age-oriented decay similar to Oscar Wilde's in *The Picture of Dorian Gray* (xxviii). Holly, the expedition's leader, continually expresses apprehension about the pernicious effects of aging. When exploring ancient Kôr, he comments in awe, "it seems that the world is very old" (121). Holly voices a Victorian preoccupation with time that resulted from Lyell's and Darwin's theories which revealed a vastly lengthened span of natural history and greater antiquity for the human race. Highly age-conscious, he describes himself several times as "middle-aged," and views the effects of time on individual humans with suspicion as a highly corrupting process. Late Victorians worried that the stress of modern life, especially upon "brain workers," exacerbated aging and was proof of generalized degeneration (Dana 405). This concern is evident in Holly when he imagines people as archeological relics: "my experience is that people are apt to fossilise even at a University if they follow the same paths too persistently" (54). Holly also asserts a consensus of opinion that aging results in immorality and malevolence, stating as "a well-known fact" that age makes humans so "cynical and hardened," death saves us "from utter moral petrifaction if not moral corruption" (161). He goes on to argue, "No one will deny that a young man is on the average better than an old one, for he is without that experience of the order of things that in certain thoughtful dispositions can hardly fail to produce cynicism, and that disregard of acknowledged methods and established custom which we call evil" (161). According to this theory, Leo is more pure than Holly, virtuous because untainted by age's polluting influence. In regard to himself, Holly claims that he has suffered "far too many worries and disappointments and secret bitternesses during . . . forty odd years of existence to wish that this state of affairs should be continued indefinitely" (82). Because he believes that age increasingly defiles him, Holly intends to refuse Ayesha's secret of youth, should they discover her whereabouts, and die within a normal human life span.

Though a generalized age anxiety permeates *She*, female aging is especially vilified. Even though the genders are purported to live in "perfect equality" (57), women are loathed and devalued when they age in Amahagger society, a culture akin to Britain in its high regard for reproductive women but denigration after menopause. The tribal leader Billali reports that when Amahagger women are young, "we worship them . . . because . . . they are the source of life"; however, after becoming "old ones," women often are killed for becoming "unbearable" (78), a telling pun. Billali not only accepts but also promotes this practice as a good lesson to younger women, even within his own family. He attests that ever since his wife was killed "in that way," though "[i]t was very sad, to tell thee the truth . . . life has been happier since" (78). Older men are not subject to such extermination, evident in his comment that his age "protects" him from younger women's advances (78). Callous disregard for older women also is obvious when Bilalli comments that such exterminations have made mature women rare in Amahagger society but then concludes that "they brought it on themselves" (78).

Of course, anxiety about female aging is evoked particularly by the 2,000 year old Ayesha. Even before he meets her, Holly is troubled by the idea of her ageless antiquity. On the way to her domain, he calls the story of her unending youth "monstrous" (82), foreshadowing her ultimate unveiling as a grotesque aberration of nature. As they draw near her domain, Holly's dream of a veiled women who reveals herself first in "the perfect shape of a lovely blooming woman" and then as "the white bones of a grinning skeleton" manifests his uneasiness about Ayesha's indeterminate age (75). Contrasting a skeleton with the Victorian trope of "bloom" that registers female sexual readiness and marital availability (King 7), Holly anticipates a fraudulent allure that merely masks decay, revealing his deep fear of being duped by the false front of the deteriorating *femme passée*.

Every depiction of Ayesha's beauty is complicated by images of a facade hiding age. The adventurers' first impressions emphasize their instinctive awareness that Ayesha is an old woman, especially their association of her body with mummies. She wears a veil to shield her irresistible beauty, but these "mummy-like" wrappings immediately remind Holly of "grave clothes" (96). When he explains to Ayesha that he has no interest in eternal youth for himself, because though death may be difficult, "harder still, to my fancy, would it be to live on, green in leaf and fair, but dead and rotten at the core," his seemingly objective statement reveals his revulsion toward Ayesha (166). As Gilbert and Gubar observe, she actually is a mummy, having been "embalmed alive" (*No Man's* 18), the only aspect that the honest, unsophisticated, and glib Job can perceive. The first time he sees her, he blurts out, "Oh God help us . . . here's a corpse a-coming sliding down the passage" (131), and he continues to view her "with the utmost disgust and horror" as "an animated corpse" (140), expressing unadulterated revulsion.

Holly's fear of Ayesha's antiquity only increases when he sees her youthful beauty unveiled. Though he intends to be impervious, telling the veiled Ayesha, "I fear not they beauty. I have put my heart away from such vanities as woman's loveliness, that passeth like a flower" (104), when she reveals herself, he is smitten, and concludes "this beauty, with all its awful loveliness and purity, was *evil*" (105). In accordance with his theory of aging, Holly expects her to be corrupted by long life and finds her to be so, commenting that some of her words are "as cynical as might have been expected from a woman of Ayesha's age and experience," and he is taken aback by her language which "jars" him (135). He also deliberates about whether Ayesha showed "evil tendencies" when she killed Leo's lover Ustane or whether she was merely following the dictates of a different system of judgment, and he concludes that the murder is a result of "the natural cynicism the arises from age and bitter experience" in one of such "great antiquity" (161).

The most alluring, and therefore most frightening, aspect of Ayesha's beauty is not youthfulness but the strange and arresting blend of youth mingled with experience which makes her more irresistible than any merely young woman could possibly be: her face is "in perfect health, and the first flush of ripened beauty, yet it had stamped upon it a look of unutterable experience, and of deep acquaintance with grief and passion" (105). Ayesha's "flush of youth" combined with the aura of her transgressive past, "the experience of two thousand years at her back," is so potent an elixir that Holly, who had thought himself past romance at forty, concludes she "was certainly worth falling in love with, if ever woman was" (107). The next time he sees her unveiled, he declares Ayesha is "the incarnation of lovely tempting womanhood, made more perfect—and in a way more spiritual—than ever woman was before" due to her amalgamation of bloom and experience (127).

Ayesha overwhelmingly rejects the sexless service model, acting as the consummate femme fatale. Elaine Showalter points out that "*She* is about . . . male dread of women's sexual, creative, and reproductive power" (83). Ayesha, however, is fearsome not only by virtue of being female, but also because her power has reached maximum potency due to experience that enables her assertive sexuality. Unapologetically seductive, she is not interested in fulfilling Victorian standards of sexlessness for older women and invites Holly to span her waist with his hands, inciting him to "worship" her (128). She unmans both Holly and Leo with her dangerous allure, making the former "faint and weak" when she says he may kiss her (128), and when she "blasts" Ustane, Leo's lover, he feels "utterly cowed, as if all the manhood had been taken out of him" (151). Leo is helpless to resist her, even though his ardor is mixed with halfhearted loathing, clear in his confession: ". . . I know I am in her power for always . . . I must follow her as a needle follows a magnet. . . . But my mind is still clear enough, and in my mind I hate her—at least, I think so. . . . I am sold into bondage" (160). Holly, also in the same position, affirms: "We could no more have left her than a moth can leave the light that destroys it. We were like confirmed opium-eaters" (160). Ayesha's nubile age is presented as an overpowering sexual force that men both crave and fear, caught into its addictive spell.

Ayesha's liminal age status also creates an opportunity for incestuous lust that occurs when fathers and sons both desire her.[29] She seduces Leo as a substitute for his ancestor Kallikrates, and though they are born sixty-six generations apart (134), by pursuing both men, Ayesha lures Leo into incestuously tinged desire. She also arouses desire simultaneously in Leo and his foster father, Holly, who, consumed with jealousy for his Adonis-like ward, despairingly asking himself, "what chance should I, middle-aged and hideous, have against his bright youth and beauty?" (108). Though Holly virtuously decides to acquiesce to the younger man, attributing this choice to "his sense of right" (108), he reports that as he later watched Leo fall under Ayesha's power, "at that very moment I was rent by mad and furious jealously. I could have flown at him, shame upon me! The woman had confounded and almost destroyed my moral sense, as she was bound to confound all who looked upon her superhuman loveliness" (152). Ayesha can simultaneously attract foster father and son due to her liminal age status, because she seems neither too young for one nor too old for the other. Though the mature siren provokes immoral desire, her experienced "bloom" is too powerful for either man to resist.

Ayesha also transgresses matronly standards not only in her sexuality but also in her competition against instead of support for younger women. Though not an actual mother, Ayesha has "quasi-maternal powers over life and death," and Haggard himself reported that he meant her to be a matriarchal figure (Gilbert and Gubar, *No Man's* 34). This virgin ruler is not a nurturing mother, however, but an abusive parent, made evident by her eugenic experiment in which she breeds deaf and mute Amahaggarians to be used as servants and then allows them to die because they are too "ugly" (104). She also thwarts the love affair of Leo and his young lover, Ustane, declaring, "Her sin is that she stands between me and my desire" (135). Holly comments, "Old as she was, Ayesha had not outlived jealousy," insinuating that perhaps she should have aged out of romance, but she thrusts herself between young lovers, preventing Leo's union with his age peer (135).

Several critics have pointed out ways in which *She* repeatedly recounts fears of the female body, but they fail to register the importance of aging to this aspect of the novel.[30] The British male is imperiled by an unhealthy, dangerous, and alarming geography depicted as an ancient and decaying female body. To reach Kôr, the trio passes through a swamp described as "poisonous," "sickly," and "scummy," filled with "stagnant" water (46). An "engulfing female Otherness" (Murphy 59), the marsh is made horrible by standing water that harbors decay, and the men take "a precautionary dose of quinine" (47) as a deterrent against contagion caused by the landscape's deterioration. They pass through a symbolic birth canal on the way to the "cup-shaped" defile (54) where Ayesha resides, entering caverns that are not only her home, but also serve as crypts, eliding womb and tomb (Gilbert and Gubar, *No Man's* 17). Kôr itself is built in a landscape described as the female body reduced to "colossal ruins" in the "vast ancient crater" of an extinct volcano (89). They later undergo a perilous journey to the pillar of fire, trekking along "a kind of rut or fold of rock that grew deeper and deeper" (179), until they reach what Ayesha describes as the "very womb of earth" (189) and Holly calls a "dreadful womb" (199) which rests in the ancient crater.[31]

Etherington argues that once the travelers go inside the mountain "the imagery becomes suddenly and dramatically male" (xxxiv).[32] The narrator describes a bridge of rock, a "tremendous spur" shaped like "the spur upon the leg of a cock" partially spanning a "mighty chasm" that "jutted out in mid air into the gulf" (179). Rather than shifting from female to male, this scene depicts two bodies joined, as the cock-like spur thrusts into the female cave, a symbol repeated by the phallic pillar of fire which regularly enters and withdraws from the cavernous chamber. The landscape remains dangerously female in the chasm which is endless, dark, and mystifying—a "dreadful place," a "hideous depth that yawned beneath" (180). This aged cleft which horrifies the men, causing them to feel "blinded, and utterly confused" (180), does not daunt Ayesha, who negotiates the space as if it is her own ancient body, "never seeming to lose her head or her balance" (180). The aging female body is evoked not only because the spur is inside a primeval and obsolete crater, but also the cavern itself is made of rock that has been "jagged and torn and splintered ... in a far past age ... as though it had been cleft by stroke upon stroke of ... lightning" (179). This gynophobic description suggests an older female body which not only has known "stroke upon stroke," but also has become "jagged and torn" by experience and time. The female body of the Earth terrifies the men, its tempestuous blasts an emblem of aging sexuality that is overwhelmingly powerful and dangerous.

Ayesha's death scene reveals the extent of her fearful antiquity. Holly surmises she has been inspired to hide her face by the statue of veiled truth in the mountain of Kôr (177). The statue's mantle is analogous not only to Ayesha's draperies but also her body itself. Even as she stands barefaced and naked before the explorers, preparing to bathe in the pillar of fire, she is still concealed, because, like the mummies in her caves, "her fair skin proves to be wrapped round an inner reality of death and putrefaction" (Etherington xviii).[33] Only when "the flame of Life" burns away her youth can Leo, Job, and Holly see reality—the horribly aged female animal that grovels before them, a sight especially unnerving and loathly because Ayesha is a woman.

Revulsion for female senescence is evident as Ayesha grows old rapidly before the men's shocked eyes. Holly describes the entire process in great detail, his sentences liberally strewn with exclamation marks and italics. She touches her head, and her hair falls out in a single stroke. Helena Michie explains that women's hair in Victorian novels often serves as a synecdoche for female sexuality, "their wantonness, their unnameable body parts" (*Flesh* 100). Holly's description of Ayesha's hair—"oh, *horror of horrors!*—it all fell upon the floor" (193)—registers his revulsion toward female aging manifested in her sudden desexualization. Age transforms Ayesha into a monstrosity that is both ancient and youthful (Murphy 57). Her hand becomes "a claw" and "a human talon," but Ayesha shrinks to the size of a "baboon" while her face remains the size of "a two-months' child" on an inappropriately large skull (193).[34] In addition, her skin turns "dirty brown and yellow, like an old piece of withered parchment" (193). As Murphy notes, age converts Ayesha "into a text that can be marked and contained . . . transformed from an unmanageable and mysterious force that acts upon others to an inert and readable surface that instead can be controlled through inscription or erasure" (239). Ayesha as readable, inscribable, and erasable text is an emblem of older women in ageist cultures who not only lose status and self determination but also often are erased into invisibility. Ayesha calls out to Leo in her death throes, "Have pity on my shame" (194), accepting this vision of female aging, interpreting her aged body as the ultimate disgrace.

The explorers all are affected permanently by the sight of Ayesha's body aging. Job's response is the most direct and dramatic, as he yells "she's shrivelling up! she's turning into a monkey!"—and then, falling prostrate "foaming and gnashing in a fit," he dies of terror (193). Leo's hair begins to turn gray as he watches, and by the time they leave the cave, his curls have become white and he has aged twenty years (196). Holly believes his sanity has been imperiled, exclaiming, "I never saw anything like it . . . and let all men pray to God they never may, if they wish to keep their reason" (194). Her metamorphosis rivets him with horrified fascination, and he exclaims that She is "hideous—ah, too hideous for words. And yet, think of this—at that very moment I thought of it—it was the *same* woman!" (194). That age transforms women into "hideous" animal-like monsters is further confirmed as he and Leo wonder whether Ayesha will be able to return. Looking at her dead, aged body, Holly reflects, "Yes ... if she comes back as beautiful as we knew her. But supposing she came back *like that!*" He then muses, "What a terrifying reflection it is ... that nearly all our deep love for women who are not our kindred depends ... upon their personal appearance. If we lost them, and found them again dreadful to look on, though otherwise they were the very same, should we still love them?" (197). Holly has the glimmer of a realization that women are dehumanized by age when female worth is defined in terms of youthful beauty, and he is alarmed as he recognizes that his devaluation of older women parallels the misogyny of the "savage" Amahagger.

Ayesha's death scene collapses into seconds what Victorians feared was happening over generations, that evolution was turning backward and the human body and culture were regressing to more primitive states by the process of degeneration.[35] As I will explain at greater length in chapter 6, degeneration became a common fear in Britain during the last two decades of the nineteenth century. In the original serial publication of *She* an illustration shows Holly standing by the veiled Ayesha, with the hunched posture and heavy brow ridge of *Homo erectus* which suggests that her very presence can cause men to degenerate.[36] As Ayesha devolves into an old woman and then a monkey-like wrinkled creature, she not only recapitulates evolutionary regression but also exposes her true nature as an "antediluvian relic, a beast and a hag" (Stott 116).[37] Gilbert and Gubar argue that *She* evokes a "primordial female otherness" that exposes male anxiety about the "ontological Old Woman ... whose mysterious autonomy brings to the surface everyman's worry about *all* women" (*No Man's* 7). Her death resolves the novel's greatest fear, that Ayesha may have "revolutionised society" and "changed the destiny of Mankind" if she had reached England (195). She was "swept back with shame and hideous mockery" from this rebellion, Holly asserts, by "the finger of Providence," a depiction characterizing older women's power as not only threatening but also a sacrilege (195). Leo and Holly feel "a wild and splendid exhilaration ... a glorious sense of ... a fierce intensity of life" in the presence of the pillar of fire (190), and they are guided by its phallic light to escape the womb/tomb of corpses, which now includes Ayesha's own. They return to the world of male authority, no longer imperiled by in the aging female body.

Holly and Leo have discovered that the "reality behind the false commandments of *She-who-must-be-obeyed* ... always was a bald, blind, naked, shapeless, infinitely wrinkled female animal" (Gilbert and Gubar, *No Man's* 21). Haggard's novel represents a rabid fear of aging female sexuality, as well as a compulsion to unmask such behavior as a fraud and annihilate it, lest vulnerable men be overpowered. Ayesha's flagrant sexuality and failure to even consider superannuation directly contravene the sexless service model.

Eliza Lynn Linton's disgust at the "artificial youth" of the ridiculous *femme passée* expresses an anxiety that permeated nineteenth-century culture as the most common trope of female aging, worries that reach hyperbolic intensity in Haggard's fantasy, but which also resonate more discreetly in realist works of fiction. Dickens's grotesquely amorous women of age, Brontë's sacrificial midlife mother and put-upon old maids, Gaskell's reluctant matchmaking spinsters, and Oliphant's queenly young matron all are written in response to a menopausal paradigm that limited and oppressed non– and post–reproductive women. Such is not always the case in Victorian fiction, however. As the next chapter will demonstrate, sometimes aging women are granted new freedoms, especially in the case of the wily and experienced remarrying widow.

Chapter 4

Marriageable at Midlife

The Remarrying Widows of
Frances Trollope and Anthony Trollope

In 1842, a cartoon appeared in *Punch* featuring a young man who lolls on a sofa, his languid gaze fixed upon the object of his desire (figure 4.1).[1] As he leans toward his *inamorata*, the lover's demeanor suggests something is amiss, his hand supporting his forehead in a gesture of weary resignation. The cause of his demur sits beside him—a corpulent middle-aged woman, clothed in a black mourning dress and white widow's cap. Her deceased husband gazes down forbiddingly on the scene from a portrait hanging in the richly ornamented parlor that now, presumably, belongs to her. The cartoon's title, "Illustrations of Humbug" addresses the gentleman's prevaricating proposal: " 'Tis true there is a slight difference in our ages, but with hearts that love, such considerations become frivolous. The world! Pshaw! Did you but love as I do, you would care but little for its opinion. Oh! say, beautiful being, will you be mine?"

This cartoon's humor rests in the well-worn stereotype of the middle-aged widow as a buffoon, desirable only for money, her ridiculous sexuality a fact of life that must be endured by avaricious suitors. Her titillated grin and eyes riveted on the parlor fire suggest an unseemly passion set alight by the young suitor's declaration. From her zeppelin-like breasts thrusting zealously above her corseted torso to her demurely mittened hands that grasp a fan, intimating an intention to ventilate her own banked flames, she is a caricature of the woman past her prime, grotesque and therefore comical in a love scene.

At the time this cartoon appeared, Frances Trollope's Widow Barnaby series was highly popular with Victorian readers. *The Widow Barnaby*, a satire on the romantically inclined middle-aged widow, was published in 1839, followed by two sequels, *The Widow Married* (1840), and *The Widow Wedded; or The Adventures of the Barnabys in America* (1843). An 1839

Figure 4.1. Cartoon. *Punch* (1842): 213. The Library of Virginia. Reproduced by permission.

review in *The Athenaeum* identifies Martha as a superb example of a long-established stereotype, an undesirable widow who schemes at love:

> As a distinct personage in our fictitious literature, The Widow occupies a place ... entirely apart and individual ... a blithe and self-seeking pursuer of every man who is marriageable and modest—an unsympathizing ogress in the ranks of her own sex—audacious and experienced in planning—resolute in obtaining—turning off her deep designs, when threatened with discovery ... making of her weeds a flower-bed under which lurks artifice and device—calling up the memories of a dead husband as a bait to ensnare a living one—loquacious—lynx-eyed–oily-tongued: something like this ... with whose bereavements satirists, prose and verse, make merry, is *the* Widow in general. ... (9)

In her tale of the scampish Barnaby, Frances Trollope draws on a stock widow figure that dates back to Renaissance and Restoration drama as the subject of misogynistic humor.[2] In the seventeenth and eighteenth centuries, older people increasingly were held in contempt, and literature and jokes of the latter century in particular routinely lampoon elderly people with the expectation that they should become sexless (Ottaway 31). According to Susannah R. Ottaway, unmarried women especially were "singled out for particularly vicious satire," represented as "sexual predators" (41). Though the independent and decisive Barnaby challenges stereotypes that limited early Victorian women, she always is presented within the conventions of this comedic tradition as a buffoon, a depiction of female midlife that Frances's son Anthony later would appropriate, transform, and transcend in his own version of the remarrying widow.

Frances Trollope had a long and distinguished writing career, producing forty-one novels as well as travel narratives, a total of 115 volumes (Ransom, "Introduction" viii), and enjoying a notoriety in her day equal to that of Jane Austen, Charles Dickens, and even her son, Anthony (Neville-Sington, "Life and Adventures" 12). By 1863, however, her novels had been eclipsed and her literary days were over. At age eighty-four she was senile, living with her son Thomas in Florence. Back home in England, Anthony was writing his fifteenth novel, *Can You Forgive Her?*, creating a subplot in which the widowed Arabella Greenow is so similar to Martha Barnaby that she is a virtual rewriting.

In September, Anthony finished chapter ten, the story of Arabella's flirtations at a beach picnic. He then took a break to make what would be his last visit to his mother. On October 6, just after Anthony had returned to England, Fanny died, and he resumed work on the novel several days later (N. Hall 257).[3] Anthony recommenced Arabella's story in chapter fourteen, and at that point she undergoes a fundamental change. Though her plot retains comedic undertones, she also becomes genuinely attractive, a midlife woman in a serious tale that recasts the atrocious widow as a worthy lover. Both Martha Barnaby and Arabella Greenow defy Victorian notions of the subordinated matron, conquering men and overcoming limitations, but while the Widow Barnaby remains a caricature, Arabella revises this persona, becoming a midlife woman who can choose a mate for pleasure rather than prudence. This choice is made possible by her age and experience and contrasts with the limited options of the novel's other younger heroines. After this initial rewriting of the widow trope, Anthony went on to further reverse the negative connotations of the remarrying widow in the story of Madame Max Goesler in *Phineas Finn* (1867–69) and *Phineas Redux* (1873–74), depicting a sexual and valorized midlife woman who achieves a liberated and companionate marriage in a serious plot with no hint of comedy.

This chapter explores Frances Trollope's adaptation of the widow stereotype and its rewriting by her son Anthony, an appropriation that can be attributed to the effects of Fanny's life and death upon her son, as well as to changes in the position of women, especially political gains, that allowed a new kind of story to be imagined in the 1860s and 1870s. Both Arabella Greenow and Madame Max Goesler demonstrate possibilities that became available to middle-aged women in second-chance plots that award them opportunities based on what they have gained due to age.[4] While Frances uses satire to claim self-determination for midlife widows, Anthony Trollope transforms that portrayal to produce increasingly progressive narratives of gain that suggest new potential for women at midlife.

I.

Though widows had to contend with behavioral proscriptions before the Victorian era, they were in a unique position of restriction in the nineteenth century. In early modern England, high death rates had made for short marriages, the average being seventeen to nineteen years among the poor and twenty-two years for the squirearchy in the early 1600s (Stone, *Family* 55). Due to falling adult mortality rates, marriages began to last longer in the eighteenth and nineteenth centuries, and by the 1880s, only about one-third of marriages ended before twenty-five years.[5] Lawrence Stone suggests that Victorian marriages were the most lengthy in history, because rising divorce rates had not yet counteracted declining mortality rates (*Family* 56).[6] While marriages endured over time in the Victorian era, remarriage became less common. Several centuries before, though remarriage was stigmatized, it was also occurred frequently. E. A. Wrigley and R. S. Schofield note that 30% of those marrying in the sixteenth century were widows or widowers (258). By the mid-1800s, the figures had dropped to only 14% of grooms and 9% of brides remarrying after death of a spouse (M. Anderson 31).[7]

Longer marriages and fewer remarriages resulted in a large number of widowed persons living in England in the nineteenth century, and the majority of the widowed were women, a fact that reflects both higher mortality rates and higher incidences of remarriage for men (Jalland 230).[8] In the second half of the century, remarriage rates for widowers of age twenty-five were approximately double that for women, and for those in their forties, men were around four times more likely to remarry as women after the death of a spouse.[9] These figures attest to divergent gender expectations for bereaved males and females which gave men chances for second unions denied to women.

In the seventeenth and eighteenth centuries, it was a commonplace that widows, deprived of their regular libidinal outlet in marriage, searched for sexual replacements, as evidenced in the Elizabethan proverb, "He that wooeth a widow must go stiff before" (Stone, *Family* 281). The prenuptial pregnancy rate for widows in eighteenth-century France was five times higher than for other single women, which indicates that just across the English Channel, widows were more sexually active than other single women (Stone, *Family* 609). In nineteenth-century England, however, while the need for companionship, sexual and otherwise, was considered an excellent reason for widowers to remarry, the same consolation was offered much less frequently to widows.

In her survey of diaries and letters of bereaved Victorians, Pat Jalland concludes that widowhood was looked at as "a final destiny, an involuntary commitment to a form of social exile" (231). Widows often faced severe financial repercussions at the death of a spouse and became dependent on extended family members. While widowers were advised to "get your wounds healed as quickly as you can" and were warned against "learning to love your sorrow instead of bearing it" (Jalland 259), widows were discouraged from seeking new marriages and their identities remained tied to their dead spouses (Jalland 256). As the widowed Emily Lopez surmises in *The Prime Minister*, "It was forbidden to her, she believed, by all the canons of womanhood even to think of love again. There ought to be nothing left for her but crape and weepers" (2.252).

By the early nineteenth century, prohibitions against female remarriage were well entrenched. The author of *The Whole Duty of Woman* (1815), designating herself merely "A Lady," advises widows that their deceased husbands must remain their primary concern, because wifely affection "burns, like the funeral lamp of old, even in charnel houses and vaults" (81). Widows are warned not to "advance yourself in a second marriage" because "this not only cancels your pretended love to your deceased husband, in violating his will and the trust reposed in you, but is a manifest defrauding of your own children, which is the highest injury of all others; for it envenoms the crime, and adds unnaturalness to deceit" (A Lady 85). While a widow's remarriage invalidates love for her deceased husband or even proves such love never existed, a similar charge would never have been leveled against remarrying widowers. Widows were isolated into an emotional suttee, their status publicly signaled by mourning dress which was much harsher than that of widowers, producing "the perception that a wife's identity and sexuality were subsumed in her husband's and died with him" (Jalland 301).[10]

Fictive narratives of remarriage that emerged in this environment easily lent themselves to satire, because a serious treatment challenged deeply engrained paradigms of proper widowly decline. The fact that mourning restrictions for widows lessened at the end of the century implies they were given a new freedom to be considered persons in their own right and allowed greater license to remarry.[11] Statistics show, however, that widows married less and less over the course of the nineteenth century and even into the twentieth.[12] This restrictive convention is apparent in the novels discussed in chapter 3—attempts at flirtation by the widows Skewton and Nickleby are hilariously grotesque, and Agnes Helstone's virtuous single-hood is a model for widowed mothers. While the Widow Barnaby's wily ways transgress restrictive paradigms for widows with comedic regularity, Arabella Greenow and Madame Max conquer the status quo as comedy gives way to serious plots of midlife affect.

II.

Most current critics read *The Widow Barnaby* as an expression of Frances Trollope's feminism, as Helen Heineman argues, "With the widow Barnaby, Mrs. Trollope created the feminine picaresque, a lady ready to pack her trunks of a moment's notice, one who enjoyed herself immensely while exploring and exploiting life's possibilities for a middle-aged woman" (*Mrs. Trollope* 157). When Frances Trollope set out to create her iconoclastic, boundary-breaking widow, however, she told her publisher she intended to write a comedy based on "efforts and pretensions resulting from vanity, a vulgar desire for fashionable homily" (qtd. in Neville-Sington, *Fanny Trollope* 266). She begins the final novel of the series, *The Widow Wedded*, with this confession: "I scruple not to confess that with all her faults, and she has *some*, I love her dearly: I owe her many mirthful moments, and the deeper pleasure still of believing that she has brought mirthful moments to others also" (1). Frances did not intend to create a paragon, but a matron who delights us with her unruly conduct.

Martha often is considered an autobiographical figure that possesses Frances's proto-feminist qualities. She sails to the United States as a famous author and purports to write a book on her travels, parodying Frances's own journey to America which produced perhaps her most enduring book, *Domestic Manners of the Americans* (Ransom, *Fanny Trollope* 124; Heineman, *Mrs. Trollope* 165). Helen Heineman argues that Martha is Frances's "first heroine to project clearly the author's own fortitude and autonomy, self-assertiveness and curiosity about the world and to embody the significance and drama of her own strenuously active life. . . . The widow was a creation that arose from the deepest wellspring of Frances Trollope's own personality" (*Frances Trollope* 88). Heineman sees Frances's message in

The Widow Barnaby as "uncomplicated and direct"—that "women could maintain their inner autonomy and gain the maximum of economic independence," and she interprets the narrator's comment that the widow is "a strange mixture of worldly wisdom and . . . female folly" as evidence of Martha's sagacity: "folly was all for show, the worldly wisdom was the real woman" (*Frances Trollope* 90).[13]

In contrast to these readings of his mother's books, Anthony Trollope's personal and public statements demonstrate he did not view her work this way. His perhaps most succinct comment on "the woman question" appears in *North America* (1862): "The best right a woman has is the right to a husband . . ." (262), and he declared in an 1879 letter that "the necessity of the supremacy of man is as certain to me as the eternity of the soul" ("To [Joline]" 821). But, though Anthony may be antifeminist in his public statements and nonfiction writing, he expressed feminist sympathies when he created heroines.

Anthony often portrays women who question traditional roles and yearn for a different kind of life, creating what Deborah Denenholz Morse calls an "ongoing fictional dialectic between belief in and subversion of Victorian ideals for womanhood" (3). Bill Overton posits two Trollopes (that is, two *Anthony* Trollopes), the official, conventional Victorian of public and private discourse, and the unofficial, contradictory novelist—a double consciousness which can best be seen, he argues, in his ideas about the role of women: "He will start out from a bland moralism—that a woman's place is in marriage, or that marriage for ambition is wrong—but these simplifications the novels soon disarm" (7). James Kincaid argues that the issue is complicated, because Trollope's platitudes about gender seem insignificant in comparison to "the dilemma of the woman faced with no satisfying alternatives" in his novels, and "the easy answers of both male supremacists and feminists alike are seen to be irrelevant" (*Novels* 29).

Critics note a shift in Trollope's attitude toward women in the early to mid-1860s, linking his female characters to an underlying feminist discourse that begins to appear during this decade, as the debate over women's rights was at its height. He met the feminist Kate Field in 1860, and she became a close friend. Margaret F. King has also established a connection between Anthony Trollope and the Langham Place Circle of feminists through his friendship with Emily Faithfull during this period (307). Jane Nardin argues that a change occurred sometime between his composition of *Barchester Towers* (1855) and *The Belton Estate* (1865), an interval that encompasses the appearance of *Can You Forgive Her?* in 1864–65. She notes, "Nearly all the techniques that Trollope uses so energetically in the later novels were pioneered in the early 1860s. The dissatisfied women of the late novels are more dissatisfied, the independent ones more independent, and the novels themselves more openly on the side of such women" (xviii). Margaret Markwick finds that though Trollope lampooned husband hunters in his early novels, after 1868 he ceases to do so (95–96)—a development we can see occurring during the progress of *Can You Forgive Her?* as he initially satirizes Arabella's career on the marriage market and ultimately endorses her quest.[4] Though he may profess conventional notions about gender, Anthony cannot escape his subterranean feminist impulses which are evident in both Arabella and Madame Max.

III.

Anthony Trollope's appropriation of the Widow Barnaby has its genesis in the influence of a literary mother upon her literary son. The correspondences between the two characters are so numerous, it is hard to believe that Anthony did not realize he was rewriting his mother's creation.[15] In his autobiography, he asserts:

> How far I may unconsciously have adopted incidents from what I have read,—either from history or from works of imagination,— I do not know. It is beyond question that a man employed as I have been must do so. But when doing it I have not been aware that I have done it. I have never taken another man's work, and deliberately framed my work upon it. (77–78)[16]

The claim that he never knowingly adopted the work of any other man hints at what he seems unable to consider—that he has appropriated the work of his own mother. Anthony would have been familiar with *The Widow Barnaby*—he comments that Frances's "best novels" were written in the 1830s, which indicates that he both read and approved of at least the first widow novel (*Autobiography* 25). Of course, one possible explanation for the similarities between Martha and Arabella is that both Frances and Anthony were merely responding to changes in the status of the remarrying widow that occurred around them. The remarkable similarities between Martha and Arabella, however, suggest that Anthony's appropriation of Frances's work goes beyond a general literary type.

That Frances influenced not only Anthony's life but also his writing is obvious. He devotes an entire chapter to her in his autobiography, an honor he confers on no other person, including his father.[17] He claims, "Filial duty will not allow me to be silent as to a parent who made for herself a considerable name in the literature of her day" (18), and he identifies himself with Frances and his brother Tom as fellow writers "with the destiny before us three of writing more books than were probably ever before produced by a single family" (19).

It is apparent that Anthony derived his celebrated writing habits from Frances. He describes her method of composition and her output in detail: "She was at her table at four in the morning and had finished her work before the world had begun to be aroused" (*Autobiography* 21). He records that she "continued writing up to 1856 when she was seventy-six years old;—and had at that time produced 114 volumes"—a total of forty-one novels (*Autobiography* 26).[18] When Anthony was nineteen, he watched his mother pursue a strict writing schedule while also nursing three of her children and her husband during fatal illnesses. He comments, "Her power of dividing herself into two parts, and keeping her intellect by itself, clear from the troubles of the world and fit for the duty it had to do, I never saw equalled" (24). Anthony's method of writing was remarkably similar. He developed the habit of getting up at 5:30 every morning, revising and writing for three hours with a goal of producing ten pages, so that, as he describes it, "I could complete my literary work before breakfast" (N. Hall 195). This regimen allowed him to divide his life as he had seen his mother do, maintaining full-time employment as a postal surveyor, until 1867, ultimately producing forty-seven novels and sixteen other works.[19]

His mother's literary influence extended beyond Anthony's writing habits, however. He met his first "literary men" while living with her, and she provided his entrance into the world of authorship, helping in the publication of his first book (*Autobiography* 58). Initially intimidated by her celebrity, he records in his autobiography that Frances "had become one of the most popular novelists of the day," while he was merely a postal clerk. He recalls giving his first manuscript, *The Macdermots of Ballycloran*, to Frances for her London publisher and convincing her not to look at it, because "I knew that she did not give me credit for the sort of cleverness necessary for such work" (51–52). The book was not a success, even though the publisher, Thomas Cautley Newby, tried to convince the public that Frances wrote it (*Autobiography* 251, n. 13). By the time Anthony did begin to prosper, several novels later, Frances had decided to put down her pen, and, he remembers: "she expressed to me her delight that her labours should be at an end and that mine should be beginning in the same field" (*Autobiography* 75). Anthony began authorship in the shadow of his mother's reputation, and from its inception his work was linked to hers both by example and influence.

Despite her professional presence in his life, Anthony does not envision himself in the autobiography as a literary descendent of Frances. Her first book, *The Domestic Manners of the Americans*, enabled the financially floundering family to reunite in a comfortable country home, and *The Widow*

Barnaby also was lucrative. Anthony does admit, "Her volumes were very bitter;—but they were very clever, and they saved the family from ruin" (*Autobiography* 21). However, he dismisses Frances as too naïvely female in her book about America: "No one could have been worse adapted by nature for the task of learning whether a nation was in a way to thrive. Whatever she saw she judged, as most women do, from her own standing point"—a point that he obviously finds deficient (*Autobiography* 21). He rejects her satiric style, commenting that "She was endowed . . . with much creative power, with considerable humour, and a genuine feeling for romance. But she was neither clear-sighted nor accurate; and in her attempts to describe morals, manners, and even facts, was unable to avoid the pitfalls of exaggeration" (*Autobiography* 27). The "pitfalls" that he and Victorian critics lambast are part of Frances's satiric style that gives power to her social commentary, a quality of which he seems unaware.[20] Anthony's comments make it clear that he was unconscious of drawing upon his mother's materials, even though a close examination shows he obviously commandeered the Widow Barnaby as the basis for Arabella Greenow.

We can only speculate about the psychological impact of Frances's death on Anthony, but there was an obvious change in his work at the time. Despite the fact that her literary powers had waned, perhaps while she was still alive he stifled his unconscious impulse to mimic her work, and only after her death could he act upon the urge, unaware he was doing so. However, though Anthony initially presents Arabella with the audacity of Martha Barnaby, eventually he transforms her into an esteemed, authoritative woman, a lot like Frances Trollope in her heyday.

IV.

Political changes between 1839, when Frances's *The Widow Barnaby* was published, and 1864, when Anthony's *Can You Forgive Her?* entered serialization, created a climate in which a remarrying widow could be presented more believably in a straight romance plot. In addition, debates over women's property and the Divorce and Marital Causes Act of 1857 amended ideas about remarriage. By both validating women's right to independent ownership and creating the specter of the remarrying divorcee, these changes gave widows more credibility on the marriage market.

The Divorce and Marital Causes Act of 1857 incorporated a gendered double standard—while men could sue for divorce on grounds of adultery, women not only had to prove adultery but also incest, bestiality, desertion, or cruelty. However, the Act did open divorce courts to the middle class. After it was passed, the number of divorces slowly increased, and by the early 1860s, when Anthony was creating Arabella Greenow, stories of divorce were much in the press. Trials became such a spectator sport that seats were hard to obtain (Horstman 87). Some had speculated that women would hesitate to seek divorces, shrinking from conflict and publicity, but in 1858, the first year the Act was enforced, 97 of the 253 divorce petitions were filed by women (Horstman 86). In the period 1858 to 1868, women initiated 40% of divorce proceedings and 92% of judicial separations (Savage 26).

Property rights and divorce reforms had significant repercussions for remarrying widows. Early in the century, though widows were allowed legal control of property, they were viewed as mere stand-ins for their dead husbands, retaining the family's holdings until inherited by their children, especially sons. With agitation for changes in property laws that followed the 1857 Divorce Act, women began to be recognized as the rightful owners and users of money and goods, and widows were no longer perceived as relics who represented their departed spouses. Consequently, it became more respectable for a widow, who now owned the property from her previous marriage not only legally, but also morally, to use it as she saw fit, even to finance a second marriage. A widow's pursuit of remarriage could be viewed as an appropriate response to her situation rather than as either unethical or ridiculous.

The Divorce Act also changed the climate for remarriage, introducing a new and scandalous phenomenon—previously married but now single men and women who were not widowers and widows. A short entry titled "Indefinite Parties" that appeared in *Punch* on September 5, 1857, one week after the Divorce Act was passed, illustrates the unsettling effect that divorce law had on the concept of remarriage: "A curious question might arise under the new Divorce Act. Suppose two divorced parties choose to be married by banns, how are they to be described? They are not bachelors and spinsters, neither are they widowers and widows; in fact, they are indescribable" (104). Before 1857, the remarriage of divorcees was unthinkable—and therefore unspeakable—but the divorced began to constitute a small but regular feature of the middle class, no longer limited to a rare occurrence among the rich.[21] Initially, the number of remarriages was small: of the 4,000 divorces that were granted between 1861 and 1876, only 696 marriages involved one divorced partner, and in only 13 were both partners divorced. However, the number of remarriages increased steadily over the century. While in 1861 only 10 divorced people remarried in all of England, 390 remarried in 1900, indicating that the stigma of remarriage for the divorced gradually waned (Horstman 156).

The emergence of the remarrying divorced had a direct influence on the status of the remarrying widow. Next to a divorced bride, a widow looking to marry would seem a paragon of virtue. In comparison to a divorcee, a widow could bestow her former husband's property on a new husband with impunity, a responsible adult acting within her legal and moral rights. Though Martha Barnaby, Arabella Greenow, and Madame Max Goesler are all fictional widows with significant amounts of property gained from previous marriages, resources which they are eager to share with new husbands, Greenow and Goesler can be imagined in a serious marriage plot because they were written in the wake of these political developments.

V.

Frances Trollope created Martha Barnaby to be a rogue who transgresses social conventions, involved in a series of adventures negotiated on the boundaries of propriety. As she travels from location to location, Martha preys on the weakness and vanity of others, humorously blind to similar traits in herself. She inhabits the hazy territory between petty fraud and actual criminality, usually only one step ahead of the law, and Victorian reviewers found her to be rather alarming. As a writer for *The Times* of January 24, 1839 describes it: "Her vulgarity is sublime"—she is "amiably disagreeable" and "delightfully disgusting," producing a feeling of "charming horror" in the reader (5). In 1852, *The New Monthly Magazine* recommends *The Widow Barnaby* as "a lady of real character and definite idiosyncrasy" due to the fact that she is "[s]howy, strong-willed, supple-tongued, audacious, garrulous, affected, tawdry, lynx-eyed, indomitable in her scheming, and colossal in her selfishness" ("Female Novelists" 24–25). Frances's contemporaries saw "the Barnaby" as a charming monstrosity.

A comparison between Arabella Greenow and Martha Barnaby makes evident that Anthony appropriated the iconoclastic and conniving aspects of his mother's creation. Lord Mucklebury describes Martha as "a widow, fair, fat, and forty" (252), and she possesses an estate in excess of 400 pounds a year.[22] Arabella is widowed at age forty and possesses an estate of 40,000 pounds (1.66–67), a multiplication of Martha's means. Martha is a forthright husband hunter from the start, made evident when she catechizes herself soon after her husband dies: "Q. What is it that I most wish for on earth? A: A rich and fashionable husband" (56). In contrast, Arabella repeatedly claims she is not looking for a new spouse, saying, "My heart is desolate, and must remain so" (1.72–73), and she professes, "One husband is enough for any woman, and mine lies buried at Birmingham" (2.75). However, her actions belie her words, and she also is on a quest to remarry, strategically flirting with two suitors.

In order to attract husbands, both Martha and Arabella flaunt their fortunes. Upon her arrival at Clifton, Martha asks for the "best rooms in the house" (78). Arabella makes a point of staying at the largest establishment in the Yarmouth row, because she "desired that all the world should see that she had forty thousand pounds of her own" (1.69). The widows also try to look more prosperous by assigning more elite-sounding names to their maids. Martha transforms Betty Jacks into "Jerningham" (75), and Arabella alters Jenny's name to "Jeannette" (1.68), designations that conform to the widows' notions of gentility.

Both widows derive great satisfaction from their new-found autonomy. The narrator describes Martha's feelings at her bereavement: "She certainly felt both proud and happy as she thought of her independence and her wealth. Of the first she unquestionably had as much as it was possible for a woman to possess, for no human being existed who had any right whatever to control her" (53). Arabella tells Kate after her husband's death, "I'm not dependent on the world,—thanks to the care of that sainted lamb. I can hold my own; and as long as I can do that the world won't hurt me." The narrator adds, "Mrs. Greenow was probably right in her appreciation of the value of her independence" (1.73). Though both make it a point to describe their great grief and cry ostentatiously in the presence of others about the loss of their dearly beloved and departed spouses, each appreciates the autonomy of widowhood made possible by property and experience.

Martha and Arabella each use their duty to young nieces as an excuse to resume their own social life early, and their explanations to the younger women are almost identical. Martha tells Agnes:

> be assured, my dear, that however much my own widowed feelings might lead me to prefer the tranquil consolations of retirement, I shall consider it my duty to live more for you than for myself; and I will indeed hasten, in spite of my feelings, to lay aside these sad weeds, that I may be able, with as little delay as possible, to give you such an introduction to the world as my niece has a right to expect. (54)

Later she adds, "it is for your sake, my dear, that I am determined, as far as in me lies, to stop the sorrow that is eating into my very vitals" (85). When Arabella puts her name down at the Assembly Room, her words may lack the high satire of Martha's, but the import and humor are the same. She tells Kate, "my dear; I know very well what I owe to you, and I shall do my duty . . . society can have no charms now for such a one as I am. All that social intercourse could ever do for me lies buried in my darling's grave. . . . But I'm not going to immolate you on the altars of my grief. I shall force myself to go out for your sake, Kate . . ." (1.72–73). By claiming a duty to present their nieces on the marriage market, both widows enable their own social circulation. Though professing to prefer the retirement provided by mourning, they relish a renewed public life.

In addition to using their nieces as a social excuse, both widows circumvent the restrictions of propriety by abandoning mourning too soon. Victorians rigidly adhered to mourning conventions in 1839 when *The Widow Barnaby* was published. By 1864 when *Can You Forgive Her?* began serialization, mourning dress was still de rigueur, as indicated by the author of *Etiquette for Ladies* who notes in 1866 that though mourning is not as strict as it used to be, the custom is still generally observed for two years (66). For Victorians, a widow's clothing indicated the sincerity of her grief, functioning to "identify the mourner, show respect for the dead, elicit the sympathy of the community, and match the mourner's sombre mood" (Jalland 302). Women, in particular, were thought to need a period of outward, public sorrow in order to adjust to the emotional aspects of widowhood. Fanny Douglas writes that some women cling to mourning because it "soothes their own feelings to express them outwardly, and the thought that by so doing they render tender homage to the dead has also its consolation" (111). In *Manners and Social Usages*, Mrs. John Sherwood adds that "mourning dress does protect a woman while in deepest grief against the untimely gayety of a passing stranger. It is a wall, a cell of refuge. Behind a black veil she can hide herself as she goes out for business or recreation, fearless of any intrusion" (189). Some widows even chose to remain in mourning for the rest of their lives.[23]

Wearing mourning for the proper period was considered essential for respectability. Sherwood argues that "Many people hold the fact that a widow . . . wears her crape for two years to be greatly to her credit" but if she changes her widows' weeds before that time it is said that she "did not care much for the deceased" (198). After cautioning against excessive mourning, Douglas asserts: "Almost worse than the woman who mourns too much is the woman who mourns too little. One can forgive her garments, but not her apologies" (114). After the proper period had expired, changing from mourning to regular dress was a necessary, though delicate, passage; it is "a matter in which every gentlewoman should decide for herself, and in which none should too rashly condemn the other. The safest principle is, that whatever the feeling instinctively dictates cannot be wholly wrong" (Douglas 110). However, Sherwood counsels the widow to use discretion by gradually effecting the process: "It shocks persons of good taste to see a light-hearted young widow jump into colors, as if she had been counting the hours. If black is to be dispensed with, let its retirement be slowly and gracefully marked by quiet costumes, as the feeling of grief, yielding to the kindly influence of time, is shaded off into resignation and cheerfulness" (196). Retiring one's mourning by degrees was an essential duty of the genteel widow.

Two years of full black mourning were required of widows until late in the century, with exacting standards of color and fabric allowed for each period after the death of a spouse, rules which both Martha and Arabella bend to their own purposes. For a year and a day dresses of dull, nonreflective black paramatta and crepe were worn, followed by dullish black silk trimmed in crepe for nine months, then three months of combined silk and wool or cotton paramatta. In the final six months widows could assume the colors of half mourning—grey, lavender, or black and white in their trimmings (Jalland 300; Cunnington and Lucas 268). Widows also wore indoor caps of white muslin trimmed in front with ruched white crape, with a long white streamer hanging down from behind by mid-century. An outdoor bonnet with veil was considered essential (Cunnington and Lucas 266–67).[24] The strictures of mourning fell heavily on bereaved women, as Sherwood observed in 1888, "everyone who has seen an English widow will agree that she makes a 'hearse' of herself" (189).

Both Martha and Arabella circumvent the restrictions of the mourning period by lying about how long their husbands have been dead. Martha tells her landlady that she has been a widow for "very nearly six months" (83), while the narrator informs us that "Mr. Barnaby, however, had been alive and well exactly three months after the period named by his widow as that of his death" (84). Arabella also doubles the time of her widowhood; when her husband has been dead for six months, she tells Cheesacre "you don't know what it is to have buried the pride of your youth hardly yet twelve months" (1.213). When she has been a widow for nine months, she refers to the "melancholy circumstance" as having taken place fifteen (1.413) and then eighteen months previously (1.414). By accelerating their widowhood, each more quickly can begin the business of finding a new spouse.

The widows use similar methods to end the isolation imposed by mourning. When Mr. Barnaby has been dead about six months, Martha puts her name down for the Assembly rooms at Clifton, subscribes to the library where gossip freely flows, and attends a ball. She does decide it may be impolitic to dance at the ball in front of her wealthy sister-in-law, but she plays cards, displaying much "vivacity" and "*enjouement*" (145). Arabella settles in Yarmouth when she has been a widow for four months and makes similar social advances, registering at the Assembly Room, receiving guests, all the while smiling "from beneath her widow's cap in a most bewitching way" (1.73), walking on the pier with Kate and Bellfield, and rowing with friends down the beach for a picnic on the sands.

Martha and Arabella also flout the spirit of mourning. Martha challenges the conventional paradigm by finding her weeds "so hatefully unbecoming in her estimation that she firmly believed the inventor of it must have been actuated by some feeling akin to that which instituted the horrible Hindoo rite of which she had heard, whereby living wives were sacrificed to their departed husbands" (57). Her defiance and comparison of mourning to suttee allege that it is unchristian or (perhaps even worse) un-British. In either case, her failure to be soothed by her attire as an act of homage to the deceased flouts propriety and indicates her resolve not to be subsumed by her dead husband's identity. She uses her bereaved state as a convenient device for arousing sympathy, while also making the most of the freedom and goods offered by her widowed state.

Martha begins to transgress mourning customs when she has been a widow only three months. During a short sojourn in Exeter she not only discards black crepe for black satin and silk, but then wears lavender half-mourning (84), and soon "there was no colour of the rainbow that did not by degrees find its way amidst her trimmings and decorations" (86). Though she assumes deep mourning again six months into her bereavement when she reaches her sister-in-law's house at Clifton, she soon moderates black satin with bright colors, so that "although in mourning, her general appearance was exceedingly shewy and gay" (123). The widow's audacity is increased by her contrast with Agnes, who continues to wear mourning at her aunt's behest, ostensibly, so Martha claims, because Agnes looks well in black, but in reality to save money by consigning her abandoned finery to the younger woman. Agnes, true to the female mourning prescription, says that her veil makes her feel "more comfortable" in public (132). Martha's accelerated mourning liberates her husband-hunting, an act of perfidy the novel exploits as high comedy.

Like Martha, Arabella defies standards of proper behavior by using her weeds to romantic advantage. At the picnic in Yarmouth, we are told, "She had not mitigated her weeds by half an inch. She had scorned to make any compromise between the world of pleasure and the world of woe" (1.80–81). However, instead of slighting mourning early, she wears her black dresses and widows caps coquettishly to appear more attractive to suitors. Her impropriety is not in gaudy colors but in the amount of attention she lavishes upon her gowns. Arabella shows her widow's weeds to Kate "with all the pride of a young bride when she shows the glories of her trousseau to the friend of her bosom," obviously not the expected attitude for a grieving widow (1.70). She also wears her widow's cap "jauntily," so that it shows "just so much of her rich brown hair as to give her the appearance of youth which she desired" (1.413). By using mourning clothes for flirtation, she undercuts its intended purpose: "there was that of genius about Mrs. Greenow, that she had turned every seeming disadvantage to some special profit, and had so dressed herself that though she had obeyed the law to the letter, she had thrown the spirit of it to the winds" (1.413). Though Arabella follows the dictates of strict mourning, wearing the required clothing and repeatedly calling attention to the excellencies of her dead spouse, she flouts its purpose, which becomes the subject of comedy, her attire even more subversive than Martha's.

Both widows' wiles are effective: six months after her husband's death, Martha has a proposal from Major Allen, and she decides to leave Clifton so that "her marriage, within seven months of her husband's death, might not take place under the immediate observation of his nearest relations" (183). This engagement is later canceled, but she becomes the bride of Mr. O'Donagough a few months later. Arabella receives a proposal from Cheesacre when she has been a widow for about five months (1.96), but acts as if the offer is an insult to her sense of propriety. However, she gives Bellfield "ground of hope" before she has been a widow a year (2.149), and he is accepted and kissed just a year from Greenow's death (2.261).

VI.

Despite their similarities, Arabella develops into a far different kind of widow than Martha. Arabella's plot in *Can You Forgive Her?* often is dismissed for serious consideration by critics who interpret her as minor comedic relief that contrasts with the more significant stories of Alice Vavasor and Lady Glencora. Edward Marsh denigrates her tale as "farce at its lowest," dispatching it outright: "luckily it is easily detachable, and I strongly advise anyone reading the book for the first time to skip it ruthlessly" (v). Many others as well view Arabella only through the stereotype of the farcical widow, missing the generic change that shifts from satire to a more realist mode that imagines new possibilities for women. Though Anthony begins his depiction of Arabella in the style of his mother's self-determining but buffoonish widow, he ultimately transforms her from caricature to a sincerely attractive midlife woman who reinvents her life according to advantages based on her experience.[25]

For the first ten chapters of the novel, Arabella is presented as a parody of the proper widow, a depiction voiced through the perceptions of her niece, Kate Vavasor. At first, Kate sees Arabella as "a good woman . . . of a bad sort" who was wrong to marry a rich man thirty years her senior. She protests against having to visit her aunt, but concludes that she has no choice. From this initial perspective, Kate describes Arabella as ready to flirt with any man, and her mourning seems outrageously vain. Her eyes are "always red with weeping, and yet she is ready every minute with a full battery of execution for any man that she sees" (1.56). Her lamentations are a "performance" in which she would "address the shade of the departed one in terms of most endearing affection" using ostentatious—and incorrect—Latin: "Peace be to his manes" (1.70). Though Kate "is surprised to see that real tears . . . were making their way down her aunt's cheeks" (1.70), she also observes that the tears are checked by a fashionable mourning handkerchief. Kate views her aunt as both boring and hypocritical, interesting only for her forty thousand pounds.

After chapter ten and in the remainder of the novel written after Frances's death, Kate's comments change from burlesque, and though her plot still has a comedic resonance, Arabella transforms into a truly admirable character. Margaret F. King notes that Arabella "becomes increasingly a figure of comic delight, even admiration—a shift signaled by Kate's changing discourse about her" (321). As chapter nineteen opens, Kate reflects upon her new perspective:

> She had laughed at Mrs. Greenow before she went to Yarmouth. . . . She had spoken of her aunt as a silly, vain, worldly woman, weeping crocodile tears for an old husband whose death had released her from the tedium of his company, and spreading lures to catch new lovers. . . . But Mrs. Greenow had about her something more than Kate had acknowledged when she first attempted to read her aunt's character. (1.197)

Kate realizes that her aunt is "clever . . . generous . . . pleasant" and now has "more appearance of true feeling than Kate had observed before" (1.197–98). As the narrator asserts, "There had come to be a considerable amount of confidence between the aunt and the niece" by the time that she and Arabella are together at Netherfields after the Squire's death (2.239).

The spirit of Arabella's mourning shifts, and as James R. Kincaid argues, her grief "is not entirely hypocritical" (*Novels* 47). Even after her engagement to Bellfield when crocodile tears would no longer be of service to her campaign on the marriage market, Arabella tells Kate that though she will remarry, she will never truly love again: "As for love, my dear, that's gone,—clear gone! . . . Some women can love twice, but I am not one of them. I wish I could" (2.241). Kate notes later that her handkerchief "still bore the deepest hem of widowhood," and she knows Arabella will continue to use it until she is remarried (2.390). The handkerchief that was a marker of hypocrisy becomes a symbol of sincerity. Despite her engagement, Arabella's grief over Greenow's death is believable by the end of the novel.

In both *The Widow Barnaby* and *Can You Forgive Her?* a rivalry between the generations is set up, developed in terms of clothing and physical appearance, a competition that denigrates Martha Barnaby but augments Arabella's attractions. In *The Widow Barnaby*, Agnes acts as a reverse foil for her aunt, emphasizing Martha's comic dowdiness, her simple elegance contrasting with Martha's audacious showiness. When they attend church for the first time in Clifton, Agnes is wearing deep mourning for her uncle—all black except for a white collar—provided from Martha's cast-offs. The widow's garb is the antithesis of Agnes's quiet and proper mourning, her excessive costume described with comedic copiousness:

> On this occasion she came forth in a new dress of light grey gros-de-Naples, with a gay bonnet of paille de riz, decorated with poppy blossoms both within and without, a "lady-like" profusion of her own embroidery on cuffs, collar, and pocket-handkerchief, her well-oiled ringlets half hiding her large, coarse, handsome face, her eyes set off by a suffusion of carmine, and her whole person redolent of musk. (129)

The two are "as strangely a matched pair in appearance as can well be imagined" (129), a juxtaposition that continues throughout the novel, highlighting Agnes's superior taste and looks. For example, when Frederick Stephenson first sees Agnes he proclaims, "In my life I never beheld so beautiful a creature. . . . Her form, her feet, her movement," while his companion, Colonel Hubert, is taken aback that she would appear with a companion who is "such a dame as that feather and furbelow lady" (133). Martha's forthright showiness is made obvious by her understated and refined niece.

Even before the shift from comedy to realism takes place in *Can You Forgive Her?*, Arabella's physical presence eclipses that of her niece, but she is presented as sensational, a sight that draws attention and borders on the inappropriate. When Arabella goes to church on her first Sunday in Yarmouth in "all the glory of her widowhood" (1.70), not only does she overshadow her niece, but she also draws attention away from the spiritual purpose of the occasion: "Kate Vavasor became immediately aware that a great sensation had been occasioned by their entrance, and equally aware that none of it was due to her. . . . How many ladies of forty go to church without attracting the least attention! But it is hardly too much to say that every person in that church had looked at Mrs. Greenow" (1.71). By out-shining her niece, Arabella blatantly transgresses behavioral prescriptions for midlife women, but she later garners respect by nurturing Kate.[26] Though her attempt to make a match between her discarded suitor, Cheesacre, and Kate adds light comedy, she eventually does make a successful match between Cheesacre and Charlie Fairstairs, an arrangement Kate praises as highly suitable (2.389). Not only are Arabella's charms presented as authen-tic, but her altruism toward the younger generation takes the remarrying widow from satire to benevolent patronage.

Anthony inverts Barnaby's self-serving actions in Arabella's behavior toward her dependents. Martha always is intent on her own advantage, never balking at the chance to use others to promote her schemes, especially her niece Agnes. Arabella, however, is truly altruistic toward Kate, who confesses, "with all her faults, I believe she would go through fire and water to serve me" (1.324). Martha gives her used clothes to her servant Jerningham as bribes for spying on men and makes Agnes wear them to save money. Arabella also passes down her cast-off clothes, but they are desirable acquisitions: "When Mrs. Greenow made a slight change in her mourning ... Jeanette reaped a rich harvest in gifts of clothes" (1.198), and the narrator tells us that Arabella "would spare neither herself nor her purse on Kate's behalf" (1.74). Martha loudly attests to her sacrifices and generosity toward her niece while giving her only a closet to sleep in and cast-off dresses, finally threatening to turn her out "neck and heels into the street" if Agnes will not agree to be Martha's factotum while she is in debtor's prison (306). Arabella's behavior toward her beneficiaries, though not entirely selfless, is motivated by genuine goodwill.

Martha and Arabella both lie as they husband-hunt, but Arabella's initial mendacity is eventually forgiven. After Martha and Major Allen discover that each has deceived the other about the extent of their fortunes, their love affair comes to a crashing end, and Martha plans her "next campaign" at Cheltenham: "She knew that the exploits she contemplated were hazardous, as well as splendid; and that, although success was probable, failure might be possible ..." (221). Her lies are presented as daring and comic, skills for marrying into money and security. Can You Forgive Her?, in contrast, downplays Arabella's dissimulation as merely a loveable foible. Other characters, as well as Arabella herself, acknowledge that she revises facts, but her lies are presented as either unimportant or understandable. Kate is aware that Arabella has dissimulated about the length of her widowhood, her intentions for remarriage, and her pursuit of suitors, but this does not prevent her shift in attitude from vilifying to admiring her aunt. Hearing Arabella's version of events near the end of the novel, Kate merely concludes that "she had a pleasure in telling her own story, and told it as though she believed every word that she spoke" (2.391). Arabella's prevarication is charming, amusing, and easily forgiven.

Perhaps the most revealing of all Martha's personal habits is her propensity to wear rouge, an offense mentioned many times by other characters as a marker of her vulgarity and mendacity. Victorians thought rouging improper, not only vain, but a visual lie. Mrs. Merrifield writes in Dress As A Fine Art, "We violate the laws of nature when we seek to repair the ravages of time on our complexions by paint" and she warns that using makeup "is not only bad taste, but it is a positive breach of sincerity" (2). Several characters in The Widow Barnaby comment disparagingly about Martha's cosmetics. When she "touched up her bloom to the point she deemed to be the most advantageous," her sister-in-law concludes she "looked precisely like a clever caricature" of herself (104). Her brother-in-law decides that he will "feel more comfortable when the rouge pots were all gone" from his house, because they are a bad influence on his daughters (108), and even Martha's fiancé O'Donagough threatens to delay their marriage unless she stops coloring her cheeks (373). Martha temporarily stops using makeup when such action serves her purposes, but she continually returns to the "paint pot," a joke that recurs throughout the novel.

In contrast, Anthony specifically points out that Arabella does not use rouge. When Bellfield accuses her of giving way too much to grief, she cries, her "soft tears . . . showing in their course that she at any rate used no paint in producing that freshness of colour which was one of her great charms" (1.207). Instead, Bellfield is lampooned as vain and performatively insincere about age when Kate notes in a letter: "He paints his whiskers, too, which I don't like; and, being forty, tries to look like twenty-five" (1.139). Despite the other wiles she may use to capture male hearts, Arabella's beauty as a midlife marriageable woman is genuine.

Martha Barnaby is caricatured sexually as the feminine grotesque, while Arabella has authentic sexual attractions. When she chooses a husband, she bases her decision on pleasure, and the text indicates that a large part of that pleasure will be sexual. As several critics have pointed out, Arabella champions desire as appropriate for the midlife woman. Jane Nardin notes that her interest in sex is not censured (134). George Levine comments on her "un-Victorian frankness that's quite satisfying" (11). Margaret Markwick argues that Trollope's novels refute a paradigm of sexlessness for Victorian women and finds in Arabella "an open acknowledgment that being in love and desiring to marry is about wanting to touch someone in an intimate way, and about enjoying being touched" (80). Deborah Denenholz Morse finds in Arabella an "obvious sexuality" (9) and stresses that while she repressed her "strongly sexual nature" to marry the elderly Greenow, in her widowhood she "embarks on a new life of freedom and sexual possibility" finally making a choice that is sensual rather than moral (10). In Arabella, Trollope acknowledges midlife female libido for women "of a certain age" who have sexual knowledge based on experience.

Early in the book, Arabella's sexuality calls her character into question. She has tarnished her reputation before her first marriage by suggestive behavior: "At thirty-four she was still unmarried. She had, moreover, acquired the character of being a flirt; and I fear that the stories which were told of her, though doubtless more than half false, had in them sufficient of truth to justify the character. Now this was very sad, seeing that Arabella Vavasor had no fortune. . . ." (1.66–67). In its mock seriousness, this passage is comedic, a tone continued when Arabella explains to Kate that coquetry can control rampant sexuality: "If I had sons and daughters I should think a little flirting the very best thing for them as a safety-valve" (1.100). She also promotes such dalliance among "old people" who should "be content to flirt together" (1.100). Randall Craig argues that "Mrs. Greenow's failure to take the accusation of flirtation seriously—in fact, she defends it—is proof of her incorrigible character and excludes her from polite society" (221), and when Arabella puts her "doctrine of flirtation" into action, the narrator does draw attention to her behavior as comedic. She and Bellfield put their heads into the same picnic hamper, described as "innocent by-play" (1.82), and when they repeat the action later in the day, "a great intimacy was thereby produced" (1.88). The narrator's denial of inappropriate behavior—"I by no means mean to insinuate there was anything wrong in this. People engaged together in unpacking pies and cold chickens must have their heads in the same hamper"—merely underscores her impropriety (1.88). Descriptions of Bellfield also suggest Arabella's frank sexual appraisal. Not only is his face "handsome" with "well arranged features," but his body is foregrounded in the observation that he is "a well-made man" down to "the exquisite shapes of his pseudo-sailor's duck trousers" (1.79). That Bellfield has been aware of Arabella's eye for his fit physique is suggested in his later comment to Cheesacre: "You're a podgy man, you see, and Mrs. Greenow doesn't like podgy men" (1.416).

After chapter 10, Arabella's flirtations abate and her sexuality is valorized. When she and Bellfield bend over an album containing pictures of Greenow in chapter 40, as her mourning bonnet brushes his whiskers, their fingers touch over a picture of the deceased. Arabella knows Charlie Fairstairs and Mr. Cheesacre are watching her, and the comment that she "was certainly a woman of great genius and of great courage" adds a humorous note of mock heroism in a scene of far more muted flirtation than her earlier behavior (1.419). When Arabella champions the idea that women should be sexually self-actualized, she is presented in a much more sympathetic light. Instead of just advising Kate to flirt, she educates her about the dangers of frigidity. She explains that lack of beauty and money are not the key impediments to attractiveness, but naïveté about desire, cautioning: "There's a stand-off about some women,—what the men call a 'nollimy tangere,' " a "touch me not" attitude that turns men away. Some women are "so hard and so stiff" that "a man would as soon think of putting his arm round a poplar tree," and women who "look as though matrimony itself were improper, and as if they believed the little babies were found about in the hedges and ditches" are "a deal too backward" (2.240). Kate's response, "Yours is a comfortable doctrine, aunt," indicates that instead of being horrified, Kate accepts her aunt's advice to seek sexual knowledge and express attraction (2.240).

Because Arabella is a midlife widow, she is in a position to indulge in romance, described with a trope of "rocks and valleys." She decides that since she first married for money, now she may "venture on a little love" (2.65). Alice and Glencora must marry prudently, because, as young women they need husbands to found their fortunes and be responsible fathers to their future children. Arabella, however, chooses the "wild" man over the "worthy," because she has married them sequentially. As a widow, a woman of age and experience, she is allowed options not available to her younger counterparts.

Arabella is aware of the limitations of her choice, however, telling Kate, ". . . I do like a little romance about them,—just a sniff, as I call it, of the rocks and valleys. One knows that it doesn't mean much; but it's like artificial flowers,—it gives a little colour, and takes off the dowdiness. Of course, bread-and-cheese is the real thing" (2.242). Because she already has acquired the bedrock of monetary stability through first marriage, the "bread and cheese" that a man like Cheesacre can offer, she can now seek pleasure, the "rocks and valleys" offered by Bellfield. However, she refuses to indulge in high-flown overstatement about romance: when Bellfield says, "Arabella, you'll make me the happiest man in the world," she responds, "That's all fudge" (2.251), deflating his extravagant praise. Her romance of "rocks and valleys" is practical and clear-sighted, not the satirical hyperbole with which Martha Barnaby bedecks her love affairs.

Arabella and Bellfield are described as a romantic couple that is specifically middle-aged and sexual. They go out walking together, and Arabella teases Bellfield that perhaps he will think her too old. He replies that "she was just the proper age for a walking companion, as far as his taste went" (2.250). When he kisses her on the high road from Shap to Vavasor, because she is still in widow's weeds and "neither he nor his sweetheart were under forty, perhaps it was as well that they were not caught toying together in so very public a place" (2.252–53). Though this warning hints that at their age they should keep intimacies private, it also specifies the explicitly sexual nature of their attraction.

Despite the shift from comedy, Arabella's denouement is similar to Martha's. Both widows chose a compromise, a flirtatious rake who will not bring money but pleasure, while allowing them a large measure of independence. This strategy hilariously challenges propriety when practiced by Martha, but is suggestively liberating in Arabella's case. Martha decides to marry the would-be missionary Patrick O'Donagough after several reverses—the failure of her plan to snag Lord Mucklebury, her arrest for debt, the refusal of the flirtatious lawyer Morrison to render legal help when he discovers her financial problems, and Agnes's resistance to her commands from prison. Vexed and humbled, she decides to make the best of the remaining possibilities and looks into the affairs of O'Donagough, a penniless but well-connected man, the illegitimate son of a lord who provides him financial bail-outs. She decides that he will do quite nicely, because not only would " 'The reverend Mr. O'Donagough' ... look very well in the paragraph which she was determined should record her marriage in the Exeter paper" (370), but he is handsome and a decade younger than she (333). In addition, with O'Donagough she will retain control of her money. They immigrate to Australia and the charming scoundrel suits Martha until his excesses at the horse races cause his death. Always dexterous and adaptable, she manages quite easily on the last page of the novel to make a similar match with another rascal, her old lover, Major Allen, who conveniently turns up in Sydney at the right moment. Martha manages to have it all her own way—obtaining a husband for her pleasure while also retaining independence.

Anthony resolves Arabella's husband hunt in a similar way. Though forthright determination ushers Arabella through problems with disarming dexterity, the marriage market does have its complications. She settles for a solution in Bellfield that is problematic yet palatable. She is aware of his limitations as a spouse, and the struggle she faces as his wife: "he'll give me a great deal of trouble. I know he will. He'll always be wanting my money, and, of course, he'll get more than he ought. ... And he'll smoke too many cigars, and perhaps drink more brandy-and-water than he ought. And he'll be making eyes, too, at some of the girls who'll be fools enough to let him" (2.241). The description of her marriage, however, is genuinely laudatory and the satire gentle: "Mrs. Greenow's own marriage was completed with perfect success" because she "took Captain Bellfield for better or for worse, with a thorough determination to make the best of his worst" (2.400). Bellfield "had been in luck" to marry her, because she would forgive him, gratify his desires, and "keep from him the power of ruining them both" (2.401). As Morse notes, "she certainly does not recognize her 'better self' in Bellfield" but "chooses a weak man whom she can master" (11).

Despite Bellfield's problematic aspects, however, Arabella's choice is liberating. Margaret F. King argues that though Trollope ultimately overrides Alice's and Glencora's yearning for independence, he allows Arabella to "combine self-direction with domesticity" (312) and prevents patriarchal ideology "from having the last—or at least the only—word" (323). Morse finds a feminist impulse in Arabella because "she embarks as a widow upon a new life of freedom and sexual possibility" (10), and her plot "images the dislocation of conventional attitudes about women in relation to courtship and marriage" (10–11). King sees Arabella's plot as a "discourse and narrative of comic—and specifically female—liberation" in which she subverts the wild man/worthy man paradigm by virtue of the fact that she can choose at all (320–21). These critics interpret Arabella as an example of Anthony's emergent feminism as she disrupts marital conventions, obtaining mastery over her affianced husband and her fate. This is not a perfect union, but a compromise between pleasure and prudence reached by a woman with the experience to make an informed choice. Based on the independent yet farcical Widow Barnaby, Arabella achieves a midlife union that is far more valorized than Martha's comedic fate.

VII.

While Anthony Trollope depicts Arabella Bellfield's marriage as a compromise for which she settles, he takes the remarrying widow further in Madame Max Goesler, whose position as a midlife woman of experience enables her to become the most liberated of his female characters. Jane Nardin finds that Marie Goesler offers "Trollope's most feminist revision of the genre" of romantic comedy, as she "successfully challenges Victorian patriarchy," and ultimately achieves greater autonomy than any other heroine in his later novels (193). In *Phineas Finn* and *Phineas Redux*, Marie changes from a vamp to a self-actualized, independent woman married to her equal, an achievement made possible by middle age.[27] Like Arabella, she initially is denigrated, but Trollope eventually writes her into an admirable, sexual, fully realized midlife heroine.

In *Phineas Finn*, Anthony begins Marie's story by stereotyping her as a middle-aged, foreign temptress, the daughter of a German Jewish attorney and the widow of a wealthy Austrian banker. She is a minor character introduced in the second half of the novel and seems only an ambitious and crass social climber (Letwin 74). Gossips conjecture that she has a second husband and has been the duke's mistress, and she distances herself from Victorian norms by repeatedly claiming to be mystified by the British (*Finn* 146). Marie initially is unladylike, foreign, and schemingly erotic. She uses her arresting eyes "in a manner which is as yet hardly common with Englishwomen . . . to intend that you should know that she employed them to conquer you" (*Finn* 2.25). Her sexuality is dangerous, enticing the aging duke (Morse 71). His desire is so obvious that Lady Glencora, who fears her son could be supplanted by a new heir, begs Madame Max to drop the seduction.

Marie is "unlike"—not a proper British woman, her clothing a metonymy for her foreign peculiarity: her "dress was unlike the dress of other women . . . unlike in make, unlike in colour, and unlike in material" and "the ordinary observer would not see that it was unlike in form for any other purpose than that of maintaining its general peculiarity of character" (*Finn* 2.25-26). The erotic nature of this "unlikeness" is made evident by a sensuous visual journey over her body: "My pen may not dare to describe the traceries of yellow and ruby silk which went in and out through the black lace, across her bosom, and round her neck, and over her shoulders, and along her arms, and down to the very ground at her feet" (*Finn* 2.26). The narrator's moving gaze fondles her body with voyeuristic pleasure cloaked as a description of mere silk. The self-conscious voice that denies itself permission to do what it nevertheless is doing signals both nervousness and pleasure about her midlife body. Only because she is a woman of age and experience can the narrator take such liberties and then later valorize her, a maneuver that would be unacceptable with a virginal female character.

However, after initially introducing her as a seductress, Anthony revises his portrayal of Madame Max. As Elizabeth R. Epperly argues, "Trollope seems to change his mind about her . . . by the end of *Phineas Finn* it is clear that Madame Max is both desirable and worthy" (29–30). Epperly finds that the change in Madame Max occurs when the reader is allowed into her consciousness and can see her "struggling for position and self-control" (28). She considers the duke's marriage proposal, described metaphorically as playing with his coronet in her lap, and seems conniving. But, as James R. Kincaid observes, her "ruthlessly unsentimental examination of her own feelings" allows her to see that the match would be ludicrous (*Novels* 211). Her decision to reject his offer is based on self-knowledge and humility, and she is never alienated by the text again.

By the end of *Phineas Finn*, Madame Max has become an appealing figure, no longer "unlike," but a woman of estimable uniqueness. She initially is described with a manly metaphor, compared to a conquering knight (*Finn* 2.25), but her unnatural masculinity changes to feminine strength when she rescues Phineas by her wits, and she is a courageous, independent woman of ability and experience, valorized rather than vilified.[28] As the novel progresses, Marie's eroticism is transformed from a threat to mature and knowledgeable sexuality. Jane Nardin interprets her as "the first of Trollope's respectable, 'serious' female characters to have access to a range of conjecture upon sexual matters greater than that of the narrator" (194). For example, when Glencora suggests that the duke may yet produce an heir, Madame Max laughs, suggesting her experience with the complicated sexuality of an elderly man such as her former husband (Nardin 194). Madame Max's mature sexuality is transformed to an asset instead of a threat.

Marie also becomes more appealing as we are given increased access to her vulnerability and awareness of her own limitations (Epperly 28). She is humanized by midlife fears about time running out for romantic possibilities with Phineas: "She had never yet known what it was to have anything of the pleasure of love. . . . Might there not yet be time left for her to try it without selfishness,—with an absolute devotion of self,—if she could only find the right companion? There was one who might be such a companion" (*Finn* 2.203). As a single woman, she has been wary of behavior that would spark censure, but has grown weary of the restriction entailed. She tells Phineas she is "the most cabined, cribbed, and confined creature in the world!" and adds, "I have been fighting my way up for the last four years, and have not allowed myself the liberty of one flirtation" (*Finn* 2.316). When Marie can no longer bear these strictures, she proposes to Phineas, which the chapter title, "Madame Max's Generosity," presents as noble rather than transgressive (Morse 79). Glencora defends the practice of women proposing, saying it is becoming common, words Juliet McMaster finds hyperbolic but also an "observation of social change, even if only of that which occurs within the world of Trollope's novels" (170). McMaster concludes: "Trollope by no means wants his readers to condemn Madame Max's offer of herself to Phineas. That is a true and courageous gesture" (169). Marie's proposal is not transgressive but admirable, an example of Trollope's lurking feminism.

At the close of *Phineas Finn*, however, Marie is not yet a suitable mate for the protagonist, so in *Phineas Redux* Anthony rewrites her yet again. He removes her foreign taint, and she no longer draws attention to her un-English origins. In *Phineas Finn*, she is "that German woman" (2.345) but in *Phineas Redux* becomes only "she with the German name" (1.123). Her Jewish background, deprecated in the first novel, is no longer mentioned in the second, all anti-Semitism channeled toward Emilius, Lizzie Eustace's bigamist husband. Instead, Marie is esteemed universally throughout *Phineas Redux*: "Credit was given to her everywhere for good nature, discretion, affability, and a certain grace of demeanour which always made her charming. She was known to be generous, wise, and of high spirit" (*Redux* 2.70). Clearly, in *Phineas Redux* Trollope valorizes her.

However, of even more portent than Marie's decorum and British assimilation is the author's legerdemain with her age (Epperly 24). Anthony employs a fictional sleight of hand in order to achieve an ideal union, freezing Marie in early midlife while the other characters grow older around her. Anthony insists that with the Phineas books he makes a special effort to register time and modify characters as they age: "In writing *Phineas Finn* I had constantly before me the necessity of progression in character,—of marking the changes in men and women which would naturally be produced by the lapse of years. . . . I knew not only their present characters but how those characters were to be affected by years and circumstances" (*Autobiography* 202–3).

He achieves this with Phineas, who evolves from a naïve political acolyte into a seasoned member of Parliament, addressing the assembly with aplomb as he conducts national business. Phineas's aging is consistent: he is twenty-five at the beginning of *Phineas Finn* (1.34), thirty at the end (2.335), and thirty-two at the start of *Phineas Redux* (1.96). Other characters are pointedly aged between the two novels as well. Violet Chiltern has become a mother, and Lady Laura has lived for several years in Dresden to avoid contact with her husband. In contrast to this careful tracking of other characters, Madame Max is not allowed to age. When she is introduced midway through *Phineas Finn*, Marie is "probably something over thirty years of age" (2.25), several years older than Phineas, but halfway through *Phineas Redux* she is "hardly yet thirty" (1.267), and later she is said to be a few months younger than Lady Laura (*Redux* 2.225), who is said to be the same age as Phineas, thirty-two (*Redux* 1.96). Instead of growing older, Marie becomes younger between the two novels.

This fictive magic makes Marie and Phineas more compatible mates according to the Victorian norm that men should marry women younger than themselves.[29] Phineas views age disparity as an impediment to becoming involved with Lady Laura when he first meets her: "he was by no means in love with Lady Laura,—who was, as he imagined, somewhat older than himself" (*Finn* 1.30). Marie is older than Phineas when she is attracted to him in the first novel, and he marries the youthful Mary Flood Jones. Anthony wrote in his autobiography that he regretted pairing Phineas with inexperience and naïveté: "I was wrong to marry him to a simple pretty Irish girl, who could only be felt as an encumbrance. . . . I had no alternative but to kill the pretty simple Irish girl which was an unpleasant and awkward necessity" (202). Phineas finds a truly companionate marriage when he learns to prefer mature experience over Mary's "sweet, clinging, feminine softness" (*Finn* 2.232).

Because a neophyte is an inadequate mate for Phineas, Trollope creates a more appropriate match in Marie. Even before the revision in her age, Madame Max appears youthful—she has "young and fresh" lips (*Finn* 2.144), Lady Laura calls her "young and pretty" (*Finn* 2.166), and Phineas tells her she is "young and beautiful" (*Finn* 2.319). Though she looks young, however, Phineas does not succumb to her charms until she becomes his junior in fact as well as appearance. As Polhemus argues, his "love changes from Mary, a cute blob of Irish dew bound to fade . . . to Marie, an active, sophisticated woman with independent spiritual and physical needs, a sharp mind, and an erotic history" ("Being in Love" 394–95). In a contest between the sophisticated versus the simple woman, Phineas ends up with the better choice, a "strong witty passionate woman mated with a man who appreciates her unconventional qualities and is himself sensitive and sexual" (Morse 39). As Glencora acknowledges in *The Prime*

Minister, bemoaning to Marie her own husband's coldness, "Think of your life and of mine. You have had lovers" (1.350). A seasoned widow, Marie is a much more appropriate partner for the socially and politically sophisticated Phineas than dependent, submissive Mary. Their marriage is one of the most successful unions in the Palliser series (Morse 39), made possible because the spouses come to their union with a past. Marie can decline the Duke's proposal because she has freedom to choose for love not money due to her previous marriage. Phineas, too, finds a more fulfilling life with a mature wife who can be his equal.

In *Phineas Redux,* Anthony creates a midlife marriage without the compromises that flaw Arabella Greenow's union with Captain Bellfield. Marie tells Phineas, "It must be an even partnership" (*Redux* 2.355). Their "easy camaraderie" is evidence of equality (Morse 79), pictured physically by their seated position, holding hands, when Phineas proposes (Morse 83). Their marriage balances "involvement and detachment," and "is the Victorian ideal transformed out of recognition," as they share "power, freedom, professional engagement, and the right to obey conscience on equal terms" (Nardin 200).

While Frances Trollope exploits and questions the trope of the remarrying midlife widow as the feminine grotesque, her son Anthony transforms and transcends the stereotype in his increasingly valorized widows, fully realized as sexual women and independent adults. Robert M. Polhemus describes the "Lot complex" that draws together older men and younger women, the men seeking to confer and continue potency and the women to appropriate patriarchal power for themselves (*Lot's Daughters* 4). Polhemus, however, discusses only young women and does not explore the next part of the story. Arabella and Marie wield authority, obtain younger husbands, share their resources, and in the latter case, establish grounds for equality because they are former daughters of Lot, having obtained their power from older husbands. Their autonomy, however, has been earned not only through the agency of older men, but by their decisions based on experience, a legacy of their midlife status.

In Arabella and Madame Max, Anthony Trollope offers alternatives to the vision of midlife widowhood upon which Punch's 1842 leering, clownish woman is based, ideas that became more possible in the latter decades of the nineteenth century. As I have discussed in the previous chapter, Eliza Lynn Linton's 1868 diatribe against the midlife flirt and H. Rider Haggard's 1886 story of frightful excess in the aging female body demonstrate ways in which older women were denigrated and feared throughout the century. Anthony Trollope's versions of female midlife suggest the new freedoms that women of all ages would slowly acquire, liberties with special significance for those doubly marginalized in Victorian culture by prejudices against their gender and their age.

Chapter 5

In the Eye of the Beholder

Victorian Age Construction and the Specular Self

t age fifty-two, Thomas Hardy was beginning to feel uneasy about aging.[1] On October 11, 1892, he wrote to his friend Arthur Blomfield: "Hurt my tooth at breakfast-time. I look in the glass. Am conscious of the humiliating sorriness of my earthly tabernacle. . . . Why should a man's mind have been thrown into such close, sad, sensational, inexplicable relations with such a precarious object as his own body!" (qtd. in F. Hardy 13–14). This moment of specular disgust was ultimately recorded in a poem:

> I look into my glass,
> And view my wasting skin,
> And say, "Would God it came to pass
> My heart had shrunk as thin!"
>
> For then, I, undistrest
> By hearts grown cold to me,
> Could lonely wait my endless rest
> With equanimity.
>
> But Time, to make me grieve,
> Part steals, lets part abide;
> And shakes this fragile frame at eve
> With throbbings of noontide. (Hardy, *Complete Poems* 81)

As Martin Seymour-Smith notes, critics have resisted reading these words as simply "making a universal statement about how men and women feel about ageing" (461–62), but instead link the poem, as well as Hardy's novel *The Well-Beloved*, to issues in his own life—marital dissatisfaction and his attraction to younger women (Millgate 330–32). Whatever the specific motivation for its creation, however, language about the body in the poem as well as the note to Blomfield—"humiliating sorriness," "precarious," "wasting," "shrunk," and "fragile"—suggest that Hardy felt disgust toward age and its manifestations. By interpreting a middle-aged man as too wasted and fragile to follow heart "throbbings" that seem inappropriately—and therefore painfully—youthful, on the surface Hardy's poem seems to condemn the aging body as unfit for love and writes it into affective decline.

Throughout his fifties, age haunted Hardy's works. When he was fifty-two, the same year of his epistolary thoughts about "the sorriness of his earthly tabernacle" quoted above, Hardy serially published *The Well-Beloved*, and the heavily revised text appeared in book form in 1897 when he was fifty-seven. At that time, Hardy was moving from writing novels to poetry, and "I Look Into My Glass," the last piece in *Wessex Poems*, was published a year after the novel. The age anxiety Hardy mentioned to Blomfield and voiced in "I Look Into My Glass" also appears in *The Well-Beloved* as mirror scenes in which the protagonist must confront his obsession about aging.

In this chapter, I use such specular moments as windows into the aging fictive psyche in order to address the question of how Victorian novels construct midlife. Thomas Hardy, Anthony Trollope, and Oscar Wilde portray middle-aged men and women peering into mirrors, calculating age's effect on their bodies, and then producing age scripts by which they live. I examine these scenes from the perspective of Kathleen Woodward's mirror stage of old age, a theory that investigates how association with or dissociation from the signs of age affects identity. Three of Anthony Trollope's novels from the 1860s and 1870s depict midlife Victorian women who determine whether or not they have aged out of affect by identifying with or distancing themselves from mirrored signs of age. While this association/dissociation pattern is repeated by men in Oscar Wilde's *The Picture of Dorian Gray* and Hardy's *The Well-Beloved*, these novels of the 1890s contain far more eccentric and fabulous depictions than Trollope's earlier female mirror scenes, demonstrating both the greater latitude of cultural age prescriptions for men and a heightened fin-de-siècle anxiety about male aging and decline. When considered from the perspective of these novels, Thomas Hardy's "I Look Into My Glass" describes the same type of specular moment, a complicated response to the experience of aging that combines grief and celebration, protesting ageist perspectives as the poet struggles to find an older persona with which he can identify.

Mirror scenes show the extent to which age can be a surprisingly protean and self-constructed category of identity in Victorian life, one that increases in urgency as the era draws to a close. When middle age was considered the prime of life, as it had been for centuries, the central dilemma of senescence was defined in terms of ensuring longevity and enjoying a "green old age." However, within the depths of nineteenth-century fictive specularity, evidence lurks for a cultural shift that transfers the problem of age to midlife, introducing danger at a much earlier stage in the life course and conferring much of the responsibility for the journey's outcome on the individual. As characters interpret specular signs of senescence, these scenes expose psychological aspects of midlife aging that reveal how fiction instructed Victorians to think about age.

I.

Hardy's description of "the humiliating sorriness of my earthly tabernacle" is typical of the specular self-judgments we often inflict upon ourselves as we age. The mirror appears to reveal self-evident and difficult truths, especially in cultures that routinely devalue aging. In the poem, the speaker constructs a decline narrative as he notes signs of age and then attaches certain meanings to them. This concept of age-as-loss is part of a powerful cultural construct, one in which we often unconsciously participate (Gullette, *Declining* 4). In her discussion of ageism in Western culture, Kathleen Woodward explores the complex psychological process behind the ways we reject agedness in ourselves as we look at our reflected image, and she posits a "mirror stage of old age" that inverts Jacques Lacan's infant mirror stage ("Instant" 59). Lacan proposed that between the ages of six and eighteen months, an infant experiences a recognition of her or his reflection in a mirror that contrasts with a simultaneous disunified existence in a "fragmented body" (2, 4). Lacan posits that "the discrepancy between the visual image and the lived experience . . . gives rise to the *I*" or perception of the self (Woodward, "Instant" 59). This mirror stage "situates the agency of the ego . . . in a fictional direction" (Lacan 2), functioning as a "drama whose internal thrust is precipitated from insufficiency to anticipation—and which manufactures for the subject, caught up in the lure of spatial identification, the succession of phantasies that extends from a fragmented body-image to a form of its totality" (Lacan 4). Through this fiction, the young child produces an idealized image of a more unified self, or the ideal ego.

In Woodward's mirror stage of old age, the elderly adult is repulsed by the mirror image and separates the inner self from the image but with the terms reversed: "the harmonious whole resides within the subject, and the *imago* prefigures disintegration" ("Instant" 60). The aging person sees the image in the mirror as something other than the "true self" and resists it. Woodward argues that this disidentification with age may be a salutary move, because it is unwise "to recognize oneself as old, to accept one's mirror image as a true measure of one's self," especially *"when one has the desire to achieve something"* in life instead of fading into death ("Instant" 62). She asks, when we face decrepitude in the mirror, "Is it not healthier (that is, life-sustaining) to reject that image?" ("Instant" 60).[2] From this perspective, a reversal of the infant mirror stage, a disidentification with the image, is a normal and advantageous response to aging, because the mirror image no longer suggests an ideal unity but an increasing degeneration that ultimately ends in annihilation.

I would like to expand on Lacan's and Woodward's ideas to argue that, while the child contrasts a fragmented body with the mirrored whole, for the elderly adult to compare an image of disintegration with an inner sense of wholeness he or she must construct an image of an earlier unity designated youthfulness, a necessary prerequisite to an imagined future of increasing fragmentation. Instead of anticipating mastery, the elderly individual suspects its loss, taking an opposite "fictional direction" than does the child. The earlier youthful self is experienced retroactively as one begins to long for an idealized past body that may not have been perceived at the time as either youthful or ideal. Rejection of the aged *imago* is reached through years of scrutinizing gradual changes, challenging and negotiating their relevance and meaning, so that, by the time one is elderly, a dialogue between the body and inner age consciousness has long been established.

Not only are mirror scenes depictions of this dialogue at work, but, by their very nature, they may themselves evoke age anxiety, because they exist in the tension between the imaginary and the symbolic—the image and the words that interpret that image. Participation in the symbolic, which earlier had allowed for mature individuality, is potentially threatened by the body's aging. With the possibility of senility or even a modicum of memory loss, thought and language can be at risk. While the mirror stage of old age inverts the identification with wholeness in the *imago*, aging also inverts the individual's relationship to the symbolic: early in life we enter that order during the mirror stage, but late in life the elderly individual may become estranged from it. In midlife the first manifestations of this problem are experienced—the first slowings of memory, the first searchings for a lost word—developments that suggest further decline. As we stand in front of the mirror and consider our own aging image, a wrinkle or gray hair can be interpreted as the signal of a mounting disintegration which includes a diminution of the very ability being used, a sign that meaningful participation in the symbolic may become impossible some day.

Mirror scenes, functioning as fictive records of moments in this life-long dialogue, reveal age anxiety at its height. As characters in Victorian novels regard their mirrored faces, they decide whether to associate with or dissociate from age in a conversation with self that becomes highly relevant to the outcome of their plot. This interplay between the mirrored image and the characters' words is an uneasy negotiation, a tension never fully resolved, comprised of conscious intentions and unconscious, culturally inscribed age scripts. In addition to these psychological factors, gender also plays a major role in ways characters view the *imago*. As we shall see, women looking into the mirror tend to evaluate themselves as objects of desire and pay a higher price for becoming older, while men usually calculate their abilities as pursuers, though *The Picture of Dorian Gray*, for a variety of reasons, challenges this generalization. Aging results from biological imperatives, is influenced by gender paradigms, and is not fully or even largely in the conscious control of an individual, but it can be affected to a surprising extent by a character's conscious articulations, as this chapter illustrates.

II.

In Victorian fiction, a gendered paradigm of midlife onset heralds the end of youth and marriageability at a much early point for females than males. Though statisticians discussed midlife as a set period for both genders—ages thirty to fifty according to the 1871 census (Benson 9)—as I have demonstrated in previous chapters, fiction represents single women aging into midlife at thirty due to the concept of spinsterhood, a category not imposed on men. Women's lives were also limited at midlife by Victorian interpretations of menopause, by the expectation that after completing this dangerous passage a woman would enter a period of healthy and happy androgyny as "the neutral man-woman" and commence "rendering herself useful" after the demands of reproduction ceased (Braxton Hicks 475). The average age of menopause was a bit under forty-five (Tilt 13), so in her middle to late forties, a woman was to become a sexless matron and grandmother, working to further the reproductive activities of the next generation through overseeing courtships.[3]

The power of specular association with or dissociation from signs of age is evident in Trollopean mirror scenes that complicate and challenge these limiting stereotypes for midlife women, showing the great extent to which individual interpretation can influence how age is manifested as well as its impact on a character's plot. Consider the case of Lady Laura Kennedy in *Phineas Redux*. In the second of the Palliser novels, Lady Laura is pursued by Phineas Finn, but she marries Robert Kennedy. They later separate because of incompatibilities, and when she becomes a widow in *Phineas Redux*, she wishes Phineas to renew his intentions of marriage. As a widow, Lady Laura faces a prejudice against her remarriage. Victorian diaries and letters show that while widowers were encouraged to remarry (Jalland 253), widowhood was seen as "a final destiny, an involuntary commitment to a form of social exile" (Jalland 231).[4] Providing they were young enough, however, many widows did take new husbands, and Lady Laura is only in her early thirties. She has another reason to question her viability as a wife, however: Lady Laura believes marital discord and separation have aged her:

> Could it be that she was entitled to hope that the sun might rise again for her once more and another day be reopened for her with a gorgeous morning? She was now rich and still young,—or young enough. She was two and thirty, and had known many women . . . who had commenced the world successfully at that age. . . . She gazed at herself in the glass, putting aside for the moment the hideous widow's cap which she now wore. . . . Though she was young in years her features were hard and worn with care . . . she now lacked that roundness of youth which had been hers when first she knew Phineas Finn. She sat opposite the mirror, and pored over her own features with an almost skilful scrutiny, and told herself at last aloud that she had become an old woman. He was in the prime of life; but for her was left nothing but its dregs. (2.271–72)

By associating with early signs of aging, Lady Laura bars herself from romantic affect. Even though she is chronologically young, she calls herself an "old woman" at thirty-two with complete conviction. Lady Laura believes herself to be making a rational, conscious decision as she ages herself out of love. What we might read as unhealthy, perhaps unconscious self-punishment and repression, a capitulation to ageist female norms, is presented by the novel as a realistic though perhaps somewhat tragic option for women over thirty. The spinster paradigm makes Lady Laura's thoughts a thoroughly tenable response in Victorian England.

When Lady Laura accepts deterioration as her identity, she begins to act the part. Though the same age as Phineas, she performs the role of an elder: "Lady Laura took upon herself the tone and manners of an elder sister,—of a sister very much older than her brother" (1.108). Phineas then begins to see her in this way: "The thing was so long ago that she was to him as some aunt, or sister, so much the elder as to be almost venerable. . . . He owed her a never-dying gratitude. But were she free to marry again to-morrow, he knew that he could not marry her. She herself had said the same thing. She had said that she would be his sister" (1.176). Because of her perceived age, both she and Phineas dismiss her romantic viability, and they assume sibling roles. By seizing an identity based on a belief in her own deterioration, Lady Laura weds herself to a future of decline. This is fully realized when she becomes lonely and bitter, refusing near the end of the novel to retain even a friendship with Phineas because he is marrying another woman, Madame Max Goesler.

This self-imposed aging-out-of-affect is not the only possibility for women in *Phineas Redux*, however. Lady Laura's premature aging contrasts with the extended youthfulness of her rival, Madame Max. While the novel seems to reign in midlife female sexuality with Lady Laura's loss of erotic viability, Marie Goesler's plot reintroduces and valorizes it. As I have discussed at greater length in chapter 4, she has devoted three years of her life to acting as companion to the ailing and elderly Duke of Omnium, and after his death experiences age anxiety as she considers her chances of marriage: "She told herself . . . that the time had now gone by, and that in losing these three years she had lost everything" (1.266). Like Lady Laura, she is thirty-two. However, though Marie worries about whether her time of romance and marriageability is running out, she does not internalize an image of herself as aged or present herself as "old" in the same way that Lady Laura does. Instead, she falls in love with Phineas and fights for him, providing evidence that frees him from unjust incarceration. Trollope felt it necessary to alter Marie's age despite her youthful looks, subtracting several years when she reappears in the second Phineas novel, revealing that he felt impelled to limit the power of self-determination over age (Epperly 24).[5] Trollope wrote his novels within the constraints of realism, and he works this fictive magic to enhance compatibility between Marie and Phineas, conforming to the Victorian convention that the ideal wife is younger than her husband.

Madame Max eventually marries Phineas as his equal, an attractive and marriageable midlife woman who is a definitive contrast to Lady Laura. She responds to her initial apprehensions about age by mustering confidence in her ability to attract and to act, taking an aggressive approach toward Phineas's incarceration and her love for him, an energy the inverse of Lady Laura's passive capitulation to decline. *Phineas Redux*'s differing marriage plots—one that figures female midlife affect as improbable and the other as a possibility—demonstrate how powerful a woman's psychological stance toward aging can be, especially just past the fateful age of thirty.

While Lady Laura's plight shows the remarkable effect a character's association with mirrored decline can have in a novel, perhaps even more surprising is the possibility that youthfulness can be regained when agedness in the *imago* is resisted. The protagonist of Trollope's *Miss Mackenzie* negotiates the complex borders between spinsterhood and marriageability, showing that, despite strong cultural prescriptions, specular dissociation can make age pliable and more self-determined for women on the margins of midlife. Even though it was Trollope's original intent to deny Margaret affective success, because he envisioned her as not romantically viable due to age, she thrives in a midlife marriage plot that takes over the novel. Trollope wrote in his *Autobiography*:

> *Miss Mackenzie* was written with a desire to prove that a novel may be produced without any love—but even in this attempt it breaks down before the conclusion. In order that I might be strong in my purpose, I took for my heroine a very unattractive old maid, who was overwhelmed by money troubles; but even she was in love before the end of the book and made a romantic marriage with an old man. (122–23)

In *Miss Mackenzie*, "unattractive old maid" becomes a fluid category that Margaret finally escapes, overcoming age stereotypes and proving herself to be a suitable romantic object.

In her mid-thirties, the unmarried Margaret Mackenzie is considered to be a spinster, and, as her sister-in-law calls her, an "old maid" (11). When she inherits a sizable income, however, Margaret's spinster status is dislodged. She stands before a mirror considering whether she is too old to marry:

> she got up and looked at herself in the mirror. She moved up her hair from off her ears, knowing where she would find a few that were grey, and shaking her head, as though owning to herself that she was old; but as her fingers ran almost involuntarily across her locks, her touch told her that they were soft and silken; and she looked into her own eyes, and saw that they were bright; and her hand touched the outline of her cheek, and she knew that something of the fresh bloom of youth was still there; and her lips parted, and there were her white teeth; and there came a smile and a dimple, and a slight purpose of laughter in her eye, and then a tear. She pulled her scarf tighter across her bosom, feeling her own form, and then she leaned forward and kissed herself in the glass. (110–11)

Margaret is six years past her portentous thirtieth birthday as she assesses the marks of age. When she is described as "shaking her head, as though owning to herself that she was old," the clause suggests not just that the "few" gray hairs show she is beginning to age, but that within her cultural context it is now appropriate for her to see herself as elderly. Margaret resists this conclusion, however. As her laugh and tear indicate, she is between two states in a liminal period where the contest can go either way—she can focus on the gray hair or "the fresh bloom," which, as Amy M. King points out, is a marker of physical and sexual viability for marriage associated with young women (8). Margaret shakes her head only "as though" she is old, dissociating from age and identifying with her still-existent youth. Especially significant is the sexuality of her self-appraisal. As she inventories her body, the cascading rhythm of clauses linked by the repeated "and" propels her toward a sensuality revealed by the mirror, culminated by a celebratory kiss of her own image. In a moment of female sexual empowerment, Margaret reads her body as a tool that affords her continued marriage market viability.

Though Margaret's spinsterhood is reversed because she has inherited a sizeable income, the novel suggests that money alone cannot trump age. Margaret has retained youthfulness:

> But luckily for her—or unluckily, as it may be—this money had come to her before her time for withering had arrived. In heart, and energy, and desire, there was still much of strength left to her. Indeed it may be said of her, that she had come so late in life to whatever of ripeness was to be vouchsafed to her. . . . All this is mentioned to show that at the age of thirty-six Margaret Mackenzie was still a young woman. (26)

In fact, Margaret has improved with age as "a woman who at thirty-five had more of the graces of womanhood than belonged to her at twenty" (8). However, age stereotypes about women past thirty are not so easily overcome as the mirror scene and her continued youthfulness suggest. A short time later Margaret reconsiders her confidence in the power of continued "bloom":

> Who was she, that she should be allowed to be in love? Was she not an old maid by prescription, and, as it were, by the force of ordained circumstances? . . . . And although in certain moments of ecstasy, as when she kissed herself in the glass, she almost taught herself to think that feminine charms and feminine privileges had not been all denied to her, such was not her permanent opinion of herself. She despised herself. Why, she knew not; and probably did not know that she did so. But, in truth, she despised herself, thinking herself to be too mean for a man's love. (137–38)

Margaret's self-confidence is not immediately powerful enough to overcome the hegemony of deeply engrained age paradigms, and unconscious forces prove more potent than conscious choices. Along with her outward change in status from spinster to marriageable woman, Margaret must negotiate an inner transformation from asexual to sexual, from a woman who was once overlooked to one now desired and pursued, all the while knowing that the change has been brought about by money. Her self concept is dominated by internalized cultural "prescriptions" of spinsterhood that seem to her sacred or "ordained." Repressed desire, shame, and other psychological freight result from this initial marriage market rejection along with internalized cultural norms that devalue aging. Unaware that she despises her own aging self, she has became reconciled to spinsterhood, and, despite an autoerotic moment, still questions her desirability. Spinsterhood had come to be a public acknowledgement of what she believed about herself, that she was a romantically untenable figure, and deservedly so. To reverse that self-judgment and the powerful cultural construct from which it arises, Margaret must struggle with the image of lack she internalized as an "old maid."

An interfering neighbor, Mrs. Stumfold, reinforces Margaret's age anxiety. The busybody warns Margaret away from being courted by Mr. Maguire, a man who has been showing her marked attention. Clearly, Mrs. Stumfold believes that youth is a more important requirement for female marriageability than fortune as she claims he is engaged to another woman, arguing her case with an intentionally offensive stress on Margaret's age:

> "Another young lady,"—with an emphasis on the world young—
> "whom he first met at my house, who was introduced to him by
> me—a young lady not above thirty years of age, and quite suitable
> in every way to be Mr. Maguire's wife. She may not have quite
> so much money as you; but she has a fair provision, and money
> is not everything; a lady in every way suitable." (157)

Though she is furious and ushers Mrs. Stumfold out of her house, the humiliated Margaret thinks: "to have been called old and unsuitable—for that was, in truth, the case . . . was not all this enough to make her cry?" (158–59). Margaret's tearful response shows how deeply entrenched is her internalization of spinsterhood. The acquisition of a modest fortune at a few years over the magic boundary of thirty does not guarantee resolution of Margaret's divided consciousness.

Margaret does marry, however. She is courted by her cousin John Ball, ten years her elder, his wooing initially motivated by her fortune. Though eventually John is proven to be the true heir of the money and can possess the fortune without also having to take the woman, he continues to pursue

Margaret. He even offers to split the inheritance with her, putting an independent life in her power. Ultimately, however, Margaret's disidentification with age triumphs, and she sees herself as a suitable love object, agreeing to marry Ball. Sir John weds her without the money, a plot twist prioritizing affect over pecuniary considerations, allowing the early-midlife "old maid" to become un-spinstered for love instead of money. Older than Lady Laura, Margaret is a spinster, not a widow, and while both factors should make her even more unmarriageable, *Miss Mackenzie* imagines the possibility that spinsterhood and its ageist and sexist paradigm can become reversed.

Self-assessments at the mirror are not infallible indicators of how a novel will end, however, and the imperatives of the Victorian marriage plot can overcome the conscious intention to age out of affect. Lady Matilda Carbury in Trollope's *The Way We Live Now* attempts to dissociate herself from age and its repercussions, developing a career as a novelist and resisting marriage, which makes her an atypical Victorian heroine, precursor to the "new woman" in many ways. A forty-three-year-old widow at the beginning of the novel, she perceives herself as relatively youthful and uses this quality to assist in "the procuring of bread and cheese" through selling her writing (1.3). Though she describes herself in a letter to Broune, her publisher, as an "old woman," this is a flirtatious ploy to sell copy, and the narrator assures us that "she was satisfied to do so by a conviction that no one else regarded her in that light" (1.3). She uses her looks "with a well considered calculation," smiling at her publishers with intimate glances so they will "give her good payments for indifferent writing" (1.3).

This system of exploiting her youthful looks has been successful, but in her mirror scene, Lady Carbury confronts the vulnerability of her looks upon which she bases this strategy:

> As she sat opposite to her glass, relieving her head from its garniture of false hair, she acknowledged to herself that age was coming on her. She could hide the unwelcome approach by art,—hide it more completely than can most women of her age; but, there it was, stealing on her with short grey hairs over her ears and around her temples, with little wrinkles round her eyes easily concealed by objectionable cosmetics, and a look of weariness round the mouth which could only be removed by that self-assertion of herself which practice had made always possible to her in company, though it now so frequently deserted her when she was alone. (1.109–10)

Lady Carbury concedes she is aging but also resists, subduing gray hair and wrinkles by cosmetics and public "self-assertion." She also attempts to dissociate her future from decline by disconnecting from romance further to avoid the stigma of aging that, she acknowledges, is inevitable:

> But she was not a woman to be unhappy because she was growing old. . . . She, however, had not looked for happiness to love and loveliness, and need not therefore be disappointed on that score. She had never really determined what it was that might make her happy,—having some hazy aspiration after social distinction and literary fame, in which was ever commingled solicitude respecting money. But at the present moment her great fears and her great hopes were centred on her son. (1.110)

A few weeks earlier, she had resolved that "The time for love had gone by, and she would have nothing to do with it" (1.14). Her look in the mirror reaffirms her plan. Dissociating from culturally scripted repercussions of age, she dismisses her affective viability and thus her sexuality, to focus her identity on writing and the marital fortunes of her children.

Despite her intentions, Lady Carbury's attempt to remain independent of the marriage plot is an undertaking doomed to failure. Her literary aspirations are tainted from the first chapter by the low quality of her work and descriptions of her machinations to achieve publication. As Helena Michie points out, her desire to work makes her suspect anyway, and would "*necessarily* remove her from the moral purity of her daughter and other leisure-class Trollope heroines" (*Flesh* 33). Her hopes for her son also obviously are misplaced. The novel gives her only marginal literary success, and she is gravely disappointed by Felix. In the end, she does "after a fashion, repent," deciding that her aspirations for a literary career and her son's wealthy marriage are all "vanity," though seeing her "error" only "with a broken light" (2.462). As she abandons her former plans, the marriage plot takes over.

Trollope resolves Lady Carbury's plot with a betrothal that is figured in surprisingly erotic terms, while at the same time disciplining her by subjection to Broune's dominance. At the beginning of the novel, when she and Broune are friends and equals, she turns down his offer of marriage because she conceives of herself as a self-sustaining woman. Later, however, when she has lost all her money and her son is involved in a scandal, Broune begins to take over her affairs, and she sees him as masterful, even omnipotent. When, at the book's end, Broune tells her she should not write novels anymore, she gives up her career. Her son is exiled to Germany to avoid his tarnished reputation, her daughter prepares to marry a man whom she does not approve, and Lady Carbury's life seems barren, her confidence shattered.

As Broune proposes for a second time, her dependence is evident when she kneels at his feet and claims she has nothing to offer. The text opines:

"Was it not a career enough for any woman to be the wife of such a man, to receive his friends, and to shine with his reflected glory?" (2.465). In a sense, Carbury gives up her individual significance, accepting an identity as the reflection of her husband, becoming, in effect, Broune's mirror. He accrues greatness through her view of him and her relation to his success: he has all the money, the status, the career, the ideas, and she is stripped of those things she has dreamed of, achieving them only at second hand. Her "vanity" in wanting independence is chastised through a marriage based on her dependency, because she attempted to achieve autonomy as a parasite, selling weak writing by charm, and marrying her son for money rather than love.

Trollope depicts a forty-three-year-old bride who is chastised and ready to reform, but he rewards her with a cautiously qualified midlife passion:

> Then he drew her towards him, and in a moment she was kneeling at his feet, with her face buried on his knees. Considering their ages perhaps we must say that their attitude was awkward. They would certainly have thought so themselves had they imagined that any one could have seen them. But how many absurdities of the kind are not only held to be pleasant, but almost holy,—as long as they remain mysteries inspected by no profane eyes! It is not that Age is ashamed of feeling passion and acknowledging it,—but that the display of it is without the graces of which Youth is proud, and which Age regrets. (2.465)

Trollope seems unable to present this moment as a straight love scene—made clear by the necessity of the words "considering their ages"—but is compelled to qualify the moment in terms of age. Their embrace is "awkward," "absurd," and "lacking grace" because the lovers are forty-three and fifty, far from the hazy, idealized sexuality that characterizes depictions of younger couples embracing in Victorian novels. However, the narrator overrides these negative descriptors with the more positive "pleasant," the almost hyperbolic "holy," then fades the scene to black with the word "mysterious" and an injunction against "profane eyes." By attributing "passion" to the couple, Trollope valorizes female midlife sexuality, showing that Lady Carbury definitely has not lapsed into Braxton Hicks's "neutral man-woman state" (475) even though she has reached the average age of menopause. Through their atypical love scene we see that Lady Carbury's "time for love" has definitely not "gone by."

The Way We Live Now demonstrates the power of the Trollopean marriage plot to override considerations of age with which Victorian heroines had to struggle. Though the extended affective and sexual viability of Madame Max, Margaret MacKenzie, and Lady Carbury contrasts with Lady Laura's

accelerated aging, these cases demonstrate that, at least within Trollope's
novels, contemplative mirror gazing grants fictive women opportunities to
question, reify or revise Victorian paradigms of midlife. Scenes of specular
angst operate similarly for men in novels by Wilde and Hardy, though,
as I will explain, their presentation of age anxiety is far more hyperbolic,
both in terms of extending youthfulness and increasing penalties for the
sin of aging.

III.

In contrast to the plight of women such as Margaret MacKenzie, Lady
Laura Kennedy, and Lady Carbury, fictive Victorian males faced far lesser
consequences for aging. Instead of being considered "spinsters" if unmarried
by thirty, they lived the carefree "bachelor" life and were not written into
sexual and affective decline as early as women. However, they were subjected
to midlife age anxiety increasingly across the century, as I have discussed in
chapter 2. Mirror scenes depict men worrying about aging and attempting
to change it in novels that represent age in exaggerated forms, reflecting
heightened fear of decline at the fin de siècle. Two notable portrayals of
male angst about senescence appear in 1890s novels that are striking both
for their male mirror scenes and for their hyperbolic treatments of age.

Specular fictive moments featuring women evince the Western convention that mirror gazing is a particularly female pastime. Sabine Melchior-
Bonnet argues that Christian artists traditionally have used women with
mirrors to symbolize sins such as "coquetry, laziness, envy, greed, [and]
untruthfulness," considered to be particularly female failings (201), and
she notes that since the thirteenth century, the fallen Eve frequently has
been "depicted brandishing a mirror" (200). Elaine Showalter describes
the "savagely 'gynecidal' visions of female sexuality" that proliferated in
Victorian paintings at the fin de siècle, expressing fear of women's new
power through images of "women kissing their mirror images" or "gazing
at themselves in circular baths" (10).

According to this tradition, men attending closely to the mirror
would be vain and even feminized. John Leech's 1852 *Punch* cartoon in
figure 1.1 satarizes a man peering into a mirror and worrying about a single
gray whisker.[6] The title "*Temus Edax Rerum*," "Time, the devourer of all
things," makes light of his consternation, and his verbal turnabout—"No!
Yes! No!—Yes!"—implies a silly self-absorption. Male mirror scenes can
be taken more seriously in novels. In *An Old Man's Love* (1884), Trollope
depicts such manly musings, though they are cursory. For example, William
Whittlestaff, "as he looked at the glass, told himself that a grey-haired old

fool, such as he was, had no right to burden the life of a young girl" (1.34), a much briefer description than the extended contemplations by women explored above. When Dickens and Trollope portray men in the throes of midlife age anxiety, they often are engaged in less feminized pursuits than specular reflection. Arthur Clennam contemplates his age difference with Pet Meagles while gazing into a fire and with Little Dorrit while sitting in his bedroom armchair (Dickens, *Little Dorrit* 239, 798). Roger Carbury's bitter ruminations about his cousin Hetta considering him "an old man" occur as he prepares to answer a rival's letter, presumably at his writing desk (Trollope, *The Way We Live Now* 668). Wilde and Hardy, however, both created extended male mirror scenes that are presented as serious contemplations on aging and conform to Kathleen Woodward's associative/dissociative pattern. Representing age in exaggerated forms, Wilde's *The Picture of Dorian Gray* and Hardy's *The Well-Beloved* reveal a heightened fear of decline projected onto the male body.

These eccentric fictions of male aging relate to the late-century apprehensions about manhood I have discussed in chapter 2. As John Tosh notes, "The fin de siècle is now . . . commonly seen as a period of crisis in masculinity, when evidence from many different directions seemed to confirm that men were under threat and losing control of themselves and others" (119). Tosh lists multiple incursions by women into privileged male domains: the new woman novel expressed dissatisfaction with the conventions of patriarchy (117), the Divorce Act of 1882 strengthened wives' legal recourse against husbands (117), and an unprecedented public female presence was evident in the form of female shoppers, students, and office workers (119). Tosh also attributes loss of masculine confidence to diminishing paternal rule over the family, lessening imperial power, especially "the physical unpreparedness of British manhood" exposed by the Boer War, and once-covert homosexuality now put on public trial (119). Fin de siècle fears about degeneration and manhood underlie tension about aging in Wilde's and Hardy's mirror scenes. The fact that men are portrayed peering into mirrors, measuring their age-related attractiveness with great seriousness, in itself, would have suggested effeminacy to some Victorians.

Wilde's *The Picture of Dorian Gray* presents a complicated case of a man dismissing himself from affective viability at a young age. Though the portrait at the novel's center is not literally a mirror, it serves a specular function, giving Dorian information about aging.[7] Wilde's novel operates within the realm of the fantastic, and Dorian calls the portrait "the most magical of mirrors" (87), because it provides a literal depiction of the psychological and moral changes within himself. All signs of age are deflected from his body onto the painted canvas, and Dorian escapes aging by a method that even he himself does not understand. Though the portrait appears to make it possible for him to dissociate entirely from age, the opposite actually occurs.

Dorian learns to fear age in his twenties, at the height of his culturally assumed beauty, when his mentor Lord Henry delivers a "strange panegyric on youth" (20), declaring it to be "the one thing worth having" (17). He warns Dorian, "You will become sallow, and hollow-cheeked, and dull-eyed" and "You will suffer horribly" (18), because with age "[w]e degenerate into hideous puppets" (19). Only after this lecture does Dorian recognize his own youthfulness and, while gazing at the painting, fear losing it:

> A look of joy came into his eyes, as if he had recognized himself for the first time. . . . The sense of his own beauty came on him like a revelation. He had never felt it before. . . . As he stood gazing at the shadow of his own loveliness, the full reality of the description flashed across him. Yes, there would be a day when his face would be wrinkled and wizen, his eyes dim and colourless, the grace of his figure broken and deformed. The scarlet would pass away from his lips, and the gold steal from his hair. The life that was to make his soul would mar his body. He would become dreadful, hideous, and uncouth. (20–21)

Like a bite in Eden from the tree of knowledge, age anxiety reveals both his beauty and its vulnerability over time.

Dorian then links age with loss of affective viability, fearfully acknowledging the fragility of his attractions as he confronts Basil:

> I am less to you than your ivory Hermes or your silver Faun. You will like them always. How long will you like me? Till I have my first wrinkle, I suppose. I know, now, that when one loses one's good looks, whatever they may be, one loses everything. Your picture has taught me that. Lord Henry Wotton is perfectly right. Youth is the only thing worth having. When I find that I am growing old, I shall kill myself. (21–22)

Even at age twenty, Dorian begins to worry about a future when he will be aesthetically, sexually, and romantically devalued, capitulating completely to Lord Henry's ageist assessment of human value to the point of predicting his own suicidal end. Associating his personal value with youthfulness, he predisposes himself to interpret the first sign of age as cataclysmic. When Dorian stares at the portrait, he intertwines age with vice, embracing them as his true identity. Though only thirty-eight years old by his death, a young man in Victorian terms, by intentionally associating himself with specular signs of age, he becomes grotesquely aged beyond his years.

Of course, these excessive fears of age are presented in the context of same-sex desire: Dorian's concern that Basil will no longer "like" him. Many critics have explored the novel as a coded gay text, but, as Alan Sinfield cautions, "The book should be viewed not as the cunning masking of an already-known queerness, but as reaching out towards formulations of same-sex experience that were . . . , as yet, nameless" (102–3). He points out that though all Lord Henry's "sexual involvements seem to be with women," and Basil "is in love with Dorian, but apparently not in a sensual way" (100), yet the novel "invokes the queer image, to some readers at least, *despite at no point representing it*" (103).[8] Dorian also is presented as, at least ostensibly, having love affairs with women throughout the novel, from his ill-fated attraction and disenchantment with Sybil Vane to "the girl whom he had lured to love him" at the end of the book (180). While I agree with Ed Cohen that ". . . Dorian fears that time will rob him of the youth that makes him the object of male desire" (81), my focus is not on whether Dorian's desire is for men, women, or both, but on his perception and construction of aging. His fear of age and loss of desirability stand apart from the nature of his love objects.[9]

An important aspect of *Dorian Gray* that divides it from the other novels with which I deal is Dorian's conflation of aging with moral corruption. In this fictional world, sin "writes itself across a man's face" and "cannot be concealed" but is seen "in the lines of his mouth, the droop of his eyelids" (122). The body itself becomes a canvas upon which one's spiritual state is represented in the most public, obvious, and unavoidable ways, a fate Dorian is able to evade as long as the hidden portrait "bear[s] the burden of his shame" (86). But, because he understands that the painting "reveal[s] to him his own soul" (87), he believes himself to be thoroughly corrupt. This preoccupation with "soul," however, is always linked to physical aging, consistently displayed in a hyperbolic fear and loathing of growing old. The signs of "sin" that so offend Dorian in the painting are always depicted in terms of age—wrinkles, drooping skin, protuberant veins, sallow coloring, and faded hair (100). Aging and sin are conflated throughout the book, by their juxtaposition and descriptions of age as corruption, to the point that Dorian cannot decide "which were the more horrible, the signs of sin or the signs of age" (105). The book is riddled with an indictment of aging, and Dorian eventually interprets age as a greater evil than moral failure.

Is Dorian's physical ruin, then, a result of his sybaritic excesses or of age itself? Does his dissipation cause accelerated aging, and can reformation cause a reversal? Dorian asks all these questions, wondering whether a change in his behavior can countermand the corruption he sees in the painting: his "nature" may "grow finer" if "[s]ome love might come across his life, and purify him" (100), transforming the cruelty revealed by the portrait. He concludes, however, "No; that was impossible. Hour by hour, and week by week, the thing upon the canvas was growing old. It might escape the hideousness of sin, but the hideousness of age was in store for it" (100). As Alan Sinfield describes it: "The ageing process is made to represent moral degeneracy" (103). Wilde was an astute social critic, and this aspect of the novel suggests that even outside his hyperbolic fictive world male aging was beginning to be perceived as personal failure.

That Dorian's true identification is with the aging image rather than with his unchanging physical body is evident in the manic triumph combined with disgust that he feels while looking at the portrait. As Dorian publicly pursues Lord Henry's New Hedonism, he initially is unconscious of any changes within himself, but after spurning Sybil Vane, he discovers an alteration in the painting—"lines of cruelty round the mouth" (74)—and is taken aback. The portrait functions as a mechanism that reveals his unconscious content, an index of subconscious guilt. Repressed self-hatred and abnegation are evident as he enjoys a "real pleasure in watching" the portrait's secret record of deterioration (87). He returns again and again, comparing the painted face of age to his own youthful mirrored countenance and becomes increasingly "enamoured" with the image, "more and more interested in the corruption of his soul" displayed there (105). The text accelerates his aging into a grotesque and reptilian metamorphosis, when, at twenty-five, Dorian sees "hideous lines that seared the wrinkling forehead or crawled around the heavy sensual mouth" (105). Staring at this image, Dorian deploys an inverted version of Woodward's mirror theory: instead of rejecting an outwardly aging body and identifying with an inner youthfulness, he embraces the age and corruption in the painted image as his true identity, even though his body does not evince it.

When Lord Henry comments at a dinner party, seemingly in jest, "The tragedy of old age is not that one is old, but that one is young" (178), he states the psychological principle of aging that functions throughout the novel, a system consistent with Woodward's mirror stage. Lord Henry and Dorian despair at the signs of age, because they associate an inner "true" self with youth. At the first sign of age in the painting, Dorian believes himself to be fatally flawed. Eventually, driven by despair, he stabs his specular self in the portrait and falls dead, "withered, wrinkled, and loathsome of visage" (184). Though the description of his face as "loathsome" may refer to an outward manifestation of the moral failings the book so incessantly invokes, the words "withered" and "wrinkled" are beyond doubt comments upon Dorian's unnaturally accelerated aging at thirty-eight. In the stabbing he acts out, whether consciously or unconsciously, his youthful determination to kill himself when he looks old.

In *Degeneration*, which was published in German the year after *Dorian Gray* and in English three years later, Max Nordau mentions Wilde in particular as a consummate example of degeneration, not only in "his personal eccentricities" of dress that reveal a "hysterical craving to be noticed" (317), but for esteeming "immorality, sin and crime" in his literature and life (319–20). His trial and resultant imprisonment for homosexuality in 1895 were seen by many to confirm the veracity of these accusations. Though seemingly opposed in view, Wilde's novel and Nordau's denunciation of it both express late-Victorian angst about decline, whether in the body or in culture, a concept that also underlies Hardy's challenge to the boundaries of aging in *The Well-Beloved*.

Two mirror scenes in Thomas Hardy's *The Well-Beloved* offer a case of male specular disidentification overriding age stereotypes that goes beyond the other depictions I have considered. Jocelyn Pierston's story demonstrates the extent to which male age boundaries can be stretched and shows that eventually even the most insistent youthful self-image is defeated. Jocelyn constantly seeks an idealized woman, the Well-Beloved, even though she has "flitted from human shell to human shell an indefinite number of times" (13).[10] Most notably, he looks for the Well-Beloved in three women, a grandmother, mother, and daughter, all named Avice. He woos each when she is in her twenties, but he, of course, becomes successively older—first twenty, then forty, and finally sixty when he falls in love with the youngest Avice. The pursuit of the ever-vanishing Well-Beloved is predicated upon Jocelyn's belief that he is an appropriate love object, a suitability always understood in terms of his youthful looks and emphasized by his constant reassurances to himself that he not only appears to be, but is, a much younger man than his chronological age indicates. As the section titles constantly reiterate with increasing irony, Jocelyn remains young, no matter what his age: he is "A Young Man of Twenty," "A Young Man of Forty," and eventually even "A Young Man of Sixty" (Ryan 177).

Mirror scenes reveal his self-construction that makes an extended youth possible for a time, even at sixty, when he would have been considered elderly in Victorian England but sees himself as a much younger man: "He was not exactly old he said to himself . . . as he beheld his face in the glass" (159). However, a glance in the mirror reminds him that he is aging, and he feels compelled to catalogue the signs of age that seem to accost him. He thinks that "his brow was not that blank page it once had been," and he notes some "pale wiry hair" and skin that is a bit "wrinkled" and "drawn" (160). These marks of time's passing are irrefutable, and though he concedes, "Time was against him and love, and time would probably win"

(160), the word "probably" evinces his continuing belief in his romantic viability, and he leaves himself the option to dissociate from age. At this point, he appears to be quite successful in distancing himself from age.

In another mirror scene that follows closely after the first, he catches a glimpse of himself in bed early one morning when his looking glass swings into a vertical position, and again he feels compelled to linger on the image:

> The recognition startled him. The person he appeared was too grievously far, chronologically, in advance of the person he felt himself to be. Pierston did not care to regard the figure confronting him so mockingly. Its voice seemed to say "There's tragedy hanging on to this!" But the question of age being pertinent he could not give the spectre up, and ultimately got out of bed under the weird fascination of the reflection. . . . Never had he seemed so aged by a score of years as he was represented in the glass in that cold grey morning light. While his soul was what it was, why should he have been encumbered with that withering carcase . . . ? (166)

At first reading, this passage seems to indicate that Jocelyn has begun to consider himself elderly, but, though he acknowledges signs of age, he also proceeds to dismiss them. His insistence that the mirror image only "appears" or "seems" to be him, only "represents" who he may be, reveals his continued distancing from the aged *imago*. Woodward's theory of a split between the image and a younger and truer inner self is especially applicable when Jocelyn draws a distinction between his "soul" and his "withering carcase" (166)—a body from which he psychologically averts himself, dismissing debility and continuing to pursue a woman forty years his junior.

As long as he resists the mirror image and constructs himself as a young man who is affectively and sexually viable, Jocelyn continues to pursue the Well-Beloved, despite his age. Michael Ryan argues that as a sixty-year-old lover, Jocelyn is "a figure of fun," but the text takes him seriously as a worthy suitor (178). The second Avice, who is twenty years younger than Jocelyn and the mother of his final Well-Beloved, considers the sixty-one-year-old man a most appropriate match for her twenty-year-old daughter, an assessment based not only on his money and social position, but also upon her perception of his youthful appearance. This estimation is shared by women of her daughter's age: "Not a young woman on the island but was envying Avice at that moment; for Jocelyn was absurdly young for three score, a good-looking man, one whose history was generally know [*sic*] here; as also were the exact figures of the fortune he had inherited from his father, and the social standing he could claim" (179). While Jocelyn's money and class are undoubtedly the chief component of his desirability, his youthfulness is not depicted as a sham or ridiculous self-deception but instead as authentic and the basis of genuine attractions.

Jocelyn's May-December romance is challenged, however, when, in spite of his conscious determination to appear young, his unconscious fears ultimately become realized. As Ryan points out, he woos the third Avice in the dark, knowing she thinks him younger than he is (178). When she sees him in the light of morning, the third Avice is taken aback, "so overcome that she turned and left the room as if she had forgotten something; when she re-entered she was visibly pale" (166). Sophie Gilmartin explores ways in which Jocelyn resists acknowledging problematic aspects of their age disparity. When he discovers that a stone carving of his name and the first Avice's has been worn by wind and tide, he "fails to see that he is being displaced and erased by time, and that just as there is a genealogical succession of Avices, there are also newer generations of Pierstons who can love those Avices. He can belong to one generation only, not all three" (Gilmartin 233). Like the petrified trees that "have their distinct and proper place in the geological time scale, so does he in a genealogical division of that time scale" (Gilmartin 233). The final Avice views Pierston as "a strange fossilized relic in human form" and "actually places him *inside* the stone, into its geological layers as an empty shell to be dug up and wondered at" (Gilmartin 234). Though she does agree to marry him, the third Avice ultimately reneges by running away with a man who is her age peer. Jocelyn's amorous pursuit is then changed not by his chronological age, but by alterations in his self-assessment resulting from Avice's conviction that he is old. Her elopement with a younger man and the sequence of events set off thereby—her mother's death and Jocelyn's catching cold at the funeral—result in his capitulation to age and a cessation of the quest. A period of fever seems to burn the vision of his own youthfulness out of him, and he gives way to decline. The emphasis here is not on illness having aged his body out of affect but on a change in his own reading of himself.

Jocelyn's sickness seems to punish male desire prolonged into old age, an inverse of the usual Victorian plot device wherein women chastise their first erotic feelings by becoming ill (Michie, *Flesh* 25).[11] Of course, Jocelyn's relinquishment of his quest is not entirely, or perhaps even wholly, in his conscious control. Biology dictates that at some point, no matter how young his mate, he must acknowledge the eventual approach of old age. However, repressed fears and ageist self-hatred come upon him so suddenly in his sickness and its aftermath, that they seem a petulant fit, an almost suicidal surrender. He no longer views himself as virile but relegates himself to old age and ceases his quest.

Jocelyn's capitulation to age becomes visible in his own self-fashioning, and he changes from presenting himself as a young to an old man. Before his illness, he is "well preserved, still upright, trimly shaven, agile in movement; wore a tightly buttoned suit which set off a naturally slight figure; in brief, he might have been of any age as he appeared . . . at this moment" (152). After his illness, however, he "changed his style of dress entirely," wearing "a homely suit of local make" thirty years out of date, letting his "iron-grey beard grow as it would" along with "what little hair he had left from . . . baldness." As a result, at sixty-two, he appears to be seventy-five (202), though a few months earlier he had been seen as "absurdly young" by women in their twenties (179).

After Jocelyn surrenders to age, the novel vilifies elderly affect by placing him in a passionless marriage with his former sweetheart Marcia, who is depicted as too old to be desirable. Both Jocelyn and his wife are transformed radically and quickly from apparent youth to elderhood, a change brought about in part by their decisions about whether or not they are old. At age sixty, Marcia has appeared thirty-five due to her skill with cosmetics learned in Paris. After Jocelyn claims to have lost his desire for female beauty, she reveals her freshly washed face, apologizing lest she "shock" him, and, without makeup, he sees her as "the image and superscription of Age—an old woman, pale and shrivelled, her forehead ploughed, her cheek hollow, her hair white as snow" (200). A great beauty at twenty, she has now been altered by "the raspings, chisellings, scourgings, bakings, freezings of forty invidious years" (200). Jocelyn responds that she is a "brave woman" with "the courage of the great women of history" to reveal her visage thus unadorned, but her valiant deed is rewarded with the revelation that his passion for her is gone now that she looks so old, and he concludes, "I can no longer love; but I admire you from my soul" (200). Her value and affective viability are completely undermined by physical age, and after this, she is depicted as elderly and debilitated. For example, Marcia is so incapacitated by rheumatism that she must be brought to their wedding in a wheelchair (204).

In this marriage, affect and age are portrayed as completely incompatible. John Kucich comments: "The couple's mutual honesty about aging puts them both beyond desire, in a companionate marriage more extremely chaste even than Victorian domestic ideals" (233). Kucich here participates in the novel's construction of age-as-loss by depicting passionlessness as the obvious and only route a marriage between sixty-year-olds can take. Jocelyn's belief that the aging Marcia is worthy of admiration but not love, as well as his own performance of agedness that surpasses his actual chronological years, are not necessarily "honesty about aging" but a construction that signals his interpretation of age as debility. Though he had been a seriously viable romantic candidate at sixty, his altered self perception causes a deterioration, fantastic in its suddenness, that places him in unalterable physical senescence as well as a culturally devalued marriage characterized by aged passivity.

Jocelyn is a sculptor and has succeeded in art and love due to a thriving ego, but at this point, he loses his former sense of self. He becomes "conscious of a singular change in himself. . . . The malignant fever, or his experiences, or both, had taken away something from him" (197). He has lost his aesthetic sense, "the sensuous side" of his nature, and female beauty now seems "a stupid quality" (198), but he greets this change with relief, telling Marcia, "Thank Heaven I am old at last. The curse is removed" (202). Having lost his appreciation for beauty, he now inhabits a reduced and insipid world, no longer able to create art or pursue love.

Michael Irwin argues that by the novel's end, Pierston is "relatively contented, sufficiently prosperous and newly married to a wife whom he . . . likes and esteems," though he does acknowledge that "this is precisely because he is dead as an artist" (49). Jocelyn's surrender to a decline narrative is a troubled ending that cannot be considered an acceptance of his lot with "relative contentment." Hardy presents deterioration as in many ways a psychological choice, not a physical inevitability. Identifying with an aged body is, as Woodward's theory suggests, ultimately harmful to Pierston's emotional well-being and sets him on a downward trajectory.

As Dorian Gray relegates senescence to sin and Jocelyn Pierston stretches age boundaries to the point of collapse, they show male midlife anxiety raised to unprecedented levels that contrast with milder forms of age apprehension in earlier Victorian novels. Applying the feminized trope of mirror gazing to men, Wilde and Hardy coalesce the masculinity and degeneration crises, projecting a hyperbolic midlife crisis onto the fin-de-siècle male body. Though cultural expectations are significant, they are not all-powerful, and individual interpretations significantly influence how age is manifested on the body and in the plot of these fictive characters.

IV.

I would like to end this chapter by returning to Hardy's poetic specular scene published a year after *The Well-Beloved*. William E. Buckler describes "I Look Into My Glass" as a meditation on the cost of life's inevitable mediocrity: "The image of middle life is, equally, an image of all the middling results of life" showing us that "what we *would* achieve or express is always so much greater than what we *actually* achieve, and what abides is a poignant reminder of what was stolen away. That is the image of himself that the poet would have us see . . . also an image of ourselves" (191–92). Though it is possible to interpret *The Well-Beloved*'s conclusion in a similar way, Pierston's age resistance portrayed in mirror scenes suggests a more complicated reading of Hardy's verses. I agree with Joanna Cullen Brown that the poem's theme is contained in *The Well-Beloved*'s description of "this curse of his heart not ageing while his frame moved naturally onward" (2), but the poem and the novel go beyond concluding only that having a young heart is the curse of age. I argue instead that they present a complicated mixture of emotions that ultimately protests ageist notions distancing older persons from the ability to love fully.

Praying that his heart will shrink "as thin" as his aging body (3–4), the poetic speaker asks to be placed in the same position as Jocelyn when he welcomes sensual evisceration. However, just as in the novel, this request is not to be taken on its surface as a satisfactory resolution of age issues. Samuel Hynes asserts that the poem teaches us to "confront reality honestly: look into your glass" (187) because Hardy, as an "old poet," is revealing his own experience of accepting age with "calm serenity," and he adds that there is "no pain or bitterness" in Hardy's poems that address aging (186). Brown finds that "I Look" contains "no self pity" in its presentation of aging, even though, "It is this glimpse of equanimity, of a fate accepted . . . that makes the last stanza so unbearable" (2). I disagree that the poem, no matter how agonizingly, presents merely an acceptance of aging.

The first eight lines appear to counsel acquiescence to age as dissolution, but in the second stanza, at the poem's center, Hardy acknowledges the impossibility of submitting placidly to age. The poet writes that if only his heart would become "thin," he would be "undistrest" by other "hearts grown cold" (3–5). With this reduced heart, he could then wait for death with "equanimity" (7–8), giving in to age, but he adds that while lingering, his heart will be "lonely" (7). A genuinely composed heart is not pierced by loneliness, and his purported desire for insensibility is doomed from the start. Therefore, the poet is stuck in the middle state of feeling love yet also believing himself to have become an inappropriate love object. I am suspicious of the poet's request to lose his ability for loving. Instead of taking the poem at face value, I read it as an expression of fear that the time for love is over, a cry for continued connection, and a protest against his own sense that love has ceased with age.

Jean Brooks writes that "Grief is the one note that suffuses 'I Look Into My Glass' " (214), but, by focusing only on the poem's sorrow, we ignore the way in which the final stanza weaves together various threads of emotion introduced throughout—grief, to be sure, as he considers acquiescing to decline, but also a protest that defends the body and heart of age. Though the speaker acknowledges Time's ability to "make [him] grieve" (9), in the next line, when he imagines himself divided in two—a youthfulness stolen away but another part that remains and feels intensely—the poetic persona proclaims both resistance to the theft and a tribute to his still-"throbbing" heart that desires expression.

There is a tone of sadness in much of Hardy's work, but this melancholy is not read as a generalized sign of acceptance for loss. When Jude Fawley anguishes over the insurmountable obstacles that prevent his university education and Sue Bridehead suffers when she first defies and then succumbs to angel-in-the-house ideology, rather than construing *Jude the Obscure* as Hardy's acquiescence to class and gender roles, critics interpret the novel as his defiance, a critique of societal circumscription. The same is true for grief over aging in the poem—Hardy is protesting not just biological senescence but cultural prescriptions of age.

Instead of being limited only to the constraint of ageist stereotypes that decree the aging body as unfit for love, in "I Look" the poet expresses his deep desire for continued romantic viability, his pain at imagining the only choice to be abandoning love. Acceptance of age in the second stanza is similar to Pierston's marriage to Marcia—settling for a pallid present that amounts to nothing more than waiting for death. Relinquishing passion and productivity to age is not presented in either the poem or novel as a palatable "solution" to issues of aging. The poem's grief is directed not only at a predestined and irredeemable decline, but also at attitudes that erect an unbridgeable gulf between affect and aging.

While Pierston ultimately gives up passion in regard to both art and affect, Hardy is not Pierston. Instead of relinquishing creativity as he aged, in his fifties, when he wrote *The Well-Beloved* and "I Look Into My Glass," Hardy shifted from creating fiction to poetry, producing a second major body of work. My analysis may seem to imply that, should life mimic art, Hardy's literary exploration of decline narratives during his late fifties signaled his intent to give up on affect and desire, but subsequent events suggest otherwise. At the age of seventy-two, Hardy became a widower, and less than two years he later married Florence Dugdale, thirty-nine years his junior. Of course, we can only speculate about the relationship between Hardy's life and his art, but he does seem to invite an equation of his literary visions of age with his later life experience with his more general assertion, "The ultimate aim of the poet should be to touch our hearts by showing his own" (Hardy, *Life and Work* 131).[12]

These fictive and poetic mirror scenes demonstrate a shift in thinking during the nineteenth century as the problem of age changed from a struggle to prolong life in "green old age" to apprehension about the onset of age in

midlife. These texts depict an emerging paradigm of middle age that relo-
cates the dangers of decline to midlife, their specular moments revealing the
significance of individual interpretations over biological imperatives. They
expose the extent to which self-determination about age and marriageability
was available in Victorian life, even if only in an imagined world.

Chapter 6

"How To Keep Young"

Advertising and Late-Victorian Age Anxiety

In 1889, Pears ran an advertisement featuring an Aboriginal man at rest on a flowered bank, with letters announcing "Pears' Soap" that float across the sky, and the words "Ev'n the black Australian dying hopes he shall return, a white' vide Locksley Hall" bordering the lower edge (figure 6.1).[1] This promotion makes little sense when viewed alone; its success is predicated upon familiarity with Tennyson's second Locksley Hall poem published three years earlier, as well as prior knowledge of other Pears' advertisements that represent Africans, Indians, and Australians being "civilized" by British soap. Critics such as Thomas Richards, Anne McClintock, and Anandi Ramamurthy have explored what McClintock aptly terms the "commodity racism" of such ads that present British products as "imperial kitsch" promising to help control the ever-widening empire (209).[2] This image of an Aboriginal man is one of many such racially focused ads, the earliest an 1884 depiction of a black child washed white by Pears that appeared frequently in Victorian publications for the next ten to fifteen years and has become familiar to many in the work of McClintock (213).[3] While critics have explored the commercial exploitation of dark skin in these ads, another concept repeatedly conflated with images of racial otherness is yet to be considered, however: manufacturers' promises not only of white but also young skin.

Though at first glance the Australia ad may not appear to involve age, this promotion is one of many late-nineteenth-century attempts to sell soap as a youth-enhancing commodity. In Pears' initial race-oriented ad, text surrounding the whitewashed child makes this strategy visible. While illustrations of a black child's skin washed white, endorsements by a renowned opera singer and a popular actress, and references to economical price and availability "everywhere" evoke issues of race, gender, and social class that have been examined in previous studies, the slogan "For improving and preserving the complexion" promises that Pears will keep consumers' skin young.[4] An apprehension that increasingly permeated late-century

Figure 6.1. Pears' Soap advertisement. August 10, 1889. The Bodleian Library, University of Oxford: Soap 5. Reproduced by permission.

advertising, age anxiety powerfully motivated the Victorian consumer and must be added to analyses of Victorian commodity culture.

As previous analyses have stressed, late-nineteenth-century manufacturers used soap as "the God-given sign of Britain's evolutionary superiority" (McClintock 207), a metaphor that has particular resonance in age-oriented advertisements. McClintock explains that soap "emerged commercially during a period of impending crisis and social calamity . . . in a social order felt to be threatened by the fetid effluvia of the slums, the belching smoke of industry, social agitation, economic upheaval, imperial competition and anticolonial resistance" (211). These conditions were interpreted by many Victorians as evidence that Great Britain was losing primacy in a wholesale degeneration. Though late-century soap ads sometimes make direct claims about the youth-enhancing effects of their product, more frequently they employ images that simultaneously provoke and allay decline anxiety. They motivate resistance to decay through evoking perceived threats to established hierarchies, but such ads also convert what had been considered a natural process to an unnatural and preventable deterioration that requires preventative commodities.

The previous chapters of this book demonstrate ways in which midlife became an increasing cause for concern in Victorian novels, but discourses of age were not confined to fiction alone, proliferating throughout society in a variety of mediums, especially commercial promotions. Victorians could choose from a multitude of anti-aging products regularly advertised on posters, distributed in pamphlets, and published in magazines. To increase longevity one could don the Harness Electropathic belt or swallow Parr's Life Pills. If hair seemed thin or gray, a vigorous application of Dr. Scott's Electric Hair Brush, massage with Koko for the Hair or dousing by Oldridge's Balm of Columbia guaranteed immediate relief, and wrinkles could be banished by a legion of skin lotions that, as the widely advertised Beetham's Glycerine and Cucumber claimed, made their users "Forever young! Always fair!"

During the last two decades of the century, an unprecedented advertising boom and mounting anxiety about degeneration combined to offer manufacturers increased impetus to exploit decline apprehensions for commercial profit. Two soap companies in particular, Pears and Sunlight, seized this opportunity and, in a heated competition for new national markets, used anti-aging as a ploy to attract the British consumer. Many of their campaigns focused on youthfulness as an imperative midlife concern, capitalizing on the degeneration fears of a mass audience. In this chapter, I explore ways in which these soap advertisements both expose and accelerate late-Victorian age anxiety by projecting fears of national decline onto the commercialized, midlife body.

I.

Putting "Locksley Hall Sixty Years After" to commercial use is a particularly provocative choice by Pears, a strategy that situates age-oriented advertising within the discourse of national anxiety about degeneration. According to Stephen Arata, during the last decades of the nineteenth century, degeneration became so widely known and accepted by the growing middle class that it functioned as "a form of 'common sense'" (16). In his 1880 book, *Degeneration: A Chapter in Darwinism*, E. Ray Lankester explains that, while natural selection can cause organisms to advance in an evolutionary progression, the same process also may reverse (29), initiating adaptation "to *less* varied and *less* complex conditions of life" that "leave the whole animal in a *lower* condition" (32). Lankester freely applies this theory to humans, citing "the Fuegians, the Bushmen, and even the Australians" as examples of populations that "exhibit evidence of being descended from ancestors more cultivated than themselves" and advises that "[w]ith regard to ourselves, the white races of Europe, the possibility of degeneration seems to be worth some consideration," a concern registered by Alfred Lord Tennyson and then co-opted by Pears (59).

Degeneration came to be understood as an inescapable product of modern urban life. In his influential text *Degeneration,* Max Nordau contends: "Parallel with the growth of large towns is the increase in the number of degenerates of all kinds" (36). Charles L. Dana attributes societal decline to an increase of a "neuropathic constitution" that arises from current incidences of "crime, alcoholism, insanity and nervous diseases," great numbers of "brain workers living on a higher mental plane than in former times," as well as "the diffusion of syphilis, the stimulating influences of modern civilisation, the press, the telegraph, the railroad; [and] the gradual increase of urban at the expense of rural populations" (405). For Dana, these social ills are clear indications of degeneration that "only a blind or sentimental optimism can deny" (405). Arata indicates that Victorians came to fear industrialization had created a "pathological" British culture (25), in short that "degeneracy was a by-product of modernity" (26), an inevitable consequence of the stress of nineteenth-century living with dire consequences for the nation that also could cause a "breakdown" in individuals (17).

The combination of national and personal decline became commercially useful to soap manufacturers, because modern life was believed not only to undermine the nation, but also to accelerate the aging process itself. Nordau asserts that in "contemporary civilization . . . the vertigo and whirl of our frenzied life" produce "states of fatigue and exhaustion" which exacerbate age (42). He reports medical opinion that glasses have become necessary at forty-five rather than the customary fifty, and the onset of gray hair is occurring in the early thirties (42), that fatal cases of heart disease and "nervous complaints" doubled in the 1880s (41), and "[o]ld age encroaches upon the period of vigorous manhood" to the extent that "[d]eaths due exclusively to old age are found reported now between the ages of forty-five and fifty-five" (42). The situation is summed up by one of the experts he quotes: "Men and women grow old before their time" in the last decades of the nineteenth century (41–42).

By quoting a line of "Locksley Hall Sixty Years After" in its Australia ad, Pears plays on regression paranoia (figure 6.1). In fact, Tennyson's poem so elaborately enumerates these fears, it serves as an excellent primer on various aspects of decline ideology that manufacturers used to sell soap as both an anti-degeneration and anti-aging commodity. In "Sixty Years After," a man muses to his grandson about the outcome of issues raised in the first "Locksley Hall" poem, denouncing modern life in the language of degeneration. He asks in despair: "Have we risen from out the beast, then back into the beast again?" (148) and pictures "Reversion ever dragging

Evolution in the mud" (200), a clear statement of his belief that the problems of urbanized, industrialized Britain arise from evolutionary inversion as "civilized" humanity regresses to a more primitive form. Throughout the poem, the speaker laments ongoing reversals in established racial, gender, and class hierarchies that he interprets as evidence of degeneration.

Racial "reversion" was commonly associated with degeneration, a fear the speaker voices in his claim that proved so useful to Pears, "even the black Australian dying hopes he shall return, a white" (70). After attributing to the Aboriginal man an internalization of his own racist theories, the speaker goes on to question whether reincarnation as a Caucasian would be an improvement, because white British superiority has degenerated: "Gone the cry of 'Forward, Forward,' lost within a growing gloom; / Lost, or only heard in silence from the silence of a tomb" (73–74). According to the poem, modern notions of progress have been revealed as sham, and ravaged British culture has nothing to offer its colonized subjects. The speaker later extends this idea to other parts of the Empire, asking similarly of India: "Those three hundred millions under one Imperial sceptre now, / Shall we hold them? Shall we loose them?" (117–18) and concludes, "Nay, but these would feel and follow Truth if only you and you, / Rivals of realm-ruining party, when you speak were wholly true" (119–20). British leaders have degenerated into prevaricating party factionists instead of cooperating to govern as the superior "civilizing" power. Some Victorians looked at imperialism itself as culturally degenerative, "an atavistic stage of economic and political development" that resulted when manufacturers, unable to find a sufficient market at home, used the colonies for commercial expansion (Brantlinger 236). Ruling over the racial "other" was fraught with peril according to degeneration theory, an idea evident in the speaker's fears that the white supremacy in which he trusts is being undermined by the British themselves.

In addition to his racial anxieties, Tennyson also presents threats to established class hierarchies in images of elite society degenerating and even reversing rank with the working class. While the upper classes have become decadent, simple agrarian workers are "kings of men in utter nobleness of mind" (122). Humble country folk are now the "Truthful, trustful," vulnerable to political machinations of "the practised hustings-liar" (123), and, as a result, "Here and there a cotter's babe is royal-born by right divine; / Here and there my lord is lower than his oxen or his swine" (125–26), evidence of class inversion. Science, which should be the educated classes' instrument to improve modern life for all, serves instead to expose a lack of social conscience, as the speaker asks, "Is it well that while we range with Science, glorying in the Time, / City children soak and blacken soul and sense in city slime?" (217–18). Urban decay, both physical and moral, indicts upper-class society for turning a blind eye when "the smouldering fire of fever creeps across the rotted floor" (223) and for ignoring "the crowded couch of incest in the warrens of the poor" (224). The speaker's grandson has been involved in a train wreck caused by a "vicious boy" putting something on the track that shatters a wheel (214), evidence that technology has become subverted from a tool of progress to an opportunity for new types of disaster, evoking nineteenth-century fears of science-gone-bad that reach back at least as far as Mary Shelley's *Frankenstein*. Within the vision of "Sixty Years After," the upper classes and their innovations pollute Britain instead of provide, corrupt instead of direct.

Along with racial and class reversion in "Sixty Years After," degeneration also causes gender paradigms to fail, evident in the moral decline of womanhood. Among the working class and poor, "Crime and hunger cast our maidens by the thousand on the street. / There the Master scrimps his haggard sempstress of her daily bread" (220–21). The seamstress was a particularly charged image for Victorians, connected both to poverty and prostitution. Impoverished needlewomen, exemplified by Elizabeth Gaskell's *Ruth*, often were portrayed as ladies fallen from genteel origins through a family's financial ruin, especially vulnerable to seduction. Sewing also was considered a common second income for prostitutes. A lace-seller reported to Henry Mayhew that "the women of the town" were often seen "sewing at their doors and windows" because "it suits the women to have some sort of occupation, which they needn't depend upon for their living" (388). Tennyson uses the seamstress as an icon for lower-class female workers caught in an inescapable cycle of poverty, admonishing the upper classes because the domestic sphere has failed to safely enclose all women.

The speaker also is alarmed that lower-class lives are a contagion infecting the English lady, as working-class immorality has become a popular theme in novels enjoyed by upper-class women. The new craze for French novels has, according to the poem, "Set the maiden fancies wallowing in the troughs of Zolaism" (145). Eleven Zola novels were translated and published in Great Britain from 1884 to 1886, immediately preceding and during the time Tennyson wrote "Sixty Years After," and their stark descriptions of working-class life frankly depict sexual liaisons, prostitution, slums, poverty, and alcoholism (Frierson 533–34).[5] Max Nordau devotes a chapter of his book to Zola, dismissing naturalism as evidence of social degeneration (497). In Tennyson's poem, novel-reading women are polluted by degenerated mass culture as they venture outside the protection of the enclosing domestic sphere, even if only in imagination.

Though fears of racial, gender, and class reversion were common late-Victorian concerns, Tennyson's stance in "Sixty Years After" was considered by some to be exaggerated and inappropriate, a dangerous and even unpatriotic critique of Britain by a major public figure. As Tennyson biographer Peter Levi comments: "I do not recollect any indictment of the Victorian age that is more terrible" (308). According to Tennyson's son Hallam, the poet intended for both Locksley Hall pieces to be "descriptive of the tone of the age" rather than his own views (329), but despite the poet's protests to the contrary, Tennyson's contemporaries were inclined to read the poem as his personal disparagement of Great Britain.[6] The poet's grandson Charles Tennyson claims that William E. Gladstone took "Sixty Years After" very seriously when it appeared between his third and fourth terms as prime minister, interpreting its lines as "a deliberate repudiation of all the social and economic progress of the last half-century," an attack "he felt . . . deeply" (494). Peter Levi argues that Gladstone felt "bound to reply" to an assault on British culture so potentially harmful (308). His critique appeared in *The Nineteenth Century*, stressing national accomplishments—the repeal of slavery, improved conditions for the poor, legislative reforms—and closes by obliquely rebuking Tennyson for his timing: "Justice does not require, nay rather she forbids, that the Jubilee of the Queen be marred by tragic tones" (Gladstone 18). Gladstone's reaction indicates that the fears voiced in this poem were significant enough to put a major political figure on the defensive. The particular anxieties Tennyson describes serve as a foundation for Pears' campaign to turn British soap into an anti-aging product that could overcome the depredations of degeneration, a strategy that subtly undergirds the Australia advertisement in figure 6.1, as well as many other soap promotions.

II.

Major innovations in the British advertising industry—conditions of material production as well as psychological strategy—created a climate in which degeneration fears became an ideal vehicle for commodifying the aging body. An unprecedented advertising boom occurred in the last decades of the Victorian era, aided by an advertising tax rescission in the 1850s that had brought commercial promotion within the budgets of more manufacturers. Technological innovations during the next several decades lead to cheaper paper, larger and faster print runs, and improved image reproduction (MacKenzie *Propaganda* 17–19; E. Turner 91). Commerce flourished and national brands began to appear, making advertising necessary to differentiate competing products in the newly available array (Ramamurthy 15). Soon, advertising proliferated on an unprecedented scale, creating jobs for newspaper publicity managers and entire independent marketing agencies in what many refer to as the birth of modern advertising (Williams 177–78).[7]

Until the last decades of the century, soap had been sold regionally, but, as nationally branded merchandise began to appear, manufacturers felt the need to expand beyond their traditional markets, and a "soap war" ensued as manufacturers vied to control the market (E. Turner 85). Since early in the nineteenth century, Pears had been sold exclusively in London and southeastern England (Ramamurthy 25), and even after 1835 when Francis Pears became a partner with his grandfather, A. F. Pears, he remained content to serve an exclusive clientele, at one point even signing each package himself in order to guarantee authenticity (Shackleton 3). In a more competitive market, however, Pears felt the necessity of expanding and took on a new partner in 1865, his ambitious young son-in-law, Thomas Barratt. To put Pears before a national audience, Barratt adopted new advertising techniques, expanding the company's promotional budget from around £80 a year to over £100,000. Concerned that these aggressive schemes would bankrupt the company, Francis left the business (E. Turner 83), but his fears were proven shortsighted, and Pears' value went from £7,000 in the 1870s to £810,000 by 1892 (Ramamurthy 26). Barratt devised innovative and controversial schemes—for example, incorporating Sir John Everett Millais's painting of his grandson blowing soap bubbles into an ad, which caused a furious public protest against the desecration of art for commercial purposes (Shackleton 3). Barratt also had "Pears' " stamped on a million French coins and distributed across England, necessitating an Act of Parliament to declare foreign currency illegal tender (Shackleton 3).[8]

In the same year that Pears left his company in the hands of his son-in-law, William Lever founded Sunlight Soap. Studying American advertising techniques, Lever began vigorously promoting his product as a nationally branded, all-purpose cleaner for household and personal use (E. Turner 84; Ramamurthy 25). By 1887, Sunlight Soap had begun to dominate the British market with even higher sales than Barratt's, and in the mid-1880s, Barratt began to look beyond England, expanding his promotions to international markets in the United States, India, and Australia (Ramamurthy 25–26), while Lever also became well-established in the U.S. (Church 640).[9] British advertisements, having saturated their home country, began to circulate around the world.

Both Barratt and Lever took on age-defiance strategies to boost sales in this heated competition, creating a market of legitimacy for soap as a product distanced from the wrinkle eradicators, hair renewers, and other potations of the disreputable patent medicine trade that, for a majority of the century, had been the sole market for such wares. Patent medicines were Britain's most heavily advertised commodities until the 1880s (Richards 172; Nevett 72), and even though they were relatively harmless, from 1868 to

1909 Parliament issued six acts censuring them (Richards 170). Though they fell out of favor during this period, dismissed as extravagant quackery by a middle class increasingly committed to respectability, patent medicines had made an important contribution (Church 633). Thomas Richards argues that after the Great Exhibition created mass consumer culture at mid-century, the British public, under the constant barrage of patent medicine advertisers, learned to reimagine "their bodies as a field for advertised commodities" (183) with an "insatiable need" (193), a desire that was transferred from nefarious potations to the nationally branded merchandise of developing drug and beauty industries at the end of the century.

While patent medicines were being discredited, anti-aging products were being redefined as reputable by Barratt's promotions that converted age remedies from humbug to credible beauty products through a rhetorical redefinition of soap. For a majority of the nineteenth century, advertisements had focused mainly on presenting basic "utility, quality, and price" information (Church 639). Claims were numerous and extravagant, often punctuated with italics and bold capitals, frequently decorated with numerous testimonials in tiny print. When illustrations appeared, they were simple line drawings of the product, its logo, or relatively uncomplicated sketches of a satisfied user. Grandiloquence, bombastic "proof," and excessive guarantees made such ads easy for increasingly sophisticated customers to dismiss as puffery.

In the 1880s, however, a powerful new strategy emerged as "associational images" began to dominate commercial rhetorical appeals, an approach that has been a staple of advertising ever since (Church 640). In her classic semiotic analysis *Decoding Advertising*, Judith Williamson explains how this strategy works. In order to differentiate a product from many others that basically are quite similar, the ad elicits a "transference of significance" (19) to a product from an image that has an established meaning within an already-known referent system (26). Meaning is "created" by the viewing subject who generates a relationship between image and product—a connection that is not necessarily logical, the viewer usually remaining unaware of these "nonsenses" and "illogical juxtapositions" which "become invisible" as they meld together (29). On a psychological level, as "we give meaning to ads . . . they give meaning to us" (41), and we become signified by the transaction, identifying with the product (45).

Though Barratt and Lever continued to run ads in the text-saturated old style, they also began to orient campaigns around images that spoke for themselves, transforming soap into an age-prevention beauty commodity. Early versions of this commercial signification that attempt to create an anti-aging market for soap capitalize on fear of race, gender, and class inversions as the already-known referent familiar in the language of degeneration. Victorian advertisements contain powerful public images of what nineteenth-century manufacturers imagined were or could be consumers' desires and dreams, creating a need which they purport to fulfill yet never fully satisfy in order to establish a continued demand for the product (Loeb viii).[10] Pears and Sunlight ads arouse and project degeneration-based decline apprehensions onto the physical body so that their products can offer to alleviate deterioration, ostensibly in the individual but by extension in the nation as a whole.

Barratt's early attempts at anti-aging rhetoric are text-dominant ads that make overt youth-enhancement claims designed to play directly on degeneration-based age fears, a strategy he continued to employ for the rest of the century. He incorporated testimony in a number of ads from "A most eminent authority of the skin, Professor Erasmus Wilson, F. R. S." who informs consumers that "a good soap is certainly calculated to preserve the Skin in health, to maintain its complexion and tone, and prevent its falling into wrinkles." He then assures that Pears is just such a soap, "a name engraven on the memory of the 'oldest inhabitant.' "[11] In later campaigns, Barratt complicates the simple logic of these assertions with an even more lucrative strategy. Though continuing to run versions of Wilson's endorsement, he makes the counterclaim in other ads that instead of being preventable, wrinkles are inevitable, that "Pears' Soap has to do with the wrinkles of age—we are forming them now," as an 1891 promotion declares.[12] The text then goes on to urge consumers to take on the task of aging well: "If life is a pleasure, the wrinkles will take a cheerful turn when they come; if a burden, a sad one. The soap that frees us from humors and pimples brings a lifeful of happiness. Wrinkles will come; let us give them a cheerful turn." Not only does Barratt promise happy wrinkles, but also, by locating the source of aging in early dissatisfaction that can be prevented by Pears, he declares his product essential for all skin problems, extending from the blemishes of youth to the lines of age, thus assuring a clientele from early adulthood to the most advanced life. In yet another promotion, the bar of soap itself becomes a metaphor for the agreeably aging body: "Every tablet of Pears' Soap is kept at least twelve months before it is sold. . . . And good soap, like good wine, improves with age. You may keep Pears' Soap for twenty years in any climate. . . . Every tablet will retain its original shape . . . —proof positive that there is no shrinkage, and that they are old and well-matured."[13] According to this ad, by washing with "well-matured" soap that represents the well-aged body, the consumer can avoid shrinking with age and become improved instead like a fine wine.

Though Barratt continued to print forthright anti-aging declarations in text-heavy ads, he also made more subtle claims in promotions that pioneered a newer, image-oriented technique. These advertisements derive their power from exploiting decline fears through a controlling image with minimal text. Pears' Australia ad in figure 6.1, which seems quite simple on its surface and makes no overt claims, exemplifies this strategy, using an associational image that, though implying results even more inflated than those of patent remedies, seem far less hyperbolic, connecting soap to whiteness and youth with a metaphor instead of making outright claims.

Pears plays on devolution alarm by presenting the Australian as a racialized "other" who evokes fears of waning colonial control and embodies a "primitiveness" to which Victorians feared they were reverting. Like the ad depicting a black child washed white, this promotion blatantly employs commodity racism to imbue soap with transformative power, depicting persons of color not only converted to civilization but also literally whitened by British goods. The ad's message is incorporated in a central image, a dream of rebirth, evoked by the aboriginal man's serene gaze and relaxed body. His work is over, hunting implements—boomerang, spears, carved shield, and food-gathering basket—on the greenery beside him as he rests peacefully in a trance-like state. Across a stygian river behind him, magnificent mountains rise heavenward toward one of Pears' frequently used logos, letters with a curving vine that grows from the top of the P, reiterated in curling decorative serifs on other letters. Though the picture is a death scene, Pears is associated with growth and rebirth suggested by the vista, bank of intricately detailed wildflowers, and herbaceous product name, an image that, along with Tennyson's words, subtly connects soap to skin coded newborn and white.

In its conflation of race and age, this advertisement functions as a commodity fiction that projects national fears of racial regression inward, locating them in physical degeneration that must be conquered. Age is given the same aura of otherness that racism imposes on dark skin. Anne McClintock's argument that soap consumption offers "regeneration" for "the threatened potency of the imperial body politic and the race" is equally true of the individual physical body in this ad as Pears implies age-reducing properties for its product (211). Instead of devolving into a person with wrinkles, the consumer can obtain the reborn skin imputed to the Australian's dream, the complexion of a Victorian at the top of a stable racial hierarchy that privileges the newborn white child. Racist and imperialist attitudes serve as the basis for an appeal to those frightened both by aging and the prospect that Britain will lose power over its colonies. Soap becomes a personal solution to aging that also reifies white superiority and denies degeneration's power to undermine the individual and the nation.

III.

Exploiting racial assumptions was only one of Barratt's degeneration-based strategies to transform Pears into an anti-aging beauty product. Though Barratt addressed multiple audiences according to specifically gendered roles, targeting mothers in ads that claim Pears is "a specialty" for infants and children, or men in promotions for "Pears' shaving stick," the majority of Barratt's anti-aging appeals are aimed at women in general and capitalize on late-Victorian gender instabilities. The female consumer became a significant entity to manufacturers in the last decades of the nineteenth century. Lori Anne Loeb argues that the Victorian lady became "the clear audience" (5) for ads when advertisers began to take them seriously as the primary "agents of material acquisition" with the most actual purchasing power in a majority of British households (9). Loeb points out that though men controlled the family purse, "the ultimate decision (to buy or not to buy)" increasingly fell upon the lady of the house (34). A dramatic rise in the number of ladies' magazines during this time put more and more advertisements before Victorian women, providing a new marketing arena for the manufactured commodities proliferating across the nation, which included a vast array of beauty and personal grooming products (Nevett 84).[14]

Because women were more culturally devalued by aging than men, anti-aging advertisements also were aimed in particular at a female audience, as advertisers capitalized on their culturally compelled desire to appear young. An early 1990s Pears ad illustrates the extent to which women were considered the primary market for complexion-focused promotions. A pamphlet titled "Baby-Skin" describes women as irresistibly compelled not only to touch and adore "baby skin" but also to desire it for themselves: "Haven't you seen a girl or woman catch sight of a dainty baby and break into smiles all over her face? . . . . You have seen her rush to the little stranger, seize his hands and toes and go into raptures over the pink and softness! That's the charm of baby-skin. . . ."[15] The ad goes on to address the question of a male market: "Every woman whose place in the world permits, and every man (though men are not supposed to tell it) wants, in proper measure, a baby-skin. Even the college athlete is not exempt. Let them use Pears' Soap. . . ." Though the ad attempts to masculinize Pears by co-opting men, the parenthetical digression acknowledges male desire to overcome aging as culturally inappropriate. In its attempt to draft male consumers for soap as anything other than a shaving product, Pears reveals a reluctant male market, while female consumers remain an easy sell. On the facing page, the pamphlet addresses an audience implicitly defined as female, accusing them of having become immune to how "ugly" they are and admonishing that they must "Look in the Glass!" to discover how they "tolerate faults of skin, which are almost always directly within our control."[16] Twinned with the baby-skin appeal, this ad teaches women that, whether or not they can see any evidence, their skin is the opposite of an infant's and has become flawed over time, a strategy that exacerbates female age consciousness in order to escalate a need for age-prevention and a never-ending market for Pears.

Another tactic Barratt instigated is the practice of wide-scale celebrity endorsement, particularly by famous women. Female celebrities made troubling advertisement luminaries, however, because their notoriety put them outside the boundary of conventional womanly behavior and their lives often transgressed gender norms. In order to use women in the public eye as effective product endorsers, Pears tames unruly celebrity women by presenting them as metaphorically subordinated. Within the confines of this strategy, famous females can evoke fear of bodily and societal degeneration safely, because, as they stir up decline anxiety they also simultaneously resolve it, both by their womanly circumspection and their wily use of commodities. In this way, Pears co-opts celebrity women as effective icons of anti-aging consumerism.

In the spring of 1887, Pears plastered omnibuses throughout London with an ad featuring the infamous Georgina Weldon as a midlife woman who triumphs over age with Pears (figure 6.2).[17] Weldon's history made her an exceptionally evocative figurehead for Pears, because she achieved notoriety for derailing patriarchal power, yet presented herself in the guise of a demure matron. Weldon achieved fame with her successful 1878 escape from her estranged husband's attempts to confine her in an asylum, purportedly because of her spiritualist activities, but motivated in reality, so Weldon later charged, by his affair with another woman. Weldon may seem an unlikely candidate for product endorsement, but she actually makes an ideal subject for an anti-aging icon as, in the words of Regenia Gagnier, both a "threatening invert of the sexes" and "unique woman of action" (34)—a female luminary who both raises and alleviates decline fear.

Several aspects of Weldon's life would have associated her with degeneration-related fears. A practitioner of spiritualism, she was part of a group vehemently attacked by degenerationists in the 1870s and 1880s as both fraudulent and evidence of a rise in insanity that was contributing to British deterioration.[18] E. Ray Lankester, a leading proponent of degeneration theory, sued a medium for fraud in 1876 (Walkowitz 173). Max Nordau charges in *Degeneration* that spiritualism is nothing more than the babblings of "the hysterical and deranged" (214), while mysticism is "a principal characteristic of degeneration" (45). Weldon also defied the traditional gender hierarchy through attending séances where women acted as mediums and "reversed the usual sexual hierarchy of knowledge and power" by presiding at "the

Figure 6.2. Pears' Soap advertisement. *The Graphic* (Mar. 31, 1888): 359. The Library of Virginia. Reproduced by permission.

center of spiritual knowledge and insight" (Walkowitz 176–77). Even more regressive behavior was Weldon's public censure of her spouse and physicians. Not only did she repeatedly perform a lecture, "How I Escaped the Madhouse Doctors" (Walkowitz 18), but the Married Woman's Property Act of 1882 eventually gave Weldon legal recourse, and she sued her husband and the doctors, even having a writ served on Harry in that bastion of male privilege, his men's club (B. Thompson 283). Georgina won, and the judge reinstated her marital rights, though Harry defied the ruling and refused to return (Walkowitz 183). However, as Gagnier points out, Weldon "seized the symbolic ground domestically by suing her husband for restoration of conjugal rights, signifying that his sexuality could be controlled by her" (32). Weldon also won £1000 in damages from L. Forbes Winslow, the asylum owner, and £500 from Dr. Semple, the physician who declared her insane, but these legal victories were only a beginning for the wily Georgina (Walkowitz 184–85). In the wake of her victorious legal battles, Weldon, who had an established public singing career, added amateur lawyering to her pursuits, instituting and acting as her own defense in over one hundred suits between 1883 and 1900 (Walkowitz 184).

Though she was an iconoclastic woman, by the time Weldon turned fifty and was featured in the Pears ad, she had become a popular figure whose crusades had won her notoriety and public acclaim (B. Thompson 287). Her suits came to be respected by lawyers, especially as unjustified confinement became a cause célèbre due to her efforts, and her campaign against asylum doctors produced reform (B. Thompson 292–93).[19] Her numerous legal suits provided a steady source of stories on slow news days, and she began to receive more attention in the press than many members of parliament. Dubbed "Don Quixote" as a courageous foe of the establishment, she received letters from a worldwide public (B. Thompson 287–88). Even when serving two prison terms for libel, Georgina emerged as a heroine. Two years before Pears' ad appeared, she was cheered by seventeen thousand applauding supporters upon her release from Holloway Prison, several of whom even unhitched her horse and pulled her carriage through the streets themselves (B. Thompson 299).

How could such a figure defy gender prescriptions yet achieve widespread approval and acclaim? Her popularity may be attributed in part to her skill at challenging female subordination graciously by pursuing a public career outside formal power structures in the nonthreatening role of an amateur (Gagnier 32). Even more important, though, Georgina cloaked her appropriation of male roles in an aura of womanliness, conducting her unorthodox activities as a lady merely defending herself. F. C. Phillips made the firsthand observation, "That she was strangely unlike most other women was evident at once. Her manner no doubt was feminine . . . but with all this there was a strange masculine thread in her character. She behaved like a woman, but she thought and expressed herself as a man" (qtd. in B. Thompson 285). Yet, Weldon's signature persona was "a sweet, gracious lady with a feminine voice who led a 'quiet, domestic life' " (Walkowitz 180). In reality, however, she was a dynamo, a formidable adversary in and out of court. A drawing of Weldon that appeared in *Vanity Fair* demonstrates this ploy (figure 6.3).[20] Featured in a series on eminent legal personalities illustrated by the well-known caricaturist Spy, she appears in a dark dress and bonnet that fully cover all but her hands and face, assuming a subservient pose, one hand clasping the other as if to hold it immobile, a sheaf of papers labeled *Weldon v. Winslow* held in her arms, only a trace of a smile on her serene and demure face. Walkowitz suggests that she is dressed to emulate a Salvation Army worker in this portrait, a reading that emphasizes her guise as a selfless worker (187). Her womanly ways are evident as she maternally cradles the legal settlement she won against the "madhouse doctor" that produced reforms for many other women.

Pears capitalized on this combination of feminine presence and clever woman of action to present Weldon as the image of Pears overturning age (figure 6.2). In the ad, she peers from beneath a ruffled hat tied closely under her chin, her shoulders and neck swathed with lace and dark fabric circumspectly closed by a plain, round broach. Her eyes look upward soberly with an almost martyr-like gaze, while the slightest of smiles suggests a steady but modest forthrightness. Her testimonial, "Mrs. Georgina Weldon writes; 24 May 1887, I am 50 today, but, thanks to Pears' Soap, my complexion is only 17," claims that her skin does not merely *appear* to be but literally *is* seventeen, due to her active pursuit of youth through wise consumerism. While her heterodoxy raises the specter of degeneration, suggesting that women can and will overturn the gendered status quo, Weldon's placid smile assures that decline can be, and indeed already has been, conquered by demure yet savvy women of action such as herself who are clever enough to purchase Pears.

Figure 6.3. Spy [Leslie Ward]. "Mrs. Weldon." Lithograph. May 3, 1884. Private collection.

Many Pears ads feature prominent actresses and singers endorsing soap, women of the stage with even more dangerous appeal than Weldon's. The celebrated Lillie Langtry, especially, makes frequent appearances in these promotions. Considered an aesthetic ideal, she may seem an obvious choice to advertise a complexion product, but because Lillie was linked to scandal, she could have been a perilous choice for a late Victorian advertiser.[21] Langtry repeatedly transgressed the boundaries of propriety and was notorious even before beginning her acting career. While married to Edward Langtry, she became the mistress of the Prince of Wales, and their shocking yet titillating love affair became public to the extent that penny-postcard stalls began to pin her picture beneath his (Beatty 108).[22] Though involved with the Prince, Langtry had affairs with other men, including James Whistler and, some have conjectured, her close friend Oscar Wilde (Beatty 118, 138). When she became pregnant in 1880, Lillie was unsure which of her lovers was responsible, though Prince Louis of Battenburg is generally accepted as the father of her daughter, Jeanne (Beatty 176). When she set out on a stage career, she was already a notorious woman. Enormously successful as an actress, Langtry earned £60,000 in the first decade of her career alone (Kent 113). Though outside the confines of polite society, she was adored, and products that either received her endorsement or were advertised with her name and image became immensely popular.[23]

Other female performers with equally tarnished reputations appear in numerous Pear's promotions, including May Fortescue and Adelini Patti who were involved in scandals in the 1880s as they appeared in Pears ads. Fortescue instituted a highly publicized breach-of-promise suit in 1884 against Lord Garmoyle when his parents protested that an actress would make an unsuitable wife. She rejected Garmoyle's private settlement offer, insisting on a publicly visible court trial to prove that she was "not simply a pretty brainless doll" (Kent 109). Patti, an Italian opera singer considered "the world's reigning diva" (Jennings 232), had an affair with a French tenor while married to a French marquis, their resulting divorce in 1885 famously decreasing her financial worth by half.[24] Obviously, Langtry, Fortescue, and Patti are troubling icons of beauty for British commerce. Women of the stage were problematic endorsers in part because the theater itself was of questionable repute. The respectability of stage entertainment faltered in mid-Victorian England, and though it had risen by the 1880s and 1890s, actresses remained only marginally acceptable, considered a "feminine version of the adventurer" (Loeb 95).[25]

Why would Pears employ such unruly women as the centerpiece of many soap advertisements? Actresses possessed an enormous appeal for Victorian women as public icons of beauty, not only because of their glamorous public images, but also due to their transgressive cultural power.[26] Kerry

Powell contends that middle- and upper-class Victorian women admired the theater because they were performers themselves, though within the confines of the drawing room (5). According to Kent, acting also possessed "a symbolic importance" for women as a profession that "incarnated fantasies, providing vicarious release in the notion that here was an area of special dispensation from the normal categories, moral and social, that defined women's place" (94). Actresses exercised the male privileges of employment, wage earning, and a "larger experience of life" (Powell 6) and confidently wielded public voices before audiences of silent men (Powell 10).

Nordau specifically links actresses' dangerous appeal to social regression, citing Henrik Ibsen's female characters as "hysterical and degenerate," and declares it "the true duty of rational wives . . . to revolt against Ibsenism" (415). He expresses nervousness about women wielding seductive power, because a "normal" man "becomes cool and more distant in his attitude" after "his erotic excitement is appeased," but if he "sees in woman an uncanny, overpowering force of nature" (168) and "trembles before this power, to which he is defencelessly exposed" then he has proven he is "degenerate" (169).

Kerry Powell describes Victorian men's conflicted response to actresses as similar to the enthrallment Nordau feared: both "infatuated" and "imperiled," they experienced "frantic admiration or even love, complicated by panic and disgust" (Powell 17). In order to deal with conflicting emotions of worship and aversion, Victorian men construed female performers as abnormal, unlike their wives and daughters, as "marginally 'feminine' if feminine at all, quite possibly inhuman" (Powell 3). Only within the confines of difference were actresses allowed a "limited freedom and a certain power" (Powell 3). Perceived as incompatible with domesticity and motherhood (18), stage women instead were associated with disease and prostitution (Powell 41), and even as late as the 1890s, "[t]he word 'actress' was . . . a euphemism for 'prostitute' in the press" (Powell 33).

The perilous attraction of the actress that incites ladies to rebellion and weakens males with seductive glamour makes them ideal for Barratt's advertising campaign in ads such as the Temple of Beauty, a promotion that tames their danger by linking them with the classical world (figure 6.4).[27] Pears uses the statue metaphor both to stir up and contain decline anxiety as five celebrity performers, Langtry on the front row holding her signature lily, Patti on the left, and Fortescue on the top step, appear as statues, their arms frozen in statuesque poses. Theater enthusiasts would have identified three of the pictured actresses specifically with Galatea, Langtry, Fortescue, and the American Mary Anderson each having played that role in W. S. Gilbert's popular comedy (Marshall 57; Loeb 96). Gail Marshall argues that Victorian actresses acquired respectability through association

Figure 6.4. Pears' Soap advertisement. 1887. The Bodleian Library, University of Oxford: Soap 4 (98). Reproduced by permission.

with classical statuary as an embodiment of the ideal, especially Galatea, and were so commonly compared to and presented as sculpture that they became "defined by" association with "the sculptural metaphor" (4). "The statuesque actress" became "a highly charged icon of sexual desirability" for Victorians (4).[28] The statue metaphor suggests gender inversion when the Victorian woman appropriates the role of Galatea, clambering down from the pedestal and "claiming the right to be her own Pygmalion," but when she remains in the unchanging classical realm, the threat is contained by her immobility, frozen into her role of subordinated female perfection (26).

Pears' ad makes no reference to youthfulness, the usual claim about "preserving" the skin unnecessary because the image contains this promise. The Grecian ideal transforms disreputable actresses into models of an ultimate, unchanging beauty that the consumer transfers onto her own skin,

enhanced by Pears, a commercialized body maintained in a perpetually
flawless state. Pears, "the secret of a good complexion," enables women
to emulate actress's autonomy, self-assertion, and ever-youthful beauty by
purchasing soap. Degeneration fears of inverted gender norms and personal decay thus are aroused and contained by Pears' celebrity endorsers
who create a continuing need for soap by simultaneously stirring up and
allaying anxiety.

                                    IV.

In the last decades of the century, Great Britain experienced economic woes,
and middle-class enthusiasm shifted from the disciplined morality of "self-
help" as a means of gaining respectability to a more hedonistic concern with
acquisition and consumption of material goods (Loeb 4). Economic historians
have discussed the period from 1873 to 1896 as the "Great Depression" of
British finances, because, though incomes had risen near mid-century, a trend
especially remarkable in the 1860s, which resulted in higher living standards
for the middle class, the new prosperity was challenged in the 1880s by a
sharp decrease in earnings (Banks, *Prosperity* 131). A protracted debate continues about whether a fall in retail prices, which slowed economic growth
and made Britain vulnerable to growing overseas competitors, constituted an
actual depression.[29] Whatever the exact nature of the economic downturn,
however, many late-century Victorians felt a challenge to the financial health
of the nation and their own households. S. B. Saul asserts, "The events of
the 1870s and 1880s . . . caused a serious decline in business confidence"
(53). J. A. Banks concludes that there was a definitive "psychological reaction to a field of narrowed opportunity" during this time (*Prosperity* 129).
Middle- and upper-class Victorians fought to maintain their standard of
living, and the need for more stringent budgets became a fact of life in all
but the wealthiest of households (Banks, *Prosperity* 138).
    Soap manufacturers capitalized on this economic climate by marketing
their products as money-saving commodities useful to consumers caught
in a financial downturn. Both Pears and Lever united anti-aging rhetoric
with the idea of thrift in order to attract the middle- and working-class
British buyer. According to Ramamurthy, Pears not only "appealed to the
growing group of white-collar works in Britain obsessed with their concern for respectability," but the lower-middle class also developed a "sense
of identity" with the brand, evinced by numerous poems and other ideas
for advertisements sent to Pears by a loyal public following (31). Lever
and Barratt used the appeal of social mobility to market their products as
commodities that protect both the consumer's pocketbook and her body

from deterioration. Their ads raise anxiety about degenerating bodies and declining economies, then palliate that fear with possibilities of class rise, while they reinforce the class hierarchies they seem to question.

Actresses were also used to target a class-based female audience in advertisements that responded to growing financial pressures. One Pears ad that appeared repeatedly in the late 1880s and early 1890s features the actress as thrifty consumer who pursues youthful beauty on a budget (figure 6.5).[30] Endorsements by Patti and Langtry praise the product, while Fortescue makes the anti-aging claim that Pears is unequalled for "preserving the complexion," but the layout is dominated by a picture of Langtry in an energetic pose, bursting through the page as she extends a cake of soap. Emerging from the advertisement into everyday life, Langtry does not appear in the guise of a glamorous actress but wears a high-necked

Figure 6.5. Pears' Soap advertisement. *The Graphic* (April 11, 1891): 423. The Library of Virginia. Reproduced by permission.

day dress, the height of fashionable respectability, a cheerful and confid-
ing friend who smilingly offers to share her favorite product with every
viewer. Lori Anne Loeb describes this type of presentation as exploiting
a "cult of personality" by joining celebrities and the public in "intimate
connections, the bond of being consumers, of enjoying the anticipation of
consumption, a pleasure that might unite seemingly disparate individuals"
(152). Langtry becomes everywoman, an approachable neighbor offering
cheerful advice to consumers who can achieve unfading beauty like hers
through the power of Pears.

   This ad also was produced in pamphlet form paired with another
frequently published ad, a testimonial from John L. Milton, identified as
Senior Surgeon of St. John's Hospital for the skin and author of "The
Hygiene of the Skin." He explains that Pears provides the best value for
the money, informing the consumer:

> It is a notorious fact that Pears' Soap is sold at a very small
> profit (I think not more than about one half-penny per tablet)
> on the wholesale cost price, consequently one or other of the
> many soaps in the market (on the sale of which a profit of three-
> pence or fourpence per tablet may be made) is sometimes either
> substituted or recommended to the buyer as "just as good."[31]

Targeting middle-class households experiencing financial strain, this ad
assures that even the woman who must carefully husband three or four
pence can join Langtry in possessing youthful beauty. By raising fears of
national financial degeneration, Pears cashes in on consumer desire to resist
age on a budget.

   Pears links age resistance with class rise in a poem titled "Mary Ray"
that contrasts Mary, the milkman's daughter, with the titled Countess of
Clare (figure 6.6).[32] While Mary's skin is flawless, "more and more beautiful
every day" (18), the countess's is "bad" and "spoilt" by freckles (12–13).
The Countess eventually becomes bankrupt through excessive and futile
attempts to cure her skin with milk baths and, indebted to the milkman,
is forced to marry him, but Mary, the wise Pears' user, weds a duke and
remains so young-looking that even at ninety years old she is mistaken for
"her own grand-daughter" (46). Sketches festooning the left margin depict
the countess's fall from flirtatious beauty in the second picture to an old,
haggard, and highly "spotted" woman in the fourth frame, the useless milk
tub behind her presided over by a maid who looks on in derisive pity. Mary
appears in the final picture, grandly dressed and escorted by her aging ducal
spouse, having retained her youthful complexion.

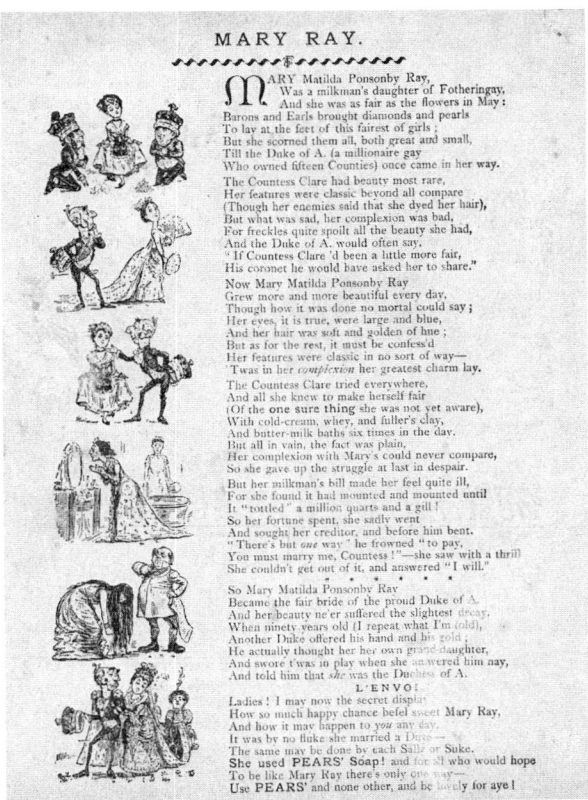

Figure 6.6. Pears' Soap advertisement. c. 1890. The Wellcome Library: EPH 162:9.
Reproduced by permission.

Though a seeming lighthearted satire, this advertisement suggests
to the middle-class female consumer that she can escape both monetary
and bodily decline through shrewd commodity consumption. However,
this tale of the milkman's daughter displacing a countess also may stir up
fear of class inversion by suggesting unbridled social mobility. It actually
reinforces class hierarchy, however, because, rather than denouncing and
attempting to overthrow the concept of rank, Mary depicts the glories of
class climbing as highly desirable and the upper echelons as limited to an
elite and lucky few. Even though this advertisement makes the frightening
suggestion that a woman can fall from rank by losing her beauty and a
lower-class upstart can rise through strategic use of beauty commodities,
the social hierarchy, though permeable, is preserved. In the process, Pears

reinforces the notion that, no matter what her class, retaining youthfulness is of utmost importance to every woman.

V.

Following Barratt's lead, William Lever also conflated fears of economic downturn with anxiety about aging to promote Sunlight Soap as a household product. Laundry had come a long way during the Victorian era from the once or twice yearly extravaganzas characteristic of eighteenth-century domestic routines, and clean white clothing, in greater supply as the cotton industry burgeoned, became a sign of respectability linked to "new habits of hygiene" and read as "signs of morality" for the middle class (Davidoff and Hall 386). Household cleaning had become more efficient in the 1860s when separate piped-in water supplies were installed in houses (F. Thompson 192). Due to companies such as Lever's, manufactured soap replaced homemade washing preparations made from wood ash or urine-based lye in the last decades of the century (Davidoff and Hall 386). Because household labor was supposed to be outside the purview of a middle-class lady, domestic servants were considered necessary to keep up standards (Banks, *Prosperity* 136). However, in the last three decades of the century servants' wages rose, female domestics' incomes increasing up to 37%, and home help became increasing difficult to find and retain (Banks, *Prosperity* 134). The combination of a straitened economy and higher servant wages resulted in decreasing domestic staffs, and the requisite three servants were reduced to two in the city or even one in the suburbs (Banks, *Prosperity* 137). Obviously, any product that claimed to make work quicker and more economical could find a ready market. Promising that Sunlight lessened time, expense, and exposure to heat, the dangerous effects of wash day, Lever guaranteed that his soap preserved consumers' youthful looks made susceptible to deterioration by doing laundry.[33]

Lever catapulted Sunlight to national prominence by launching a campaign directed specifically at retaining youthfulness with the question, "Why does a woman look old sooner than a man?" (figure 6.7).[34] This ploy helped make Sunlight the highest-selling brand of laundry soap in Britain (Church 640). The slogan is interspersed with text that raises anxiety about female aging, pinning its causes on housework. "Why does a woman's health so often break down at an early age?" is answered by a scenario that figures all women as domestic workers who, on laundry day, must undergo "a terrible ordeal" that would "break down" anyone's health, regardless of gender. Washing clothes, women become overheated "until every pore is open," drinking in the "filthy steam that comes from

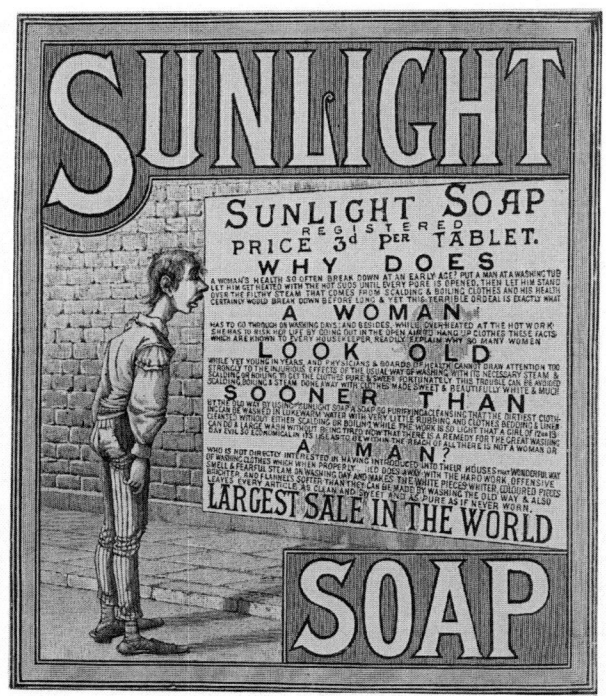

Figure 6.7. Sunlight Soap advertisement. *The Graphic* (Summer Number 1889): 28. The Library of Virginia. Reproduced by permission.

scalding & boiling clothes." Then she must "risk her life by going out in the open air to hang up clothes," endangering both health and youthful good looks, with the result that "many women look old while yet young in years." Sunlight Soap circumvents these dangers by requiring only lukewarm water and a minimum of scrubbing, saving a woman from age-inducing labor. A young man with his mouth hanging open reads the poster-like text with wide-eyed attention, in apparent astonishment at the wonder of Sunlight's amazing properties.

This promotion ran not only in magazines during the 1890s but also was printed in an elongated folding card along with another frequent Sunlight ad that features Queen Victoria and aims to unite all woman as soap consumers, from the higher classes represented by the Queen to the lower who are struggling financially.[35] Next to a silhouette of Victoria, ornate lettering asserts that Sunlight has been conferred "the appointment of soapmakers to her majesty." Along with the royal endorsement is a claim that while "Queens will have only the best of everything," "Sunlight

Soap is so cheap, everybody can afford to use it, in fact as the 'best is the cheapest' nobody can afford *not* to use it." Even the lowly are urged to take advantage of this opportunity to be treated like a queen.

This campaign uses a psychological strategy similar to Barratt's ad that features Lillie Langtry as the viewer's friend, creating a commonality between Queen and subject, so that even poor households can use the same soap that bathes the Queen, her clothes, and her castle. The line "Used all over the civilized world" reinforces the idea of British superiority, assigning the power of refinement to English soap exported around the globe. However, while Lever's images of class unity suggest that distinctions are overcome by Sunlight, instead of overturning hierarchies, he buttresses them by underscoring the Queen's position at the top of a stable social ladder, urging British subjects to emulate royal household standards. In addition, though Lever ostensibly includes every woman, from highest to lowest, as the target consumers for his product, the arduous laundry duties Sunlight proposes to palliate would have been undertaken by servants, even in the middle class, an assumption made clear in many other of Lever's promotions.

The Sunlight ad in figure 6.8 explicitly addresses the middle-class housewife as she supervises servants, though its surface claim is a pitch made to all women.[36] Announcing that "every woman is interested" to know she can stop doing laundry "the Old and Hard Way" and instead use "the Sunlight Labour-saving Way," the pamphlet's cover pictures two women wearing simple dresses and aprons talking under a washing line. Their clothing and muscular bodies indicate working-class status, while the slogan "How To Keep Young" suggests Sunlight's anti-aging potential. On its inside pages, the ad presents Sunlight as "a boon and a blessing for every housewife who buys it, no matter what her social grade." The ad goes on to substitute soap for labor, claiming, "When spring cleaning is in progress, the best 'outside help' to call in is Sunlight Soap," because with this product "the usual army of additional labourers" required for spring cleaning can be replaced by only two. Soap becomes another servant, keeping social ranks in order and saving wages in the process. In both of these ads, soap delivers the lady of the house from degenerative influences, whether or not she is the one doing the cleaning, and averted economic deterioration parallels forestalled age decline.

Pears and Sunlight ads worked and reworked the connection between soap and Victorians' desire to stay young. A later Lever promotion even makes a longevity claim, avowing that Sunlight "reduces the hours of labour" and "increases the hours of ease," thereby enabling the washing woman to "make the most of time" because "to save time is to lengthen life," and the promise that Sunlight "preserves the clothes" also metaphorically stresses the attenuated life span of its savvy consumer.[37] In the competition between

Figure 6.8. Sunlight Soap advertisement. November 1893. The Bodleian Library, University of Oxford: Soap 6 (14a). Reproduced by permission.

Barratt and Lever, each age-oriented ploy provoked another attempt to peddle soap as a youth-enhancement product, creating a higher profile for age anxiety while also offering its remedy in commodity consumption.

VI.

The increasing concern with midlife aging so evident in nineteenth-century novels was accelerated by fin-de-siècle advertisements such as these. Of course, soap purveyors were focused on profit and had no intent to change age ideology, but their promotions that conflated generalized fears of degeneration with age anxiety created an even higher profile for midlife. Their proliferation throughout Great Britain in a mass media saturation of the national imagination had lasting effects. While manufacturers used age apprehension to increase the market for their products, they also raised age consciousness to new levels, further augmenting the unacceptability of

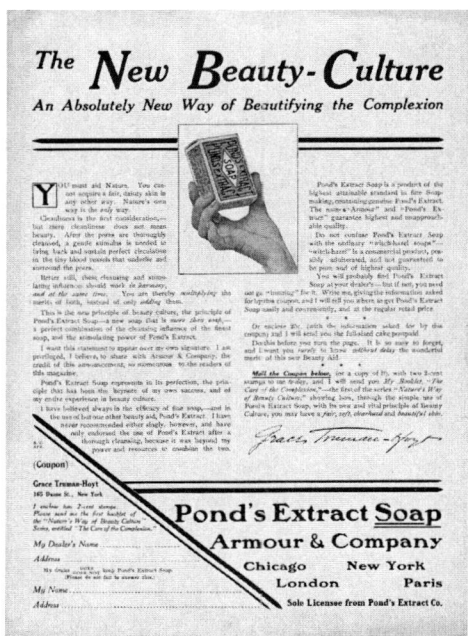

Figure 6.9. Pond's Extract Soap advertisement. *The Delineator* (April 1906). The Wellcome Library: EPH 134:22. Reproduced by permission.

the first signs of senescence in midlife. However, though advertisements increased age anxiety, they also suggested new possibilities, promising to put age defiance in the control of individual consumers. By the turn of the century, commodities that would have been classified as patent medicines a few decades earlier had become part of "the new beauty culture" promoted by an international beauty industry. The growing acceptance and increased marketability of soap as a complexion improvement product at the beginning of the twentieth century is clear in a 1906 Armour & Company advertisement. The only way to "acquire a fair, dainty skin," Armour claims, is through "the *new* principle of beauty culture, the principle of Pond's Extract Soap," with Chicago, New York, London, and Paris listed under the company name as their multiple international headquarters (figure 6.9).[38] Advertisers like Barratt and Lever created a need for age defiance commodities that boomed at the turn of the century and spread throughout Western culture. Now, over one hundred years later, our desire for such products only continues to increase, as consumers are offered more expensive and increasingly technological innovations with which we are urged to reject, resist, and defy age.

Chapter 7

Afterword
The Future of Midlife

Why write a study of Victorian midlife fictions? In *Aging By The Book,* I have argued that midlife germinated in nineteenth-century soil and grew from Victorian roots, is still evident in the artifacts of its print culture, and forms the basis for a pervasive middle-ageism that now affects every adult in the West. Our current decline-oriented concept of midlife is a fairly recent, culturally bound, widespread, flourishing notion that we must de-naturalize in order to understand its persistent influence. We must decide how we wish to respond, rather than continuing as unconscious, acquiescent victims to its debilitating paradigm. My study demonstrates that Elliott Jaques's 1965 term "midlife crisis," an ideology that has pervaded world culture, was not unprecedented, but has a Victorian history.

After establishing itself in the nineteenth century, midlife continued to thrive. When Edward took the throne in 1901, Great Britain's position was analogous to the man and woman at the top of the "steps of life," poised near the peak of international prestige and authority, but already facing decline. Youthfulness was a British craze by 1920; while the Victorian or Edwardian young lady had put her hair "up" to appear more mature, during World War I the "bob" and "Eton crop" became popular, emphasizing youthful femininity (Gilleard 157). Across the Atlantic, power was building in the American ex-colony, and British midlife was affected profoundly by U.S. youth culture, especially from the 1960s on (Gilleard 156–57). The elderly were pushed even more to the margins, creating what Chris Gilleard designates as a "ghettoization of old age" (157) with a simultaneous focus on age as "individualized experience," a process over which we can and should exert control, at least as far as possible (Gilleard 158).

According to Gilleard, during the 1980s "a 'post-youth' transformation of consumer culture" made midlife "the new cultural battlefield" (158). "Self-generativity" placed priority on preserving (or attaining) a young-looking fit physique, and the (un)aging body "was fast becoming a template against which to judge individual 'moral worth' " (Gilleard 159). Gilleard identifies "linked aspects" of a developing "culture shift" in the Reagan-Thatcher era: increased emphasis on individuation, focus on fitness rather than just behavior and clothing, a "maturing" feminist presence that critiqued age along with other cultural paradigms, and increasing commodification of daily life through self-help literature and products (158). Aging became a major consumer market, and advertisements began to feature "a newly aestheticized old age" for the middle and upper class (Gilleard 158). As medically enhanced youthfulness gained increased acceptance, plastic surgeries increased dramatically (Gilleard 161). No longer featured mainly in jokes, the aging began to be depicted by the mass media with fewer but more positive images of mainly white, upper-class, healthy elders who were both physically and economically "fitter than ever before" (159).

Changing demographics produced new life course patterns in the twentieth century. Peter Laslett argues that by the 1980s the "third age" became "a settled feature of the social structure," his term that designates the last decades of life as an extended period of healthy elderhood rather than deterioration and debility (79). James Fries was the first to recognize the life span's new rectangular shape caused by a relatively uniform longevity as most members of twentieth-century age cohorts lived into their 80s (Laslett 59; Gilleard 160). Aging is becoming an evermore pressing issue in the twenty-first century, as the elderly become a larger percentage of the population. Alexandre Kalache, Sandhi Maria Barreto, and Ingrid Keller report a worldwide doubling of elders in the next few decades: people over 60 years old will increase from 606 million at the turn of the century to 1.2 billion by 2025, and while the global population is projected to double by 2050, the number of elderly people will multiply by 300% (30).

Feminist cultural critics have stood at the vanguard of new age studies, particularly as scholars who came of age in the 1970s have reached and gone beyond their middle years. Feminists have been motivated to critique ageism due to the media's unremitting focus on women's bodies that has made the dominant Western image of age female (Gilleard 160). Following the landmark writings of Betty Friedan and Gloria Steinem, whose books call for a radical, activist old age, Kathleen Woodward and Margaret Morganroth Gullette have offered especially cogent analyses of ageism as a burgeoning cultural construction that must be challenged.[1] Woodward points out that Friedan's call for elders willing to take risks and encounter aging as a time of adventuresome and meaningful generativity was met with ridicule by some reviewers ("Against Wisdom" 213). She protests against easy assumptions of "wise" elderhood which cloak such palliative dismissal, arguing instead for an active, "wise anger" that confronts stereotypes ("Against Wisdom" 187). In her latest book, *Aged By Culture*, Gullette explores increasing ageism, outlining her own history with age studies, a journey from encouragement to militancy. She calls for new attitudes in personal lives as well as society as we "learn to name all the current enemies of the life course, even inside ourselves and within our disciplines" and dedicate ourselves to "institute new resistances" (*Aged* 196).

I would like to contrast these rigorous cultural critiques with a recently published memoir, Nora Ephron's *I Feel Bad About My Neck,* as one example among many I could have chosen to demonstrate the depressing and self-defeating results of allowing internalized ageism to go unexplored and unchallenged. The infamous line in Ephron's 1989 Oscar-nominated movie, *When Harry Met Sally,* "I'll have what she's having" is spoken by an obviously middle-aged woman in response to Meg Ryan's publicly faked orgasm. A companionable, satisfied aging permeates the movie, from the midlife woman eager to achieve the sexual pleasure modeled by Ryan to vignettes of elderly couples who glowingly report on their long, happy marriages. Perhaps the positive picture of aging in *When Harry Met Sally* results from Ephron's subject position in her forties as she wrote this script. No echo of its easy sentimentality remains in her memoir published at sixty-five in which a woman's neck becomes a synecdoche not only for an age-deformed body but a deteriorating life. Despite the book's humor, a bleak tone pervades its pages. Ephron professes to know the facts as she wonders, "Why do people write books that say it's better to be older than to be younger? It's not better" (129) and asserts "the honest truth is that it's sad to be over sixty" (128). Though she concludes, "What is to be done? I don't know" (136), her photo on the back of the book jacket delivers the final word, as Ephron coyly hides, pulling up her collar to shield her neck and lower face from view.

Recent studies expose such attitudes as counterproductive and exacerbating to the aging process itself. While ageism is rampant, the facts of aging can be encouraging, as healthier lifestyles and new medical options present us with stronger, longer-living bodies. Research even recognizes that older brains have some advantages over younger models. Gene D. Cohen reports on the "developmental intelligence" of elders (xix), their "flexible and subtle thinking" as well as adaptable ideas that privilege relativity over rigidity, skills that result from long years of cognitive processing not available to younger thinkers (xx). Cultivating knowledge about the strengths of aging can be essential to maximum functioning in later life. Thomas Hess's work indicates that a person's attitudes toward and perceptions about aging can influence their ability to perform tasks, that how we experience and use our aging bodies is dependent to a large degree on the meanings we assign to age (379). Responses like Gullette's and Woodward's make more sense than Ephron's vapid humor, because they not only are more productive—saner, healthier, and happier—but also evince genuine compassion for our shared humanity and mortality, working to make the world a more nurturing and hospitable environment. Their questions, challenges, and "wise anger" are far superior to acquiescent, self-loathing decline that yields only solipsistic sadness.

As Gullette argues, it is not enough merely to counter decline with progress narratives, however. Age theorists must draw attention to age ideology and interrogate the current "master narrative" that equates aging with deterioration (*Declining* 217, 244). With *Aging by the Book,* I call for age-sensitive readings that recognize the constructed nature of this aspect of identity, analyses that challenge instead of uncritically accept ageist Western visions.

It is not possible simply to ignore age panic: one must decide how much to intervene in the body's decline. Drugs now lower cholesterol and build up bone tissue lost to osteoporosis, options that seem reasonable choices, unhealthy to refuse. But, how about women using HRT to minimize menopause symptoms or men buying Viagra to make possible what has become impossible? Frivolous interventions or advisable health practices? Why not intervene in the veneer of age with lasar skin resurfacing, botox injections, face lifts or even more radical anti-aging surgeries that suck out, lift up, smooth over, or replace the effects of time? As we are offered more and more possibilities, the line that divides the sensible from the silly must be drawn on an individual basis. Increasingly, age is becoming a negotiation, and we may feel forced to consider and reconsider options and attitudes, running from one pole of narcissism to another as we try to find healthy ground between ageist defeat and delusional artificiality.

In the years that this book has lived with me, I have been constantly reminded of one obvious and startling fact: the funny thing about age is, when you designate the elderly as "other," lesser than your youthful self, you establish a price for happiness which you ultimately will not be able to pay. What are the results of marginalizing your future self? We must face the repercussions of this question instead of continuing to deny its power, eagerly rushing with plugged ears to the next new thing in age prevention. As Woodward points out, we have no English equivalent of "feminism" to designate ageism's challengers ("Against Wisdom" 209). It is my hope that *Aging By The Book* will contribute to this growing and yet-to-be-named discipline, exposing the deterministic paradigms we use to limit our aging selves. I want to leave my readers with a new impetus to ask this question of themselves and produce a better future for us all.

Notes

Chapter 1. Introduction:
The Rise of Midlife in Victorian Britain

1. [Leech, John.] "*Tempus Edax Rerum.*" Cartoon. *Punch* (1852): 216. The Library of Virginia. Reproduced by permission.

2. I am indebted to the work of Margaret Morganroth Gullette for her observation that "midlife . . . was slowly invented in the nineteenth and early twentieth centuries" ("Puzzling Case" 142). Though a majority of Gullette's work explores the concept of "midlife decline" in the twentieth and twenty-first centuries (a term I first encountered in her work and which I use extensively in this book), two of her essays discuss midlife valorization in Victorian England and have been particularly helpful to my project, "The Puzzling Case of the Deceased Wife's Sister: Nineteenth-Century England Deals with a Second-Chance Plot" and "Male Midlife Sexuality in a Gerontocratic Economy: The Privileged Stage of the Long Midlife in Nineteenth-Century Age-Ideology," both discussed further in chapter 2. Though the term "middle years" has designated the midsection of the life course for centuries—the Oxford English Dictionary cites examples beginning in 1450—Gullette argues it took on new meaning in the last decades of the nineteenth century, and she has come to prefer the term as one that avoids the pejorative connotations now associated with "middle-age" and "midlife" (*Aged By Culture* 28, 95–96).

3. Aristotle viewed the life course as having three stages—growth, stasis, and decline—and though he believed bodily development peaked at thirty to thirty-five, he defined life's true apex as age forty-nine, the end of the seventh span of seven years, when the mind and speech were most fully developed (Dove 28). See also Cole, *The Journey of Life,* 6.

4. For Jaques, midlife crisis is initiated when the possibility of one's own death becomes real due to aging, but the focus of his study is an exploration of the ways in which this pressure sets off a resurgence of creativity (502).

5. "Age anxiety" is another term of Gullette's that I use at length. See, for example, Gullette's description of work and love as "the twin engines of age anxiety" ("Midlife Discourses" 22).

6. Though, along with many other age theorists, I often use "middle age" and "midlife" interchangeably, the latter term more clearly connotes decline, an idea about the middle years that was emerging before being specified by this word at the fin de siècle.

7. Jon Benson asserts, "Psychologists, economists, sociologists, gerontologists, geographers and historians have all begun to recognise that age (along with gender, race, region, religion and class) could—and often did—constitute a crucial determinant of economic, social and cultural life" (1). Prominently absent are literary critics. Writing in 1997, Benson comments that only a few scholarly books about midlife have appeared, and they are, for the most part, "written by (and for) psychiatrists, social workers and health-care professionals" (4). The situation is slowly improving; perhaps most notable is Gullette's latest book, *Aged By Culture,* which was published in 2004 and deals extensively with current constructions of midlife in Western cultures.

8. An example of the need for work on midlife aging in the nineteenth century occurs in the excellent collection of essays edited by Herbert Tucker, *A Companion to Victorian Literature and Culture,* published in 1999. An entire section, "Passages of Life," is devoted to aging across the life span, but its chapters cover only childhood, adolescence, and old age, with no treatment of the middle years.

9. For example, Richard A. Shweder argues, "Until recently the European-American way of thinking about mature adulthood as midlife or middle age, a powerful cultural 'fiction' in its own right, has been the exception rather than the rule on a worldwide scale" (x).

10. Judith Butler herself points out that the body poses such a problem in *Gender Trouble.* Identifying critics' objection that "the materiality of the body is vacated or ignored or negated . . . disavowed, even" in her book, she wrote *Bodies That Matter* in order to take the material into more thorough consideration (Osborne and Segal 32).

11. For the difficulty of defining the onset and cessation of midlife see also Margie E. Lachman and Jacquelyn Boone James, "Charting the Course" (2–3) and Jon Benson, *Prime Time* (6).

12. While chronological definitions are favored in the West, they often vary from one discourse community to another. Historian Jon Benson compared numerical estimates of middle age from a variety of twentieth-century British sources between 1915 and 1984—articles in *The Lancet,* the *British Medical Journal,* as well as academic studies and government reports. He found multiple age ranges specified for middle age: thirty to fifty-five, thirty-five to fifty, forty to fifty-five, forty to sixty, forty-five to sixty-four, and forty-nine to sixty-three (7). Taking another approach, cultural psychologist Richard A. Shweder attempts to span the range of definitions, specifying thirty to seventy as " 'middle age' or 'midlife' in the cultural discourse of contemporary middle-class European-Americans" (vii).

13. See also Troyansky, "The Eighteenth Century," 198–99; Cole and Edwards, "Nineteenth Century," 260; Covey, *Images of Older People,* 19.

14. Figure 1.2: Anon. "As in a map here man may well. . . ." Engraving. London. c. 1630. Folger Shakespeare Library: ART Box A265, No. 1. Reproduced by permission. This print also appears in Antony Griffiths, *The Print in Stuart Britain.* Griffiths dates the print in the 1630s, saying that it appears in Jenner's catalog of 1662, but "The men are all dressed in the latest French fashion, and the costume suggests a date in the 1630s" (92).

Figure 1.3: Nolpe, Pieter. "The women's looking glass. . . ." Engraving. London. c. 1660. Folger Shakespeare Library: ART Box A265, No. 2. Reproduced by permission.

15. The prints are not the only configuration of the life course popular in past British representations of aging. For example, Shakespeare described the life span in Jacques's "Seven Ages of Man" speech, with a midlife peak in the fifth "age" characterized by the "wise saws" of the justice (*As You Like It*, 2.7.157). Susannah R. Ottaway, Thomas R. Cole, and others discuss cyclical and circular depictions of the life course, but the idea of the middle years as an apex, however, seems to be a major interpretation that held sway for centuries prior to the nineteenth.

16. See Stephen Katz for a fuller description of the rise and fall of longevity literature.

17. Margaret Morganroth Gullette presents the Victorian era in terms of "progress narratives" of idealized sexuality for middle-aged men and heterosexual couples, but she pinpoints the creation of midlife as "a new age category" of decline between 1900 and 1935 (*Declining* 3, 243). She argues that by the 1920s and 1930s midlife had become a source of trauma for both males and females, especially in regard to the "troubling, unwanted" body of middle age ("Midlife Discourse" 27). She notes an "explosion of discourse" in the 1970s that established midlife as decline with a simultaneous worshipping of youthfulness (*Declining* 3, 39). Mike Hepworth and Mike Featherstone agree, maintaining that "idealized standards of perpetual youth, fitness, and beauty" came to dominate Western culture in the twentieth century to the point that the desire to retain youthfulness is an assumed norm and "any tendency to accept the visible signs of ageing . . . runs the danger of being interpreted as an outer reflection of an unworthy self, signs of low self-esteem and even moral weakness" (6). See also Gullette, "The Puzzling Case" and "Male Midlife."

18. In addition, eighteenth-century mathematicians began to calculate life expectancy (Troyansky, "The Older Person" 51), and parish priests to keep accurate records of births and death (Ariès 16).

19. A literature of longevity related stories about people such as "Old Parr" who was reputed to have died in seventeenth-century London at age 152. See, for example, *Beauty's Mirror* (125); Gullette, "Male Midlife" (61); and Ottaway, *The Decline of Life* (23).

20. See discussion of menopausal onset in chapter 3, page 74 and endnote 1.

21. Of course, retirement varied by social class and gender—both male and female agricultural laborers traditionally worked until they were no longer physically able, sometimes well into old age, but as Britain changed from an agrarian economy, larger numbers of elderly people became unemployed. Large-scale retirement for middle-class workers did not become common until the twentieth century (Thane, "Social Histories" 99).

22. See also MacKenzie, "Imperial," 178.

23. See chapters 2 and 6 for further discussion of degeneration.

24. See chapter 3 for a more extensive discussion of this statistical average for menopause.

25. See also Cole and Edwards, "Nineteenth Century," 244–46.

26. For discussions of this aspect of advertisements, see Loeb, *Consuming Angels* and Wicke, *Advertising Fictions*.

27. See figure 6.1 for an example of a Pears' soap ad that was published on the front of Fergus Hume's *The Mystery of a Hansom Cab*.

28. See also Ruth Yeazell's discussion of ways in which eighteenth- and nineteenth-century novels "take their most typical form as narratives of courtship" (ix).

Chapter 2. *"No Longer The Man He Was": Age Anxiety in the Male Midlife Marriage Plot*

1. "Bald, Grey or Sparse of Hair?" Tatcho Advertisement. April 1907. The Bodleian Library, University of Oxford: Beauty Parlour 1. Reproduced by permission.

2. From 1891 to 1911, the retirement rate for males aged 45 to 54 remained relatively stable at 3 to 4% and for ages 55 to 64 at 10 to 11 percent, but census figures report a continual rise in retirement rates after 65: 35% in 1891, 39% in 1901, and 44% in 1911 (Quadagno 152).

3. As Mark W. Turner notes, some critics have objected to the conflation of Hughes and Kingsley that began with David Newsome's *Godliness and Good Learning*. See Mark Turner, *Trollope and the Magazines*, 153, 180.

4. For further analysis see Warren, "Popular Manliness."

5. For further discussion, see Mary Poovey, *Uneven Developments*, 4.

6. Examples are found in Hewitt, "The New Woman in Relation to the New Man," and Hamilton, "New Women and 'Old' Men: Gendering Degeneration."

7. The Labouchere Amendment to the Criminal Law Amendment Act of 1885 made an act of "gross indecency" between men a criminal offense, whether it occurred in public or in private, legislation used to prosecute Oscar Wilde and sentence him to prison in 1895 (Showalter 14). John Tosh argues that as a result of gender polarization created by the two-sex model, men began "to locate the sexual energy required for both pleasure and procreation primarily in themselves . . . by prioritizing penetrative sex, and (less certainly) by increasing still further the odium attached to homosexual acts," which set the scene for pathologizing and criminalizing gay men (69).

8. For example, among the professional classes, the number of live births fell from an average of 6.4 for each married woman in the population before 1861 to 3.5 between 1881 and 1891 (Banks, *Victorian Values* 40, 98).

9. Of course, there was no unified theory to which all physicians adhered. See Michael Mason for a detailed discussion of variations between physicians in regard to sexuality based on differences of class, education, and categories of practice (177–80). Roy Porter and Lesley Hall note conflicting views of Victorian sexuality surrounding the Contagious Diseases Act of 1864 and amendments in 1866 and 1869 that stirred up debate between those who held " 'natural impulse' theory of

male sexuality" and others who argued the necessity of sexual restraint outside of marriage for both men and women (138).

10. Prominent British physician Edward J. Tilt describes the typical male in whom, at puberty, the "sexual apparatus is, in general, fully effective and all-sufficient to ensure its permanent activity until extreme old age" (8). Gullette has found that in nineteenth-century American and British longevity texts, "late-life virility was promised to practically all men who had a late life" ("Male Midlife" 62). She argues that medical treatises presented potency as a prized possession that lasts until death and made "the central promise that there would always be enough of the needful for sex at any appropriate point in the life course, and so there would very likely be some left for the end" (Gullette, "Male Midlife" 65). In many texts, impotence was more closely linked to excess than age.

Many physicians advocated limiting sexual activity at any age as a way of maintaining bodily strength, not only because sexual abstention expends less physical energy, but also unejaculated semen was believed to reabsorb into and stimulate the body (Gullette, "Male Midlife" 66), and "virile longevity" was the "inevitable long-term reward" (Gullette, "Male Midlife" 68). Roy Porter and Lesley Hall report that in the nineteenth century medical tracts began to emphasize sexual pathology rather than pleasure, as they had in the past, and introduced the idea that excessive sexual activity was unhealthy, even within marriage (128).

Anxiety about impotence became quite common by the early twentieth century, made evident in Lesley Hall's report that Marie Stopes was receiving thousands of letters in the 1820s and 1830s asking for advice about impotence, and doctors referred to it in their writings as a common malady, though men reported that they received unhelpful and deficient information ("Age-Old" 24–25).

11. Though some, such as F. B. Smith, have argued that William Acton's writings are not characteristic of Victorian thought, as Robert Darby points out, these objections center around his infamous statement about passionless in women, first brought to the attention of modern readers in the 1960s by Steven Marcus in *The Other Victorians*. However, more recent work has established Acton's significance as an authority on Victorian sexual matters. Not only did *Functions and Disorders* go through six editions, but both Lesley Hall and James Paget have established that his work was well known by Victorians, and he was used as a standard reference (Darby 159). Porter and Hall note the "considerable and enduring circulation" of his ideas (144) and discuss the "risk of setting up new and . . . misleading generalizations" by wholesale dismissal of his work (141–42). However, they also discuss the "considerable circulation" of George Drysdale's *Elements of Social Science* which advanced the theory that women and men had equally strong sex drives (Porter and Hall 149–50). See also L. Hall "The English Have Hot Water Bottles"; Crozier, "William Acton and the History of Sexuality"; F. B. Smith, "Sexuality in Britain 1800–1900."

12. All quotations of *Functions and Disorders* reference the 4th edition of 1883 unless otherwise noted.

13. See Porter and Hall, *The Facts of Life*, for a discussion of the dangers of excess and continence according to Acton (142–43).

14. American clergyman Sylvanus Stall published *What A Man of 45 Ought To Know* in 1901—a book widely circulated in Great Britain and well received by medical and clerical authorities—in which he posits a male menopause similar to the "change of life" in women (Featherstone and Hepworth, "History" 251). He argues for a "sexual hush in the life of men" (40) between fifty and sixty-five when "disintegration and decay begin their slow and, at first, imperceptible change" (24). He declares that if women lose their ability to reproduce, it is "only reasonable to expect" that men do the same (31), but he also asserts that at midlife "the attractive forces" become "a repellent force," especially in women (207). For men, in contrast, sexuality is not "immolated" entirely at midlife, but moderated (95), because sex is "followed by a period of lassitude or weariness more pronounced and more prolonged than anything he has previously experienced" (78). A man who remains sexually active after forty is "not likely to retain virile powers until he is sixty" (152), and after fifty, sex shortens men's lives: "Each time that he allows himself this gratification is a pellet of earth thrown upon his coffin" (84). Virile and elderly males are not only "exceptional cases," but also are following unhealthy and even evil practices (28). That this menopausal model for men was emerging before Stall's publication is made evident in fiction. As I explain in chapter 3, Victorian novels depict women acting in accord with a model of sexlessness, but, as I have shown in this chapter, men may also appear in this guise.

15. William Acton believes this particular disparity promotes unity between marital partners as they age: "Women age much more rapidly than men, and as the reproductive functions should cease in both partners about the same time, some such interval as this is evidently desirable" (85). As I discuss more fully in chapter 3, John Edward Tilt, author of the most popular nineteenth-century British treatise on menopause, sets the average age of healthy menstrual cessation in the mid-forties, and Acton assumes that men also should cease to reproduce in their mid-fifties, timed simultaneously with a younger wife's menopause.

16. See Gullette's essay "The Puzzling Case of the Deceased Wife's Sister" for an example of a novel that is an exception to this trend. Gullette argues that in Dinah Mulock Craik's novel *Hannah* the midlife couple is valorized as both respectable and sexual. She points out that "the novel not only implies but in one place actually states that mature (here called 'second') love is a better—more reliable, satisfying, knowledgeable—kind of love than first love" (149).

17. This aspect of the novel has received little attention, the extensive body of critical analysis focusing on race, class, and gender. Notable exceptions are Robert Polhemus's discussion of the "Lottish specter of incest that haunts this narrative" in *Lot's Daughters: Sex, Redemption, and Women's Quest for Authority* (163), and Esther Godfrey's discussion of class and age differences that can be read as empowering Jane and subverting Rochester's authority in "*Jane Eyre*, from Governess to Girl Bride."

18. Early critics condemned the book as indecent for several reasons, not the least of which is Rochester's tendency to tell sexual tales to a naïve young woman (Berg 13).

19. Lady Charlotte, Douglas's age peer, is constantly subjected to "little shades of ridicule" for her "girlish giggle" (1.209–10) and the "long young ringlet" (1.87) she flirtatiously twirls. Referring to her as "the youthful-elderly," the narrator

depicts her as vainly deluded in her belief that the duke is surprised she has a married daughter (1.301). While the midlife man exists in a truly liminal state between age extremes, a woman of similar years has already passed into dotage.

20. Anthony Trollope also wrote about middle-aged men and younger women in his short stories—for example, in "Mary Gresly" (1869) a married midlife man falls in love with a younger woman, though he never lets it be known. In "Catherine Carmichael" (1878), a man near fifty makes an incompatible marriage with a woman in her twenties. When her first husband dies, Catherine is able to wed a younger suitor, depicted as her natural mate.

21. Trollope turned sixty in 1875, the year *The Way We Live Now* was published in two volumes, and during this period he was beginning to feel his age. In the fall of 1873, he had become deaf in one ear and wrote to a friend, "Why should anything go wrong in our bodies? Why should we not be all beautiful? Why should there be decay?—why death? . . ." (Glendinning 435). He also mentioned to another friend, G. W. Rusden, in the winter of 1875–76, "After a man has done making love there is no other thing on earth to make him happy but hard work" (Glendinning 441). He wrote to Cecilia Mettkerke in 1876: "In spirit I could trundle a hoop about the streets, and could fall in love with a young woman as readily as ever; as she doesn't want me, I don't—but I could" (Glendinning 448).

22. With the phrase "age of bachelors," Elaine Showalter quotes Brian Harrison, *Separate Spheres*, 97.

23. In 1881, the year before he died, Trollope had finished writing *The Fixed Period*, a Utopian novel about a country in which all citizens were euthanized at the end of their sixty-seventh year, Trollope's own age at the time. Trollope claimed of the book, "It's all true—I *mean* every word of it" (Mullen 639). Richard Mullen argues that this statement has been incorrectly read to mean that Trollope supported a Utopia based on killing off the elderly, but "his aim was to show through the islanders' rebellion that the scheme was not only wrong, because opposed to human nature and Christian teaching, but unworkable" (639). For an analysis of the implications of empire in *The Fixed Period* juxtaposed with Trollope's travel book, *Australia and New Zealand*, see Blythe, "*The Fixed Period:* Euthanasia, Cannibalism, and Colonial Extinction in Trollope's Antipodes."

24. As much as I would like to make an argument for vulgar jests between Whittlestaff and Baggett here, the *Oxford English Dictionary* does not support such an assertion, identifying the first use of "box" as slang for female genitalia in 1940s America. Nevertheless, there are still comedic aspects that hint at sexual control between the two when Baggett objects to being told "that the key of your bedroom door is in the master's pocket" (1.210), the comedy and ageism increased because she is repeatedly described as "the old woman."

25. Trollope visited South Africa in 1877 and published an account of the journey the next year titled *South Africa*. His descriptions reveal him to be only a slightly more sympathetic imperialist than his character Gordon. For example, he notes British dishonesty in the colony and registers indigenous Africans' sense of identity and loyalty, even as he labels their subversion of British rule "theft":

> The honesty of the white man may perhaps be indifferent, but such as
> it is it has to be used . . . to prevent, as far as it may be prevented, the

systematized stealing in which the Kafirs take an individual and national pride. The Kafirs are not only most willing but most astute thieves, feeling a glory in their theft and thinking that every stone stolen from a white man is a duty done to their Chief and their tribe. . . . They come to the Fields instructed by their Chiefs to steal diamonds and they obey the orders like loyal subjects. (364)

He also describes practices similar to those described by Gordon, representing British punishment as fair and as becoming increasingly humane by law: "They will pick up stones with their toes and secrete them even under the eyes of those who are watching them. I was told that a man will so hide a diamond in his mouth that no examination will force him to disclose it. They are punished when discovered with lashes and imprisonment;—in accordance with the law on the matter. No employer is now allowed to flog his man at his own pleasure" (365).

    26. See also Tosh, *Manliness and Masculinities in Nineteenth-Century Britain*, 119.

Chapter 3. "The Neutral Man-Woman": Female Desexualization at Midlife

    1. From the medieval era through the eighteenth century, the average age of menopause was generally considered to be between forty-five and fifty years old (Ottaway 36), though medical texts rarely mentioned it (Ottaway 38). Edward John Tilt reports that "the average date of cessation" in the nineteenth century was forty-five years, nine months in 1082 cases observed by three physicians in Paris and London but goes on to explain that because women with "ovario-uterine diseases" are counted in this survey, he concludes that "the average *normal* date of cessation in England is more likely to be under forty-five" (12).

    2. Teresa Mangum points out that Victorian children's literature directed ridicule toward "old" women who attempt coquetry as well as those who are "embarrassingly girlish" ("Little Women" 75–76, 85).

    3. Elizabeth Kincaid-Ehler comments on the absence of menopause in nineteenth-century fiction, positing that "wildly vacillating behaviors may have been understood at that time to be a code for menopause; however, we cannot recapture the connections because we cannot be certain that we are correctly deciphering that code" (24).

    4. When exploring Victorian constructions of menopause, it is important to note that a dearth of helpful information still exists for midlife women about this part of the life cycle. As Heather E. Dillaway wrote in 2006, "there are still major gaps in our knowledge about women's experiences of reproductive aging. . . . We lack a comprehensive definition of what menopause is, when it occurs, how women transition through the different stages of reproductive aging, and how long the entire process lasts" (31).

    5. Tilt credits the French medical professor Joseph Recamier as beginning the science of gynecology, "the youngest branch of medical literature," in 1816 (ii).

6. See Poovey, *Uneven Developments*, 35–37.

7. For similar theories about menopause in America, see Markson, "Sagacious, Sinful, or Superfluous?," and Barbre, "Meno-Boomer and Moral Guardians."

8. For studies that use anthropological and biocultural approaches to establish cultural differences in menopausal symptoms, see Davis, "The Cultural Constructions of the Premenstrual and Menopause Syndromes"; Lock, "Deconstructing the Change: Female Maturation in Japan and North America"; Kearns, "Perceptions of Menopause by Papago Women"; Wright, "Variation in Navajo Menopause"; Beyene, *From Menarche to Menopause*.

9. See Roy Porter and Lesley Hall for extensive references regarding nineteenth-century theories of hysteria and problematic female sexuality (129, 141, 319, 324).

10. In the preface to the first edition of *The Change of Life in Women in Health and Disease*, Tilt designates the forties as the menopausal decade, and in the preface to the fourth edition sets ages forty-five to fifty-five as the time span he will focus on because of "the many diseases by which it may be chequered" (iii).

11. For similar theories in Victorian American culture see Barbre, "Meno-Boomer and Moral Guardians," 28.

12. J. Braxton Hicks, one of the most prominent London obstetricians of the Victorian era, is well known today for the prelabor uterine contractions which bear his name. See Michael Mason for an explanation of differences between general practitioners and Royal college physicians such as Braxton Hicks and Tilt who practiced medicine at hospitals and formed the intellectual, academic research base of medicine (180).

13. Quotation from the 3rd edition of 1871.

14. At the end of the Victorian period, Sylvanus Stall even goes so far as to argue that heaven has ordained postmenopausal women to be sexually repulsive: "... God now makes her less attractive, and her manner and bearing consequently become such as to render her repellent to the sexual approaches of her mate" (207). Stall was an American clergyman, but his book, widely circulated in the United States and Great Britain, was well received by both medical and clerical authorities (Featherstone and Hepworth, "History" 251).

15. See Roe Sybylla's analysis of menopause's cultural construction and her comparison of Victorian ideas about sexlessness, masculinization, and disease at "the change" which are opposite to late twentieth-century menopausal theories. Sybylla, "Situating Menopause Within the Strategies of Power: A Genealogy."

16. Dickens's condemnation of midlife women is especially interesting when considered in conjunction with his personal life in his mid-forties. When he separated from his wife Catherine, who was also in her forties, he fell in love with the much younger actress Ellen Ternan (Johnson 880, 920), developments that suggest biographical speculations beyond the scope of this study.

17. Elizabeth Kincaid-Ehler notes that spinsters and married women of menopausal age often are bracketed together in nineteenth-century fiction, represented as sexless (29).

18. Brontë was not married until eight years later.

19. Auerbach, *Communities of Women;* Niles, "Malthusian Menopause: Aging and Sexuality in Elizabeth Gaskell's *Cranford*"; and Fasick, *Vessels of Meaning.*

20. Nina Auerbach reads the argument between Brown and Jenkyns over *Dickens v. Johnson* as a debate about pomposity and "literary and human right" (308). Niles argues it is "a contestation over views of aging and sexuality" (297), because Johnson, as avatar of "moral restraint," allies Miss Jenkyns with Malthus's system of celibacy to reduce population growth, a quality which Captain Brown, a reader of "low" literature, shows himself sadly lacking by producing two daughters whom he finds it hard to support (298).

21. Laura Fasick argues the Jenkyns "urgently need to carve out roles for themselves that do not depend upon caring for others because in a society that defines women as caretakers they have no one to take care of but themselves" (93). Fasick asserts, "The central issue in *Cranford* . . . is the single woman's struggle to define herself when female singleness violates society's prescriptions" (94). See also Niles's more optimistic argument that for the single women of Cranford "menopause is . . . a paradoxical source of strength" (295), because, as nonreproductive women, they do not contribute to the nation's troubling overpopulation, and are also economically independent instead of a burden on society (295). Spinsterhood becomes "a viable alternative" to marriage that produces overpopulation, and the novel's "model of nonreproductive sexuality" challenges denigrating portrayals of postmenopausal women (Niles 296).

22. Julie Fenwick notes that Deborah becomes a "surrogate son" to her father after Peter runs away from home and that "the masculinized Deborah is unmarriageable" (414).

23. See Nile's analysis of Matty as a nonreproductive but substitute mother to Martha's baby who "offers a solution to Malthus's problem of population through communal intervention" (301).

24. An interesting contrast to my reading is Niles's argument that "the narrative itself subtly approves" of this nonreproductive marriage because it brings an infusion of youthfulness to the spinsters and the bride (303–4).

25. See Julie M. Fenwick's analysis of imperialism in *Cranford* as "a dubious investment" that brings little material good to the country while disrupting maternity (421).

26. See Stubbs, *Women and Fiction;* O'Mealy, "Mrs. Oliphant, Miss Marjoribanks, and the Victorian Canon"; Rubik, *The Novels of Mrs. Oliphant;* Winston, "Revising *Miss Marjoribanks*"; Schaub, "Queen of the Air or Constitutional Monarch?"

27. Several critics have discussed Lucilla's lack of consciousness. For example, Q. D. Leavis argues that Oliphant is "constantly stressing the contrast between how she conceives of herself and how she appears to others" (12). Elizabeth Jay writes that Lucilla is "at one and the same time the most and least self-conscious of heroines, always unaware of that larger audience of readers able to perceive the brightly lit stage upon which she so often 'rehearses' her miniature dramas, as also of her cage" (Introduction xiii).

28. Ann L. Ardis points out that *She* was published several years before the New Woman became a controversial figure in print, but that the novel "anticipates all the questions to be asked of the New Woman once she makes her appearance

on the socioliterary scene" (140). For further discussion of Ayesha as New Woman, see Ardis, *New Women, New Novels*, 140–42, and Murphy, *Time is of the Essence*, 54–57. In many ways, Ayesha actually reifies Victorian gender paradigms instead of challenging them. She enjoys having men worship her for her beauty and blatantly acknowledges the basest form of marriage market barter: "man can be bought with woman's beauty, if it be but beautiful enough; and women's beauty can be bought with gold, if only there be gold enough" (135). In the scene before the pillar of fire, she promises to subordinate herself to Leo when he becomes eternally youthful like she is. Norman Etherington finds these examples of her capitulation to conventional Victorian gender stereotypes evidence that H. Rider Haggard was resisting the New Woman by writing her back into sequestration (xxxi).

29. Elaine Showalter describes her as "an incestuous maternal figure, who must die before she consummates her relation with the younger Leo" (87).

30. For example, in the hotpotting episode, Mohamed is killed when a super-heated pot is thrust over his head. Sandra M. Gilbert and Susan Gubar describe this as a "cross between cooking and decapitation" wherein the victim is "devoured by a fiery female symbol," and "a vessel associated with domesticity . . . become[s] as deadly as woman's anatomy seen in the worst male nightmares" (*No Man's* 14). Elaine Showalter also points out the killing of older women may be by hotpotting, "an image of castration and decapitation" that suggests the Amahagger may also cannibalize their mothers once they are no longer reproductive (86).

31. For further discussions of the landscape as female in *She*, see Gilbert and Gubar, *No Man's Land* (14–17); Stott, *The Fabrication of the Late-Victorian Femme Fatale* (95–96); Showalter, *Sexual Anarchy* (85–86).

32. Showalter also describes their journey "into a body that seems disturbingly sexual, both male and female" (85) and argues, "They penetrate Kôr . . . as if it were a masculine body, through rear cave entrances . . ." (86).

33. See Stott, *The Fabrication of the Late-Victorian Femme Fatale*, for a discussion of the voyeuristic aspects of this scene (121–22).

34. Teresa Mangum points out a similar theme in Haggard's *King Solomon's Mines* in his depiction of the witch Gagool as "merciless and mad, as monkey-like and savage in a terrifying reversal of Darwinian evolution in which a human paradoxically ages into the worst sort of racist stereotype—primitive, bestial infancy" ("Little Women" 79).

35. The travelers' journey to Kôr also reflects degeneration fear as they move back through human and geologic time. The potsherd that guides them traces the Vincey family history from Egypt to Greece and Rome and finally to England, recapitulating the "progress of civilization" as understood by Victorians. Holly, Leo, and Job reverse this history by traveling from Cambridge to the coast of Africa and Kôr where Leo's Egyptian ancestor Killakrates rests in state (Etherington xviii). They travel to the dawn of geologic time in the center of a volcano that holds "the Fire of Life" which has burned since the Earth's beginning (Etherington xviii). In addition, they recapitulate the individual birth process in reverse, going through a symbolic birth canal toward the womb (Murphy 58).

The Amahagger also are associated with degeneration, as the descendents of a highly developed civilization which has been demolished and whose people have regressed into "semi-savages" (Etherington xxvii). This "bastard brood of the mighty

sons of Kôr" (121) shows marked signs of evolutionary regression in their cannibalism and adulteration of a formerly pure language to "a bastard Arabic" (Murphy
45). In contrast, the British men are descended from civilizations understood as
superior, especially Leo with his Egyptian ancestors, part of the classical world
that Victorians venerated and from which they believed their society descended
(Murphy 45).

36. *The Graphic* (November 27, 1886): 577.

37. Ann L. Ardis argues that Haggard's description of evolution turned
backward in Ayesha's physical deterioration is a warning that if the New Woman
comes to power, Victorians risk a similar "social and racial devolution" (142). In
Holly's worries about the consequences if Ayesha should travel to England, Ardis
finds "Haggard's cultural displacement" of Britain's fin-de-siècle fears about the
New Woman's effect on politics and the result of her erotic freedom (141). Because
Victorians associated matriarchy with primitive societies and patriarchy with advanced
culture, Ayesha as female ruler suggests "cultural decline" (Murphy 55). She does
"not merely signify an earlier step on the evolutionary ladder," according to Murphy,
but "embodies the regressive tendencies so feared by late-century Victorians" especially in her association with the New Woman that indicates "a return to chaotic
primitivism" (57). For further discussion of Ayesha as New Woman, see Gilbert and
Gubar, *No Man's Land* (6–7). For more on Ayesha and degeneration, see Gilbert
and Gubar, *No Man's Land* (21), and Stott, *The Fabrication of the Late-Victorian
Femme Fatale* (115).

Chapter 4. *Marriageable at Midlife:*
The Remarrying Widows of
Frances Trollope and Anthony Trollope

1. "Illustrations of Humbug.—No. 1." Cartoon. *Punch* (1842): 213. The
Library of Virginia. Reproduced by permission.

2. In the earliest extant English comedy, *Ralph Roister-Doister* (1550's), Con-
stance Custance is a widow made ridiculous by Ralph's amorous advances. The tradition continues in Restoration drama with the Widow Blackacre in William Wycherley's
The Plain Dealer and Lady Wishfort in Richard Congreve's *The Way of the World*,
plays which "engendered an enduring stereotype of the early modern widow as a
woman who anxiously sought a husband at any cost" (Todd 54–55). The convention
persists in the eighteenth-century novel with women like the Widow Wadman who
is an incongruous object of love in Laurence Sterne's *Tristram Shandy*.

3. "Work Sheet" on *Can You Forgive Her?* The Trollope Business Papers,
The Bodleian Library.

4. The term "second-chance plot" comes from Margaret Morganroth Gullette.
See *Declining to Decline* and "Puzzling Case."

5. In the 1730s, 24% of marriages were terminated by the death of a spouse
within 10 years, and 56% within 25 years, but by the 1850s the numbers had
dropped to 19% and 47%, and in the 1880s only 13% of marriages ended before
10 years and 37% before 25 years (M. Anderson 29).

6. The average length of British marriage continues to decrease. Michael Anderson reports that by the 1980s divorce had caused marriage duration rates to fall to those caused by death in the 1820s (30). In fact, in *The Family, Sex and Marriage In England 1500–1800* Lawrence Stone looks at modern divorce as "little more than a functional substitute for death," arguing that the "decline of the adult mortality rates after the late eighteenth century, by prolonging the expected duration of marriage to unprecedented lengths, eventually forced Western society to adopt the institutional escape-hatch of divorce" (56).

7. The numbers were still as high in the latter part of the eighteenth century, with 15% of men and 20% of women marrying as widowers and widows (Wrigley and Schofield 258).

8. In the second half of the nineteenth century, of the total male population, widowers made up 4% at ages 35–44, 7% at 45–54, and 14% at 55–64, while, for women, the numbers of widows in similar age ranges were 8%, 15% and 30% respectively, double the male rate in every age cohort (M. Anderson 30).

9. In 1851, the marriage rate per 1,000 of population of widowers was 36% at age twenty-five and 14% at age forty, while for widows the rate was 15% at twenty-five and 4% at forty (Farr 79–80). The discrepancy continued later in the century—William Farr reports that in 1870–72, 30% of widowers remarried at age twenty-five and 15% at forty, while only 16% of widows remarried at twenty-five and 4% at forty (79–80).

10. For more details see Taylor, *Mourning Dress: A Costume and Social History.*

11. Lessened mourning customs developed throughout the second half of the century. An 1880 manual states: "Formerly mourning was worn both for a longer period and of a much deeper character than is usual at the present time" (Campbell 85). In 1894, Fanny Douglas claims "mourning is . . . not carried quite to the extremity it once was" (110). See Richard Davey, *A History of Mourning*, and Douglas, *The Gentlewoman's Book of Dress.*

12. Michael Anderson states, "By the mid-nineteenth century about 14 per cent of males and 9 per cent of women who married were widowed. The figures fell slowly for the rest of the century, reaching 8.9 per cent and 6.6 per cent respectively in the early 1900s, 7.3 per cent and 4.6 per cent in the early 1930s and 6.4 per cent and 5.4 per cent in the early 1950s" (31).

13. For further discussion of Frances as feminist reformer see Ayres (ed.), *Frances Trollope and Novel of Social Change* as well as Heineman, *Frances Trollope;* Heineman, *Mrs. Trollope;* Button, "Reclaiming Mrs. Frances Trollope: British Abolitionist and Feminist"; Kissel, *In Common Cause;* Kissel, "More Than Anthony's Mother"; Kissel, "What Shall Become of Us All?"

14. Richard Barichman, Susan MacDonald and Myra Stark argue that his novels "present his understanding of the conditions that produce frantic husband hunting and give it far-reaching social significance" (209). Juliet McMaster says his depiction of the women's cause became more sympathetic as his career progressed, so that he was "no longer a reactionary" by the end of the Palliser series (166). Robert M. Polhemus argues that "The sixties brought new frankness and objectivity about love, sex, and women to Britain" which is reflected in Trollope's love plots

(*Changing* 90). Barickman, MacDonald, and Stark also note that "from the sixties on, when women's rights had become the subject of much public debate, jesting references to the subject are scattered through Trollope's novels," but readers "find Trollope sympathetic to women and concerned about the same problems troubling Victorian feminists" (195–96).

15. For further correspondences between Anthony's and Frances's work, see Neville-Sington, "The Life and Adventures of a Clever Woman" (22–23).

16. He goes on to say, "I think that an author when he uses either the words or the plot of another, should own as much, demanding to be credited with no more of the work than he has himself produced" (*Autobiography* 77–78).

17. Biographies of Frances Trollope and Anthony Trollope, as well as book-length literary analyses, usually comment on the relationship between the two. See the following: N. Hall, *Trollope: A Biography*; Heineman, *Francis Trollope*; Heineman, *Mrs. Trollope*; Nardin, *He Knew She Was Right* (11–13); Neville-Sington, *Fanny Trollope*; Overton, *The Unofficial Trollope* (11–12, 25); Ransom, *Fanny Trollope: A Remarkable Life*; Sadleir, *Trollope: A Commentary* (37–116); and Ayers (ed.), *Frances Trollope and the Novel of Social Change*.

18. Teresa Ransom, in her introduction to the Pocket Classics edition of *The Widow Barnaby* published by Alan Sutton, claims forty-one books in 115 volumes.

19. See also Bill Overton, *The Unofficial Trollope* for more commentary on her influence in this regard (12).

20. An unsigned review in *The New Monthly Magazine* rails memorably against this aspect of her writing: "Satire is, perhaps, *the* characteristic of Mrs. Trollope's writings—satire of a hard, poignant, persevering sort. . . . It wears an almost vicious look—goes about seeking whom it may devour—snaps at strangers—bites as well as barks, and, when it does bite, makes its teeth meet" ("Female Novelists" 20).

21. The idea caused an uproar among the clergy even before the Act was passed, and they strenuously objected to the possibility that they would be forced to remarry the adulterous party of a divorce. The Attorney General agreed that clergymen could refuse to perform such marriages on the basis of conscience but stipulated that churches could not be forbidden for their use (Stone, *Road* 381).

22. Martha is actually thirty-five at the time of her husband's demise. Pamela Neville-Sington mentions that Frances uses this mellifluous phrase again in both *Hargrave* and *The Lottery of a Marriage* (*Fanny Trollope* 267).

23. Mrs. John Sherwood mentions in 1888 that Queen Victoria is still wearing her widow's cap, though Albert had been dead for over two decades (195).

24. Widowers, in contrast, added black mourning-cloaks to their regular clothes until 1850, and after that date used only black gloves, hatbands, and cravats (wide neckties) to indicate their mourning (Jalland 301).

25. Anthony credited his own early, unsuccessful play, *The Noble Jilt*, as the source for *Can You Forgive Her?*, and his dark interpretation of the widow figure in the play derives many details from *The Widow Barnaby*. Margaret De Wynter (later to become Alice in *Can You Forgive Her?*) is pursued by two suitors, the worthy Count Upsel (John Gray) and the wild Steinmark (George Vavasor). This plot is paralleled by the story of a widow, Madame Brudo, who is pursued by the

conventional, wealthy VanHoppen (Cheesacre) and the rascally Belleroach (Bellfield). Madame Brudo is, in several senses, Anthony's first rewriting of Mrs. Barnaby—like Martha she makes much of her widow's grief when anyone is around to hear, she claims she will never remarry while obviously angling for suitors, she declares a hypocritical because fabricated love for her niece, she plays her two suitors against each other, and her maid is a go-between in the love affairs. Though both Madame Brudo and Martha transgress mourning strictures and remarry too early, Brudo is even more precipitous, marrying only three months after her spouse's death while the Widow Barnaby weds after seven.

An important parallel between Frances's novel and Anthony's play is the depiction of Madame Brudo as manipulative, insincere, and ridiculous, but in this version the widow has exaggerated failings and no appeal. Brudo is not triumphantly self-determined like Barnaby. Instead, she argues for female dependence, telling her niece that women "are born to be slaves. They cannot throw off the yoke. Tis better for them twice to submit than once to rebel" (182). Even though the play was meant to be a comedy, Madame Brudo is simply not funny, lacking Martha's flagrantly excessive charm.

As the basis for Anthony's later novel, small elements which are original to the play show up in *Can You Forgive Her?* The men are aware of the widow's sexual appraisal of them—Belleroach criticizes VanHoppen for being "podgy" and tells him, "Madame Brudo does not prefer a podgy man," as Bellfield will later tell Cheesacre (101). Madame Brudo is like her later incarnation Arabella Greenow in that she does accept the wild man Belleroach over the worthy man VanHoppen. Instead of choosing freely, however, Brudo seems merely to acquiesce to Belleroach's insistence. The name alterations Anthony made when converting the play to a novel demonstrate the change from the failed comedic play to the novel of serious midlife affect. VanHoppen, the pompous, posturing burgomaster of Bruges, remains pompous and posturing as Cheesacre, a farmer who can provide both cheese and acres—in the form of Oileymead, a farm overly abundant in its housekeeping, produce, and the "rich heaps" of manure that fertilize the soil. But Belleroach becomes Bellfield, the name changing from "beautiful fish," a quarry to be landed, to "beautiful field"—a free and lovely space. Arabella herself, no longer Madame Brudo—brooding and brutish—is named Greenow—a midlife woman starting over with possibilities for growth and new life because she is "green now." Though Madame Brudo is Anthony's first appropriation of some aspects of the widow Barnaby, not until he creates Arabella does he capture the true Barnaby spirit of comedic audacity and self-determination.

26. See chapter 3 for an extended discussion of paradigms for female midlife.

27. Anthony Trollope viewed *Phineas Finn* and *Phineas Redux* as "but one novel, though they were brought out at a considerable interval of time and in different forms" (*Autobiography* 203).

28. Several critics comment on Marie's masculine attributes. Jane Nardin notes that she has qualities which are often attributed to men such as "aggression, foresight, and courage" (193). She enjoys the usually male prerogatives of a business life, involvement in political debate, financial independence, and living alone (Barickman, MacDonald, and Stark 230–31; Morse 69). She also "claims male privileges of sexual

aggression" when she proposes to Phineas (Nardin 195). Madame Max "refuse[s] to be frustrated and confined by the limits of her sex" and is "entirely independent, fully resourceful, and self-reliant" in financial affairs and later in finding evidence to acquit Phineas (McMaster 178). Shirley Robin Letwin calls Madame Max "the most perfect gentleman in Trollope's novels" (74), and Morse identifies her as the "heroic suitor" (40).

29. David M. Buss finds that the older man and younger woman marriage is a cross-cultural norm, that "men universally prefer younger women as wives" even though "the strength of this preference varies somewhat from culture to culture." In a study of thirty-seven societies, he found that the average age differential was "2.5 years younger" (51).

Chapter 5. In the Eye of the Beholder: Victorian Age Construction and the Specular Self

1. This chapter is a revised version of "In the Eye of the Beholder: Victorian Age Construction and the Specular Self," *Victorian Literature and Culture* 34.1 (2006): 27–45.

2. Kathleen Woodward argues that while it may be healthy to deny the mirrored image of oneself as the aged other, this creates a double bind—rejecting the image in the mirror causes one to judge the elderly as inferior and ultimately to reject one's own aging self ("Instant" 60), capitulation to the most radical sort of decline and ageism. Therefore, though we feel—in the words of Simone de Beauvoir—"instant repulsion" at age, we also are repulsed by our own repulsion ("Instant" 44). Woodward concludes, however, that "perhaps blindness to one's own mirror image is the most profound insight," even though that state results in an "inhumane blindness" to all elderly people ("Instant" 62).

3. Edward John Tilt states that "the average *normal* date of cessation in England is . . . likely to be under forty-five" in women who do not suffer from any kind of uterine disease (12). See chapter 3 for a more extensive discussion.

4. See chapter 4 for a more extensive discussion of Victorian remarriage.

5. For a more detailed discussion of this development, see chapter 4.

6. See figure 1.1, chapter 1.

7. In the preface, Oscar Wilde depicts the portrait as a type of mirror when he writes, "It is the spectator, and not life, that art really mirrors," a recognition that the viewer projects meaning onto art, revealing the self (xxiii). Critics point out that Wilde is here prefiguring recent theoretical recognition of the reader's function in constructing textual meaning, and, I would add, in imposing significance on the self that is revealed. See Gillespie, *Oscar Wilde and the Poetics of Ambiguity* and Price, "A Map of Utopia," 75.

8. Stephen Arata points out Wilde's careful ambiguity about Dorian's unconventional and transgressive behaviors, noting his comment in a letter to the *Scots Observer*, "What Dorian Gray's sins are no one knows. He who finds them has brought them" (65).

9. Because of its gay subtext, *The Picture of Dorian Gray* may seem too atypical an example to be used in a discussion of generalized male age anxiety. As I discuss in chapter 2, male fears about age and affect appear across a wide range of Victorian novels.

10. As Helena Michie points out, Pierston never loves an actual woman, because he discovers his love for the first Avice only after her death, and then he desires her daughter and granddaughter only as her reproductions (*Flesh* 112). Pierston never can possess the Well-Beloved because his quest is for something unattainable, a projection of himself.

11. See chapter 2, p. 50 for a similar situation in Dickens's *Little Dorrit*.

12. Hardy was quoting Leslie Stephen. See Hardy, *Life and Work*, 131.

Chapter 6. "How To Keep Young": Advertising and Late-Victorian Age Anxiety

1. "Even the black Australian dying. . . ." Pears' Soap advertisement. August 10, 1889. The Bodleian Library, University of Oxford: Soap 5. Reproduced by permission.

2. For further discussion of race in Victorian advertisements, see McClintock, *Imperial Leather*; Ramamurthy, *Imperial Persuaders;* Richards, *The Commodity Culture of Victorian England*.

3. Versions of this advertisement ran in popular periodicals including *The Graphic* and *The Illustrated London News* in the mid-1880s and have been recently reproduced in several studies (McClintock 213; Ramamurthy 27; DeVries 25). As Anandi Ramamurthy notes, "The image must have been extremely popular since numerous copies of it exist in archives around the country, both in black and white and in colour" (28).

4. This particular version is reprinted in DeVries (25) and Ramamurthy (27).

5. Tennyson's poetic condemnation was part of a general outcry against Émile Zola's work, a censure that contrasted with, and was perhaps reinforced by, high sales figures for his novels. According to Algernon Swinburne, Zola's work "turned the stomach" due to "details of brutality and atrocity" that should not be mentioned outside of medical literature (Decker 1141). George Saintsbury avowed that "M. Zola frequently revolts us by his unvarnished allusions to things which lie outside the pale of modest decency" (qtd. in Decker 1142). His British publisher, Ernest Vizetelly, was thrown into prison for indecency (Frierson 533–36).

6. Tennyson noted on the manuscript that this is "a dramatic poem, and the Dramatis Personae are imaginary" (H. Tennyson 329). He more forcefully insisted on this point in a letter to Charles Esmarch of 18 April 1888, when he wrote, ". . . I must object and strongly to the statement in your preface that I am the hero in either poem. . . . There is not one touch of autobiography in it from end to end" ("To Charles Esmarch" 366–67). Tennyson's grandson Charles, though acknowledging his grandfather's statements that the poem is not biographical, comments, "there is hardly a line of *Sixty Years After* that does not express emotions which he had

experienced at one time or another" (C. Tennyson 493). He reports that during 1886, when the poet was dealing with the death of his son, "His natural tendency to gloom and despondency reasserted itself and he became more and more oppressed with doubts about the usefulness of his own work and the future of humanity." Tennyson voiced opinions about Britain that are identical to the speaker's, according to Charles, and he quotes his grandfather as saying: "When I see society vicious and the poor starving in great cities . . . I feel that it is a mighty wave of evil passing over the world, but that there will be yet some new and strange development which I shall not live to see. . . . You must not be surprised at anything that comes to pass in the next fifty years. All ages are ages of transition, but this is an awful moment of transition" (491).

Critics are divided about whether or not the poem is a statement of Tennyson's own complaints about Britain. F. E. L. Priestley notes that "ideas" in the poem "are practically identical with ones voiced by Tennyson in the early 1830s" (532). However, he also argues that Tennyson carefully "makes the chronology deliberately a fictional one" by setting the sequel sixty years after the first poem, when he actually wrote it forty years later, "so that it refers to his imagined character and not to himself" (524). Leonée Ormand believes that "undoubtedly some of his ideas are expressed" in the poem (194). Linda K. Hughes reads the poem's cultural critique as "a sign of increasing internal pressures in Tennyson as he himself approached life's end" (214). James R. Kincaid sees it as "a vivid illustration of the general inability of . . . [Tennyson's] . . . late poems to find peace" (*Tennyson's Major Poems* 146). Robert Barnard Martin believes "Tennyson's sorrow infects" the poem and "contributes to the deep feeling of estrangement between the narrator and the world in which he lives" and argues that "the emotions are biographically his even if the events of the poem are not" (559), seeing "the narrator" as "more precisely, Tennyson's voice speaking through him" (559–60).

7. For example, see Gagnier, "Mediums and the Media" (30); Williams, "Advertising: The Magic System" (177); McClintock *Imperial Leather* (210–11); E. Turner, *The Shocking History of Advertising* (132).

8. See also Dempsey, *Bubbles: Early Advertising Art From A. & F. Pears' Ltd.*

9. See Ramamurthy's *Imperial Persuaders* for an account of Lever's exploitation of the African palm oil market through racist rhetoric and policies in the early twentieth century (52–56).

10. See Loeb's *Consuming Angels* for an in-depth analysis of the effects of advertising on female consumers.

11. Pears' Soap advertisement. *The Graphic* (August 19, 1882): 191. Other examples appear in *The Graphic* from 1886 to 1891.

12. Pears' Soap advertisement. *The Graphic* (October 10, 1891): 439.

13. Pears' Soap advertisement. *The Graphic* (August 10, 1895): 180.

14. In 1846, only four periodicals were being published for a specifically female readership, but by the end of the century, fifty women's magazines were in print (Nevett 78).

15. "Baby-Skin." Pears' Soap advertisement. c. 1890. The Wellcome Library: EPH 161:16.

16. Look in the Glass!" Pears' Soap advertisement. c. 1890. The Wellcome Library: EPH 161:16.

17. "I am 50 Today." Pears' Soap advertisement. *The Graphic* (March 31, 1888): 359. The Library of Virginia. Reproduced by permission. This ad also is discussed by Walkowitz, *City of Dreadful Delight* (188) and B. Thompson *The Disastrous Mrs. Weldon* (304).

18. Early psychiatrists, known as alienists, labeled spiritualists as insane "religious maniacs," grouping them with others they believed "disturbed the moral order" such as "[p]aupers, alcoholics, pedophiles, patricides . . . baby stealers, blasphemers, [and] shoplifters" (B. Thompson 229).

19. In the confinement scandal, *The British Medical Journal* blamed husbands, comparing them to Brontë's Rochester, who locked his wife in an attic, while spiritualists accused madhouse doctors of enjoying the "sadistic pleasures of the hunt" (Walkowitz 183). Weldon herself alleged a sexual conspiracy between medical men and husbands that amounted to "traffic in women" (Walkowitz 183), strengthened by her discovery that her own husband's long-standing liaison included a thirteen-year-old son (B. Thompson 273). Walkowitz argues that Weldon evoked fear of abusive male authority in the medical establishment and the home by calling on "the outlines of a familiar plot" from sensation novels (181), but that she rewrote the customary conclusion, gaining more legal power for women to defend themselves (183).

20. "Spy" [Leslie Ward]. "Mrs. Weldon." Lithograph. May 3, 1884. Private collection. This portrait appeared along with the essay "Ladies—No X. Mrs. Georgina Weldon" in *Vanity Fair* 31 (May 3, 1884): 243 and also was sold as a separate print. For a discussion of another, less flattering, 1884 portrayal of Weldon as a woman's rights activist in the "downscale" publication *Moonshine*, see Walkowitz, *City of Dreadful Delight*, 187.

21. Painter and playwright Walford Graham Robertson expressed an internationally held opinion when he recorded his initial impression of her before she become famous: "For the first time in my life I beheld perfect beauty" (qtd in Marshall 12).

22. The Prince was so ostentatiously public about his passion that he built the Red House in Bournemouth for their assignations (Beatty 87).

23. Her clothing set immediate style trends: when she wrapped black velvet into a small turban, adding a feather, within days the "Langtry Hat" was offered in shop windows to an eager public (Beatty 79). Robertson reports "universal worship" of Lillie manifested in products such as the "Langtry bonnet, the Langtry shoe, even the Langtry dress-improver," items that were "widely stocked and as widely bought" by Victorian women (qtd. in Marshall 12), and numerous manufacturers used her image to endorse their products.

24. Patti and her lover, Nicolini, went on to live extravagantly in her Welsh castle, marrying in 1886 (Rosselli 105–6).

25. As illustrated by the furor over private theatricals in Jane Austen's *Mansfield Park* (1814), the theater fell from respectability early in the nineteenth century when its genteel audience began to wane (Kent 98). Though Queen Victoria and Prince Albert's patronage in the 1840s temporarily shored up popularity, the stage

increasingly became associated with the lower classes and the music-hall acts that dominated the theater (Kent 98–99). In the 1860s, upper-class interest in the stage revived due to new social comedies that required a knowledge of gentility, and by the 1870s, upper class clientele started attending performances that were timed to begin after the fashionable dinner hour and featured higher ticket prices, more orderly queuing, and required evening dress (Kent 104, 107). Even Queen Victoria began to show revived interest in the theater, and, despite her protracted mourning for Albert, had plays performed in various royal residences (Loeb 95).

During this time, several actresses were admitted to the highest levels of society through marriage, but for the most part, Langtry and others like her were not accepted in polite company. Between 1884 and 1914, nineteen actresses married English nobles, creating a new, but very limited "actressocracy" (Kent 115). An 1884 article in *The Times* argues that Fortescue's £10,000 breach-of-promise award, a sum worthy of a countess, proves that actresses had ceased to be "social cyphers" (qtd. in Kent 109–10). Christopher Kent argues, however, that though one upper-class hostess may have claimed that in 1884 actors were considered gentlemen, a more accurate analysis is probably that of critic T. H. S. Escott who accused society of countenancing actresses as a bit of amusing wickedness, and the "equality" conferred on them was false (Kent 109).

26. Margaret D. Stetz asserts that women in the 1880s often were "actively dissuaded by friends, family, clergy, and even by novelists and essayists from setting foot in the theatre at all" (15), but they also were well-informed about actresses and the theater due to the popularity of publications about plays and backstage life (16) which created a feminine taste for the theater and unprecedented access to its workings (17).

27. "The Temple of Beauty." Pears' Soap advertisement. 1887. The Bodleian Library, University of Oxford: Soap 4 (98). Reproduced by permission. The Temple of Beauty ad is reproduced and discussed by Loeb, *Consuming Angels* (96–97).

28. Gail Marshall uses Lillie Langtry as an example, because she appears as an idealized statue in Graham Robertson's autobiography, a poem by Oscar Wilde, and a Frederic Leighton painting, versions in which her "scandalous reputation is safely absorbed into . . . Classical references" (12).

29. In 1969, S. B. Saul concluded that the term inaccurately reflects the complex financial environment of the fin de siècle and should be "banished" (55). After surveying the "impressively detailed literature" that has continued to accrue, Richard English and Michael Kenny have more recently argued "it remains clear that in many areas Britain was losing ground to its competitors" from 1870 to 1914, especially the United States and Germany (283).

30. "I have found it matchless. . . ." Pears' Soap advertisement. *The Graphic* (April 11, 1891): 423. The Library of Virginia. Reproduced by permission.

31. Pears' Soap advertisement. c. 1890. The Wellcome Library: EPH 161:25.

32. "Mary Ray." Pears' Soap advertisement. c. 1890. The Wellcome Library: EPH 162:9. Reproduced by permission. Although I am unable to date this advertisement precisely, its layout and style are identical to Pears' "An Unpacific Yarn" that ran in *The Graphic* from 1887 until the early 1890s.

33. For a discussion of Sunlight using fear of age to sell soap, see also Loeb, *Consuming Angels*, 117–18.

34. "Why Does A Woman Look Old Sooner Than a Man?" Sunlight Soap advertisement. *The Graphic* (Summer Number, 1889): 28. The Library of Virginia. Reproduced by permission.

35. "How To Keep Young." Sunlight Soap advertisement. October 1895. The Bodleian Library, University of Oxford: Soap 6. The Queen Victoria ad also appears in *The Graphic Christmas Number* (1895): 33.

36. "How To Keep Young." Sunlight Soap advertisement. November 1893. The Bodleian Library, University of Oxford: Soap 6 (14a). Reproduced by permission.

37. Sunlight Soap advertisement. *The Graphic* (October 5, 1901): 463.

38. "The New Beauty Culture." Pond's Extract Soap advertisement. *The Delineator.* April 1906. The Wellcome Library: EPH 134:22. Reproduced by permission.

Chapter 7. Afterword: The Future of Midlife

1. See Friedan, *The Fountain of Age* and Steinem, *Doing Sixty and Seventy*.

Works Cited

Achenbaum, W. Andrew. *Crossing Frontiers: Gerontology Emerges As A Science.* Cambridge: Cambridge UP, 1995.

Acton, William. *The Functions and Disorders of the Reproductive Organs in Youth, in Adult Age, and in Advanced Life.* 2nd ed. London: John Churchill, 1858.

Adams, James Eli. *Dandies and Desert Saints: Styles of Victorian Manhood.* Ithaca: Cornell UP, 1995.

Anderson, Michael. "The Social Implications of Demographic Change." *The Cambridge Social History of Britain 1750–1950.* Ed. F. M. L. Thompson. Vol. 2. Cambridge: Cambridge UP, 1990. 1–70.

Anderson, Nancy Fix. *Woman Against Women in Victorian England: A Life of Eliza Lynn Linton.* Bloomington: Indiana UP, 1987.

Arata, Stephen. *Fictions of Loss in the Victorian Fin de Siècle.* Cambridge: Cambridge UP, 1996.

Ardis, Ann L. *New Women, New Novels: Feminism and Early Modernism.* New Brunswick: Rutgers UP, 1990.

Ariès, Philippe. *Centuries of Childhood: A Social History of Family Life.* New York: Alfred A. Knopf, 1962.

Armstrong, Nancy. *How Novels Think: The Limits of British Individualism from 1719–1900.* New York: Columbia UP, 2005.

Ashwell, Samuel. *A Practical Treatise on the Diseases Peculiar to Women, Illustrated by Cases, Derived from Hospital and Private Practice.* Philadelphia: Lea and Blanchard, 1845.

Auerbach, Nina. *Communities of Women: An Idea in Fiction.* Cambridge: Harvard UP, 1978.

Austen, Jane. *Persuasion.* 1818. Harmondsworth, Middlesex: Penguin, 1985.

Ayers, Brenda, ed. *Frances Trollope and the Novel of Social Change.* Westport, CT: Greenwood Press, 2002.

Banks, J. A. *Prosperity and Parenthood: A Study of Family Planning among the Victorian Middle Classes.* London: Routledge, 1954.

———. *Victorian Values: Secularism and the Size of Families.* London: Routledge, 1981.

Barbre, Joy. "Meno-Boomer and Moral Guardians: An Exploration of the Cultural Construction of Menopause." *Menopause: A Midlife Passage.* Ed. Joan C. Callahan. Bloomington: Indiana UP, 1993. 23–35.

Barickman, Richard, Susan MacDonald, and Myra Stark. *Corrupt Relations: Dickens, Thackeray, Trollope, Collins, and the Victorian Sexual System*. NY: Columbia UP, 1982.

Barnes, Robert. "The Climacteric Perturbation." *Women From Birth To Death: The Female Life Cycle in Britain 1830–1914*. Eds. Pat Jalland and John Hooper. Brighton: Harvester Press, 1986. 291–92.

Bateson, Mary Catherine. *Composing A Life*. New York: Penguin, 1990.

Beatty, Laura. *Lillie Langtry: Manners, Masks and Morals*. London: Chatto & Windus, 1999.

Beauty's Mirror. A Companion to the Toilet Being a Collection of the Most Approved Rules for the Management of the Human Figure. London: C. and P. Mudie, 1830.

Belkin, Roslyn. "Rejects of the Marketplace: Old Maids in Charlotte Brontë's *Shirley*." *International Journal of Women's Studies* 4.1 (1981): 50–66.

Benson, Jon. *Prime Time: A History of the Middle Aged in Twentieth-Century Britain*. London: Longman, 1997.

Berg, Maggie. *Jane Eyre: Portrait of a Life*. London: Twayne, 1987.

Beyene, Yewoubdar. *From Menarche to Menopause: Reproductive Lives of Peasant Women in Two Cultures*. Albany: SUNY Press, 1989.

Blythe, Helen Lucy. "*The Fixed Period* (1882): Euthansia, Cannibalism, and Colonial Extinction in Trollope's Antipodes." *Nineteenth-Century Contexts* 25 (2003): 161–80.

Botelho, Lynn. "Old Age and Menopause in Rural Women of Early Modern Suffolk." *Women and Ageing in British Society Since 1500*. Eds. Lynn Botelho and Pat Thane. Harlow, England: Longman, 2001. 43–65.

Botelho, Lynn, and Pat Thane. "Introduction." *Women and Ageing in British Society Since 1500*. Eds. Botelho and Pat Thane. Harlow, England: Longman, 2001. 1–12.

Brantlinger, Patrick. *Rule of Darkness: British Literature and Imperialism, 1830–1914*. Ithaca: Cornell UP, 1988.

Braxton Hicks, J. "The Croonian Lectures on The Difference Between the Sexes in Regard to the Aspect and Treatment of Disease." *The British Medical Journal* (April 21, 1877): 475–76.

Brontë, Charlotte. *Jane Eyre*. 1847. Oxford: Oxford UP, 1980.

———. *Shirley*. 1849. Oxford: Oxford UP, 1981.

———. "To Miss Wooler." 30 Jan. 1846. Letter 224 of *The Brontës: Their Lives, Friendships and Correspondence*. Ed. Thomas James Wise. Vol. 2. Oxford: Porcupine Press, 1980.

Brooks, Jean. "The Homeliest of Heart-Strings." 1971. *Thomas Hardy Poems: A Casebook*. Eds. James Gibson and Trevor Johnson. London: Macmillan, 1979.

Brown, Joanna Cullen. *A Journey into Thomas Hardy's Poetry*. London: W. H. Allen, 1989.

Buckler, William E. *The Poetry of Thomas Hardy: A Study in Art and Ideas*. New York: New York UP, 1983.

Buss, David M. *The Evolution of Desire: Strategies of Human Mating*. New York: Basic Books, 1994.

Butler, Judith. *Gender Trouble: Feminism and the Subversion of Identity*. New York: Routledge, 1990.

Button, Marilyn D. "Reclaiming Mrs. Frances Trollope: British Abolitionist and Feminist." *CLA Journal* 38 (1994): 69–86.

[Campbell, G. E. B.]. *Etiquette of Good Society*. London: Cassell, 1880.

Cardwell, Margaret. Appendix A. *Great Expectations*. By Charles Dickens. 1861. Oxford: Oxford UP, 1994. 481–82.

Childs, Donald J. *Modernism and Eugenics: Woolf, Eliot, Yeats, and the Culture of Degeneration*. Cambridge: Cambridge UP, 2001.

Church, Roy. "Advertising Consumer Goods in Nineteenth-Century Britain: Reinterpretations." *Economic History Review* 4 (2000): 621–45.

Cohen, Ed. "Writing Gone Wilde: Homoerotic Desire in the Closet of Representation." *Critical Essays on Oscar Wilde*. Ed. Regenia Gagnier. NY: G. K. Hall & Co, 1991. 68–87.

Cohen, Gene D. *The Mature Mind: The Positive Power of the Aging Brain*. New York: Basic Books, 2005.

Cole, Thomas R. *The Journey of Life: A Cultural History of Aging in America*. Cambridge: Cambridge UP, 1992.

Cole, Thomas R., and Claudia Edwards. "The Nineteenth Century." *A History of Old Age*. Ed. Pat Thane. London: Thames & Hudson, 2005. 211–61.

Covey, Herbert C. *Images of Older People in Western Art and Society*. New York: Praeger, 1991.

Craig, Randall. "Rhetoric and Courtship in *Can You Forgive Her?*" *ELH* 62 (1995): 217–35.

Craik, Dinah Mulock. *Hannah*. 1871. New York: Harper and Brothers, nd.

Croskery, Margaret Case. "Mothers without Children, Unity without Plot: *Cranford*'s Radical Charm." *Nineteenth-Century Literature* 52.2 (1997): 198–220.

Crozier, Ivan. "William Acton and the History of Sexuality: The Medical and Professional Context." *Journal of Victorian Culture* 5 (2000): 1–27.

Cunnington, Phillis, and Catherine Lucas. *Costume for Births, Marriages and Deaths*. London: Adam & Charles Black, 1972.

Dana, Charles L. Rev. of *Genius and Degeneration*, by William Hirsch. *Science* 5.144 ns (1897): 404–6.

Darby, Robert. "William Action's Antipodean Disciples: A Colonial Perspective on His Theories of Male Sexual (Dys)function." *Journal of the History of Sexuality* 13.2 (2004): 157–82.

Davey, Richard. *A History of Mourning*. London: McCorquodale & Co., 1889.

Davidoff, Leonore, and Catherine Hall. *Family Fortunes*. Rev. ed. London: Routledge, 2002.

Davis, Dona. "The Cultural Constructions of the Premenstrual and Menopause Syndromes." *Gender and Health: An International Perspective*. Eds. Carolyn F. Sargent and Caroline B. Brettell. Upper Saddle River, NJ: Prentice Hall, 1996.

Decker, Clarence R. "Zola's Literary Reputation in England." *PMLA* 49 (1934): 1140–53.

Dempsey, Mike, ed. *Bubbles: Early Advertising Art From A & F Pears' Ltd.* Glasgow: William Collins Sons, 1978.

Dever, Carolyn. "Everywhere and Nowhere: Sexuality in Victorian Fiction." *A Concise Companion to the Victorian Novel.* Ed. Francis O'Gorman. Oxford: Blackwell, 2005.

DeVries, Leonard. *Victorian Advertisements.* Philadelphia: J. B. Lippincott, 1968.

Dickens, Charles. *American Notes and Pictures From Italy.* Oxford: Oxford UP, 1987.

———. *Bleak House.* 1853. New York: W. W. Norton, 1977.

———. *David Copperfield.* 1849–50. Oxford: Oxford UP, 1997.

———. *Dombey and Son.* 1846–48. Oxford: Oxford UP, 2001.

———. *Great Expectations.* 1860–61. Oxford: Oxford UP, 1994.

———. *Hard Times.* 1854. New York: W. W. Norton, 2001.

———. *Little Dorrit.* 1855–57. Harmondsworth, Middlesex: Penguin, 1967.

———. *Nicholas Nickleby.* 1838–39. London: Penguin, 1986.

Dillaway, Heather E. "When Does Menopause Occur, and How Long Does It Last?: Wrestling With Age- and Time-Based Conceptualizations of Reproductive Aging." *NWSA Journal* 18.1 (2006): 31–60.

Douglas, Fanny. *The Gentlewoman's Book of Dress.* London: Henry and Co., 1890.

Dove, Mary. *The Perfect Age of Man's Life.* Cambridge: Cambridge UP, 1987.

Eliot, George. *Middlemarch.* 1871–72. New York: W. W. Norton, 1977.

The Elixir of Beauty; A Book for the Toilet-Table. London: H. G. Clarke, 1848.

English, Richard, and Michael Kenny. "Conclusion: Decline or Declinism?" *Rethinking British Decline.* Eds. Richard English and Michael Kenny. New York: St. Martin's Press, 2000.

Ephron, Nora. *I Feel Bad About My Neck: And Other Thoughts On Being A Woman.* New York: Knopf, 2006.

Epperly, Elizabeth R. "From the Borderlands of Decency: Madame Max Goesler." *Victorians Institute Journal* 15 (1987): 24–35.

Etherington, Norman. Introduction. *The Annotated She.* By H. Rider Haggard. Ed. Etherington. Bloomington: Indiana UP, 1991. xv–xliii.

Etiquette For Ladies. London: Frederick Warne and Co., 1866.

Farr, William. *Vital Statistics: A Memorial Volume of Selections from the Reports and Writings.* London: Office of the Sanitary Institute, 1885.

Fasick, Laura. *Vessels of Meaning: Women's Bodies, Gender Norms, and Class Bias from Richardson to Lawrence.* DeKalb: Northern Illinois UP, 1997.

Featherstone, Mike, and Mike Hepworth. "The History of the Male Menopause: 1848–1936." *Maturitas* 7 (1985): 249–57.

———. "Images of Ageing." *Ageing in Society: An Introduction to Social Gerontology.* Eds. John Bond, Peter Coleman, and Sheila Pace. London: Sage, 1993. 304–32.

"Female Novelists." Rev. *New Monthly Magazine* 96 (1852): 19–27.

Fenwick, Julie M. "Mothers of Empire in Elizabeth Gaskell's *Cranford.*" *English Studies in Canada* 23 (1997): 409–26.

Formanek, Ruth. "Continuity and Change and 'The Change of Life': Premodern Views of the Menopause." *The Meanings of Menopause: Historical, Medi-*

cal, and Clinical Perspectives. Ed. Ruth Formanek. Hillsdale, NJ: Analytic Press, 1990.

Foucault, Michel. *The History of Sexuality.* Vol. 1. New York: Random House, 1978.

Friedan, Betty. *The Fountain of Age.* New York: Simon & Schuster, 1993.

Frierson, William C. "The English Controversy over Realism in Fiction (1885–1895)." *PMLA* 43 (1928): 533–50.

Gagnier, Regenia. "Mediums and the Media: A Response to Judith Walkowitz." *Representations* 22 (1988): 29–36.

Galabin, A. L. "Disturbances at the Menopause." 1893. *Women From Birth To Death: The Female Life Cycle in Britain 1830–1914.* Eds. Pat Jalland and John Hooper. Brighton: Harvester Press, 1986. 297–98.

Gardner, John. *Longevity: The Means of Prolonging Life After Middle Age.* 3rd ed. London: Henry S. King, 1875.

Gaskell, Elizabeth. *Cranford.* Oxford: Oxford UP, 1998.

Gilbert, Sandra M., and Susan Gubar. *The Madwoman in the Attic: The Woman Writer and the Ninetenth-Century Literary Imagination.* New Haven: Yale UP, 1984.

———. *No Man's Land: The Place of the Woman Writer in the Twentieth Century.* Vol. 2. New Haven: Yale UP, 1988.

Gilleard, Chris. "Cultural Approaches to the Ageing Body." *The Cambridge Handbook of Age and Aging.* Ed. Malcolm L. Johnson. Cambridge: Cambridge UP, 2005. 156–64.

Gillespie, Michael Patrick. *Oscar Wilde and the Poetics of Ambiguity.* Gainesville: UP of Florida, 1996.

Gilmartin, Sophie. *Ancestry and Narrative in Nineteenth-Century British Literature: Blood Relations from Edgeworth to Hardy.* Cambridge: Cambridge UP, 1998.

Gladstone, W. E. " 'Locksley Hall' and the Jubilee." *The Nineteenth Century* 119 (1887): 1–18.

Glendinning, Victoria. *Trollope.* London: Hutchinson, 1992.

Godfrey, Esther. "*Jane Eyre*, from Governess to Girl Bride." *SEL* 45.5 (2005): 853–71.

Greg, W. R. "Why Are Women Redundant?" *National Review* 14 (April 1862): 434–60.

Griffiths, Antony. *The Print in Stuart Britain: 1603–1689.* London: British Museum P, 1998.

Gullette, Margaret Morganroth. *Aged by Culture.* Chicago: U Chicago P, 2004.

———. *Declining to Decline: Cultural Combat and the Politics of the Midlife.* Charlottesville: UP of Virginia, 1997.

———. "Male Midlife Sexuality in a Gerontocratic Economy: The Privileged Stage of the Long Midlife in Nineteenth-Century Age-Ideology." *Journal of the History of Sexuality* 5 (1994): 58–89.

———. "Midlife Discourses in the Twentieth-Century United States: An Essay on the Sexuality, Ideology, and Politics of 'Middle-Ageism.' " *Welcome to Middle Age! (And Other Cultural Fictions).* Ed. Richard A. Shweder. Chicago: U of Chicago P, 1998. 3–44.

———. "The Puzzling Case of the Deceased Wife's Sister: Nineteenth-Century England Deals with a Second-Chance Plot." *Representations* 31 (1990): 142–66.

Hager, Kelly. "Estranging *David Copperfield*: Reading the Novel of Divorce." *ELH* 63.4 (1996): 989–1019.

Haggard, H. Rider. *She*. 1886–87. *The Annotated She*. Ed. Norman Etherington. Bloomington: Indiana UP, 1991.

Hall, Catherine. "A Response to the Commentators." *Journal of British Studies* 42 (2003): 538.

Hall, Lesley. "The Age-Old and Hidden Torments of Impotence." *British Journal of Sexual Medicine* 22.6 (1995): 24–26.

———. " 'The English Have Hot Water Bottles': The Morganatic Marriage between Sexology and Medicine in Britain since William Acton." *Sexual Knowledge, Sexual Science: The History of Attitudes to Sexuality*. Eds. Roy Porter and Mikulas Teich. Cambridge: Cambridge UP, 1994. 350–66.

Hall, N. John. *Trollope: A Biography*. Oxford: Clarendon P, 1991.

Hamilton, Lisa K. "New Women and 'Old' Men: Gendering Degeneration." *Women and British Aestheticism*. Eds. Talia Schaffer and Kathy Alexis Psomiades. Charlottesville: UP of Virginia, 1999. 62–80.

Hardy, Florence Emily. *The Later Years of Thomas Hardy: 1892–1928*. London: MacMillan, 1930.

Hardy, Thomas. *The Complete Poems of Thomas Hardy*. Ed. James Gibson. New York: Macmillan Publishing, 1978.

———. *The Life and Work of Thomas Hardy*. Ed. Michael Millgate. London: Macmillan, 1984.

———. *The Well-Beloved*. 1897. Oxford: Oxford UP, 1991.

Hareven, Tamara. "Changing Images of Aging and the Social Construction of the Life Course." *Images of Aging: Cultural Representations of Later Life*. Eds. Mike Featherstone and Andrew Wernick. London: Routledge, 1995. 119–34.

Harrison, Brian. *Separate Spheres: The Opposition to Women's Suffrage in Britain*. London: Croom Helm, 1978.

Heineman, Helen. *Frances Trollope*. Boston: Twayne, 1984.

———. *Mrs. Trollope: The Triumphant Feminine in the Nineteenth Century*. Athens: Ohio UP, 1979.

Hepworth, Mike, and Mike Featherstone. *Surviving Middle Age*. Oxford: Basil Blackwell, 1982.

Hess, T. M. "Attitudes Toward Aging and Their Effects On Behavior." *Handbook of the Psychology of Aging*. Eds. J. E. Birren and K. W. Schaie. 6th ed. San Diego: Academic Press, 2006. 379–406.

Hewitt, Emma C. "The New Woman in Relation to the New Man." *Westminster Review* 147 (1897): 335–37.

Horstman, Allen. *Victorian Divorce*. London: Croom Helm, 1985.

Hughes, Linda K. *The Manyfacèd Glass: Tennyson's Dramatic Monologues*. Athens, Ohio: Ohio UP, 1987.

Hynes, Samuel. "How To Be An Old Poet: The Examples of Hardy and Yeats." *Reading Thomas Hardy*. Ed. Charles P. C. Pettit. Houndmills, Basingstoke, Hampshire: MacMillan Press, 1998. 172–87.

Irwin, Michael. " 'Gifted, Even In November': The Meanings of *The Well-Beloved.*" *The Achievement of Thomas Hardy.* Ed. Phillip Mallet. Houndmills, Basingstoke, Hampshire: MacMillan Press, 2000. 41–57.

Jalland, Pat. *Death in the Victorian Family.* Oxford: Oxford UP, 1996.

Jalland, Pat, and John Hooper. *Women From Birth To Death: The Female Life Cycle in Britain 1830–1914.* Brighton: Harvester Press, 1986.

Jaques, Elliott. "Death and the Mid-Life Crisis." *International Journal of Psycho-Analysis* 46 (1965): 502–14.

Jay, Elisabeth. Introduction. *Miss Marjoribanks.* By Margaret Oliphant. London: Penguin, 1998.

Jennings, Harlan. "Her Majesty's Opera Company in Kansas City." *The Opera Quarterly* 21.2 (2005): 227–41.

Joerissen, Peter, and Cornelia Will. *Die Lebenstreppe: Bilder Der Menschlichen Lebensalter.* Köln, Germany: Rheinland-Verlag, 1983.

Johnson, Edgar. *Charles Dickens: His Tragedy and Triumph.* Vol. 2. New York: Simon and Schuster, 1952.

Joseph, Gerhard. "Prejudice in Jane Austen, Emma Tennant, Charles Dickens — and Us." *SEL* 40.4 (2000): 679–93.

Kakar, Sudhir. "The Search for Middle Age in India." *Welcome to Middle Age! (And Other Cultural Fictions).* Ed. Richard A. Shweder. Chicago: U of Chicago P, 1998. 75–98.

Kalache, Alexandre, Sandhi Maria Barreto, and Ingrid Keller. "Global Ageing: The Demographic Revolution in All Cultures and Societies." *The Cambridge Handbook of Age and Aging.* Ed. Malcolm L. Johnson. Cambridge: Cambridge UP, 2005. 30–46.

Katz, Stephen. "Imagining the Life-Span: From Premodern Miracles to Postmodern Fantasies." *Images of Aging: Cultural Representations of Later Life.* Eds. Mike Featherstone and Andrew Wernick. London: Routledge, 1995.

Kearns, Bessie Jean Ruley. "Perceptions of Menopause by Papago Women." *Changing Perspectives on Menopause.* Eds. Ann M. Voda, Myra Dinnerstein, and Sheryl R. O'Donnell. Austin: U of Texas P, 1982.

Kent, Christopher. "Image and Reality: The Actress and Society." *A Widening Sphere: Changing Roles of Victorian Women.* Ed. Martha Vicinus. Bloomington: Indian UP, 1977. 94–116.

Kincaid, James R. *The Novels of Anthony Trollope.* Oxford: Oxford UP, 1977.

———. *Tennyson's Major Poems: The Comic and Ironic Patterns.* New Haven: Yale UP, 1975.

Kincaid-Ehler, Elizabeth. "Bad Maps For An Unknown Region: Menopause from a Literary Perspective." *Changing Perspectives on Menopause.* Eds. Ann M. Voda, Myra Dinnerstein, Sheryl R. O'Donnell. Austin: U of Texas P, 1982. 24–38.

King, Amy M. *Bloom: The Botanical Vernacular in the English Novel.* Oxford: Oxford UP, 2003.

King, Margaret F. " 'Certain Learned Ladies': Trollope's *Can You Forgive Her?* and the Langham Place Circle." *Victorian Literature and Culture* 21 (1993): 307–26.

Kissel, Susan S. *In Common Cause: The "Conservative" Frances Trollope and the "Radical" Frances Wright.* Bowling Green, OH: Bowling Green State U Popular P, 1993.

———. "More Than Anthony's Mother: Frances Trollope's Other Contributions to British Literature." *Kentucky Philological Review* 20 (1989): 12–17.

———. " 'What Shall Become of Us All?': Frances Trollope's Sense of the Future." *Studies in the Novel* 20 (1988): 151–66.

Kucich, John. "Moral Authority in the Late Novels: The Gendering of Art." *The Sense of Sex: Feminist Perspectives on Hardy.* Ed. Margaret R. Higonnet. Urbana: U Chicago P, 1993.

Lacan, Jacques. *Écrits: A Selection.* Trans. Alan Sheridan. New York: W. W. Norton, 1977.

Lachman, Margie E., and Jacquelyn Boone James. "Charting the Course of Midlife Development: An Overview." *Multiple Paths of Midlife Development.* Eds. Margie E. Lachman and Jacquelyn Boone James. Chicago: U of Chicago P, 1997.

The Ladies' Hand-Book of the Toilet; A Manual of Elegance and Fashion. London: H. G. Clarke and Co., 1843.

Ladies—No X. Mrs. Georgina Weldon." *Vanity Fair* 31 (3 May 1884): 243.

A Lady. *The Whole Duty of Woman, A Guide to the Female Sex, From the Age of Sixteen to Sixty, Shewing Women, Of All Conditions, How to Behave Themselves for Obtaining Not Only Present But Future Happiness.* Stourbridge: Heming and Tallis, 1815.

Lankester, E. Ray. *Degeneration: A Chapter in Darwinism.* London: Macmillan, 1880.

Laqueur, Thomas. *Making Sex: Body and Gender From the Greeks to Freud.* Cambridge: Harvard UP, 1990.

Laslett, Peter. "Necessary Knowledge: Age and Aging in the Societies of the Past." *Aging in the Past: Demography, Society, and Old Age.* Eds. David I. Kertzer and Peter Laslett. Berkeley, CA: U of California P, 1995.

Leavis, Q. D. Introduction. *Miss Marjoribanks.* By Margaret Oliphant. London: Zodiac P, 1969.

[Leech, John.] *"Tempus Edax Rerum."* Cartoon. *Punch* (1852): 216.

Letwin, Shirley Robin. *The Gentleman in Trollope: Individuality and Moral Conduct.* Cambridge: Harvard UP, 1982.

Levi, Peter. *Tennyson.* New York: Charles Scribner's Sons, 1993.

Levine, George. "Can You Forgive Him? Trollope's *Can You Forgive Her?* and the Myth of Realism." *Victorian Studies* 18 (1974): 5–30.

Levinson, Daniel J., Charlotte N. Darrow, Edward B. Klein, Maria H. Levinson, and Braxton McKee. *The Seasons of a Man's Life.* New York: Knopf, 1978.

Linton, Eliza Lynn. *"La Femme Passée."* *The Saturday Review* 26.49 (1868): 49–50.

Lock, Margaret. "Deconstructing the Change: Female Maturation in Japan and North America." *Welcome to Middle Age! (And Other Cultural Fictions).* Ed. Richard A. Shweder. Chicago: U of Chicago P, 1998. 45–74.

Loeb, Lori Anne. *Consuming Angels: Advertising and Victorian Women*. New York: Oxford UP, 1994.

MacKenzie, John M. "The Imperial Pioneer and Hunter and the British Masculine Stereotype in Late Victorian and Edwardian Times. *Manliness and Morality: Middle-Class Masculinity in Britain and America: 1800–1940*. Eds. J. A. Mangan and James Walvin. New York: St. Martin's P, 1987. 176–98.

———. *Propaganda and Empire: The Manipulation of British Public Opinion, 1880–1960*. Manchester: Manchester UP, 1984.

Mangan, J. A. "Social Darwinism and Upper-Class Education in late Victorian and Edwardian England." *Manliness and Morality: Middle-Class Masculinity in Britain and America: 1800–1940*. Eds. J. A. Mangan and James Walvin. New York: St. Martin's P, 1987. 135–59.

Mangan, J. A., and James Walvin. Introduction. *Manliness and Morality: Middle-Class Masculinity in Britain and America: 1800–1940*. Eds. J. A. Mangan and James Walvin. New York: St. Martin's P, 1987. 1–6.

Mangum, Teresa. "Growing Old: Age." *A Companion to Victorian Literature and Culture*. Ed. Herbert F. Tucker. Oxford: Blackwell Publishers, 1999. 97–109.

———. "Little Women: The Aging Female Character in Nineteenth-Century British Children's Literature." *Figuring Age: Women, Bodies, Generations*. Ed. Kathleen Woodward. Bloomington: Indiana UP, 1999. 59–87.

Markson, Elizabeth W. "Sagacious, Sinful, or Superfluous? The Social Construction of Older Women." *Handbook on Women and Aging*. Ed. Jean M. Coyle. Westport, CT: Greenwood, 1997. 53–71.

Markwick, Margaret. *Trollope and Women*. London: Hambledon Press, 1997.

Marsh, Edward. Introduction. *Can You Forgive Her?* By Anthony Trollope. London: Oxford UP, 1973. v–xi.

Marshall, Gail. *Actresses on the Victorian Stage: Feminine Performance and the Galatea Myth*. Cambridge: Cambridge UP, 1998.

Martin, Robert Barnard. *Tennyson: The Unquiet Heart*. Oxford: Clarendon P, 1980.

Mason, Michael. *The Making of Victorian Sexuality*. Oxford: Oxford UP, 1994.

Mayhew, Henry. *London Labour and the London Poor*. London: Griffin, Bohn, and Company, 1861.

McClintock, Anne. *Imperial Leather: Race, Gender and Sexuality in the Colonial Contest*. New York: Routledge, 1995.

McMaster, Juliet. *Trollope's Palliser Novels: Theme and Pattern*. New York: Oxford UP, 1978.

Melchior-Bonnet, Sabine. *The Mirror: A History*. Trans. Katharine H. Jewett. New York: Routledge, 2001.

Merrifield, Mrs. *Dress As A Fine Art*. London: Arthur Hall, 1854.

Michie, Helena. *The Flesh Made Word: Female Figures and Women's Bodies*. Oxford: Oxford UP, 1987.

———. *Victorian Honeymoons: Journeys to the Conjugal*. Cambridge: Cambridge UP, 2006.

Millgate, Michael. *Thomas Hardy: A Biography*. New York: Random House, 1982.

Mitchell, B. R. *Abstract of British Historical Statistics*. Cambridge: Cambridge UP, 1962.

Montez, Lola. *The Arts of Beauty*. London: James Blackwood, [1858].

Morse, Deborah Denenholz. *Women in Trollope's Palliser Novels*. Ann Arbor: UMI Research P, 1987.

Mullen, Richard. *Anthony Trollope: A Victorian in his World*. London: Duckworth, 1990.

Munich, Adrienne. *Queen Victoria's Secrets*. New York: Columbia UP, 1996.

Murphy, Patricia. *Time is of the Essence: Temporality, Gender, and the New Woman*. Albany: SUNY Press, 2001.

Nardin, Jane. *He Knew She Was Right: The Independent Woman in the Novels of Anthony Trollope*. Carbondale: Southern Illinois UP, 1989.

Nevett, T. R. *Advertising in Britain: A History*. London: Heinemann, 1982.

Neville-Sington, Pamela. *Fanny Trollope: The Life and Adventures of a Clever Woman*. London: Viking, 1997.

———. "The Life and Adventures of a Clever Woman." *Frances Trollope and the Novel of Social Change*. Ed. Brenda Ayres. Westport, CT: Greenwood Press, 2002.

Newsome, David. *Godliness and Good Learning: Four Studies on a Victorian Ideal*. London: John Murray, 1961.

Niles, Lisa. "Malthusian Menopause: Aging and Sexuality in Elizabeth Gaskell's *Cranford*." *Victorian Literature and Culture* 33.1 (2005): 293–310.

Nordau, Max. *Degeneration*. 1892. Lincoln: University of Nebraska Press, 1993.

Norton, The Hon. Mrs. [Caroline Sheridan]. *Old Sir Douglas*. 3 Vols. London: Hurst and Blackett, 1868.

An Officer's Widow. *The Etiquette of the Toilette-Table: Manual of Utility, Elegance, and Personal Comfort, Adapted for the Every-Day Use of Both Sexes*. London: W. R. M'Phun, 1859.

Old Physician. *Health Without Physic; or Cordials For Youth, Manhood, and Old Age*. London: Effingham Wilson, 1830.

Oliphant, Margaret. *Miss Marjoribanks*. 1865–66. London: Penguin, 1998.

O'Mealy, Joseph H. "Mrs. Oliphant, Miss Marjoribanks, and the Victorian Canon." *The Victorian Newsletter* 82 (1992): 44–49.

Ormand, Leonée. *Alfred Tennyson: A Literary Life*. Houndsmill, Basingstoke, Hampshire: Macmillan P, 1993.

Osborne, Peter, and Lynne Segal. "Gender as Performance: An Interview with Judith Butler." *Radical Philosophy* 67 (1994): 32–39.

Ottaway, Susannah R. *The Decline of Life: Old Age in Eighteenth-Century England*. Cambridge: Cambridge UP, 2004.

Overton, Bill. *The Unofficial Trollope*. Sussex: The Harvester Press, 1982.

Park, Roberta J. "Biological Thought, Athletics, and the Formation of a 'Man of Character': 1830–1900." *Manliness and Morality: Middle-Class Masculinity in Britain and America: 1800–1940*. Eds. J. A. Mangan and James Walvin. New York: St. Martin's P, 1987. 7–34.

Patten, Robert. L. "From Sketches to Nickleby." *The Cambridge Companion to Charles Dickens.* Ed. John O. Jordan. Cambridge: Cambridge UP, 2001.

Polhemus, Robert M. "Being in Love in *Phineas Finn / Phineas Redux*: Desire, Devotion, Consolation." *Nineteenth-Century Fiction* 37 (1982): 383–95.

———. *The Changing World of Anthony Trollope.* Berkeley: U of California P, 1968.

———. *Lot's Daughters: Sex, Redemption, and Women's Quest For Authority.* Stanford, CA: Stanford UP, 2005.

Poovey, Mary. *Uneven Developments: The Ideological Work of Gender in Mid-Victorian England.* Chicago: Chicago UP, 1988.

Porter, Roy, and Lesley Hall. *The Facts of Life: The Creation of Sexual Knowledge in Britain, 1650–1950.* New Haven: Yale UP, 1995.

Powell, Kerry. *Women and Victorian Theatre.* Cambridge: Cambridge UP, 1997.

Price, Jody. *"A Map of Utopia": Oscar Wilde's Theory for Social Transformation.* New York: Peter Lang, 1996.

Priestley, F. E. L. "Locksley Hall Revisited." *Queens Quarterly* 81 (1974): 512–32.

Quadagno, Jill S. *Aging in Early Industrial Society: Work, Family, and Social Policy in Nineteenth-Century England.* New York: Academic P, 1982.

Ramamurthy, Anandi. *Imperial Persuaders: Images of Africa and Asia in British Advertising.* Manchester: Manchester UP, 2003.

Ransom, Teresa. *Fanny Trollope: A Remarkable Life.* New York: St. Martin's P, 1995.

———. Introduction. *The Widow Barnaby.* By Fanny Trollope. Phoenix Mill, England: Alan Sutton, 1995. v–ix.

Richards, Thomas. *The Commodity Culture of Victorian England: Advertising and Spectacle, 1851–1914.* Stanford: Stanford UP, 1990.

Roebuck, Janet. "When Does 'Old Age' Begin?: The Evolution of the English Definition." *Journal of Social History* 2 (1979): 416–29.

Ross, Alex. *Hints on Dress And on the Arrangement of the Hair.* London: Ross and Company, [1861].

Rosselli, John. "Patti, Adelina." *Oxford Dictionary of National Biography.* Ed. H. C. G. Matthew. 60 Vols. Oxford: Oxford UP, 2004. 105–6.

Rubik, Margarete. *The Novels of Mrs. Oliphant: A Subversive View of Traditional Themes.* New York: Peter Lang, 1994.

Ryan, Michael. "The Climacteric Period." 1841. *Women From Birth To Death: The Female Life Cycle in Britain 1830–1914.* Eds. Pat Jalland and John Hooper. Brighton: Harvester Press, 1986. 287–89.

Ryan, Michael. "One Name of Many Shapes: *The Well-Beloved.*" *Critical Approaches to the Fiction of Thomas Hardy.* Ed. Dale Kramer. London: Macmillan Press, 1979. 172–92.

Sadleir, Michael. *Trollope: A Commentary.* London: Oxford UP, 1927.

Saul, S. B. *The Myth of the Great Depression, 1873–1896.* London: Macmillan, 1976.

Savage, Gail L. " 'Intended Only for the Husband': Gender, Class, and the Provision for Divorce in England, 1858–1868." *Victorian Scandals: Representations of Gender and Class.* Ed. Kristine Ottensen Garrigan. Athens: Ohio UP, 1992.

Schaub, Melissa. "Queen of the Air or Constitutional Monarch?: Idealism, Irony, and Narrative Power in *Miss Marjoribanks.*" *Nineteenth-Century Literature* 55:2 (2000): 195–225.

Seymour-Smith, Martin. *Hardy.* New York: St. Martin's Press, 1994.

Shackleton, Tim. Introduction. *Bubbles: Early Advertising Art From A & F Pears' Ltd.* Ed. Mike Dempsey. Glasgow: William Collins Sons, 1978.

Shahar, Shulamith. "Old Age in the High and Late Middle Ages: Images, Expectation and Status." *Old Age from Antiquity to Post-Modernity.* London: Routledge, 1993. 43–64.

Sherwood, Mrs. John. *Manners and Social Usages.* New York and London: Harper & Brothers, 1888.

Showalter, Elaine. *Sexual Anarchy: Gender and Culture at the Fin de Siècle.* New York: Viking, 1990.

Shweder, Richard A. "Introduction: Welcome to Middle Age!" Ed. Richard A. Shweder. *Welcome to Middle Age! (And Other Cultural Fictions).* Chicago: U of Chicago P, 1998. ix–xvii.

Sinfield, Alan. *The Wilde Century: Effeminacy, Oscar Wilde and The Queer Movement.* New York: Columbia UP, 1994.

Slater, Michael. *Dickens and Women.* Stanford, CA: Stanford UP, 1983.

Small, Helen. *The Long Life.* Oxford: Oxford UP, 2007.

Smith, F. B. "Sexuality in Britain 1800–1900: Some Suggested Revisions." *A Widening Sphere: Changing Roles of Victorian Women.* Ed. Martha Vicinus. Bloomington: Indiana UP, 1977. 185–87.

Smith Rosenberg, Carroll. *Disorderly Conduct: Visions of Gender in Victorian America.* New York: Oxford UP, 1985.

Soloway, Richard A. "Population and Demographics." *Victorian Britain.* Ed. Sally Mitchell. New York: Garland Publishing, 1988.

Stall, Sylvanus. *What A Man of Forty-Five Ought to Know.* London: Vir Publishing, 1901.

Steinem, Gloria. *Doing Sixty and Seventy.* San Francisco: Elders Academy Press, 2006.

Stetz, Margaret D. *Gender and the London Theatre 1880–1920.* High Wycombe, Buckinghamshire: Rivendale P, 2004.

Stolberg, Michael. "A Woman's Hell? Medical Perceptions of Menopause in Preindustrial Europe." *Bulletin of the History of Medicine* 73 (1999): 404–28.

Stone, Lawrence. *The Family, Sex and Marriage In England 1500–1800.* New York: Harper and Row, 1977.

———. *Road to Divorce: England 1530–1987.* Oxford: Oxford UP, 1990.

Stott, Rebecca. *The Fabrication of the Late-Victorian Femme Fatale: The Kiss of Death.* London: Macmillan Press, 1992.

Stubbs, Patricia. *Women and Fiction: Feminism and the Novel 1880–1920.* Sussex: Harvester Press, 1979.

Sybylla, Roe. "Situating Menopause Within the Strategies of Power: A Genealogy." *Reinterpreting Menopause: Cultural and Philosophical Issues.* Eds. Paul A. Komesaroff, Philipa Rothfield, and Jeanne Daly. New York: Routledge, 1997. 200–21.

Taylor, Lou. *Mourning Dress: A Costume and Social History*. London: George Allen & Unwin, 1983.

Tennyson, Alfred. "Locksley Hall Sixty Years After." *Tennyson: A Selected Edition*. Ed. Christopher Ricks. Berkeley: U of California P, 1989. 640–51.

———. "To Charles Esmarch." 18 April 1888. *The Letters of Alfred Lord Tennyson*. Eds. Cecil Y. Lang and Edgar F. Shannon, Jr. Vol. 2. Oxford: Oxford UP, 1990. 366–67.

Tennyson, Charles. *Alfred Tennyson*. [Hamden, Conn.]: Archon Books, 1968.

Tennyson, Hallam. *Alfred Lord Tennyson: A Memoir By His Son*. Vol. 2. New York: MacMillan, 1897.

Thane, Pat. "The Age of Old Age." *A History of Old Age*. Ed. Thane. London: Thames & Hudson, 2005. 9–29.

———. *Old Age in English History: Past Experiences, Present Issues*. Oxford: Oxford UP, 2000.

———. "Social Histories of Old Age and Aging." *Journal of Social History* 37.1 (2003): 93–111.

Thompson, Brian. *The Disastrous Mrs. Weldon: The Life, Loves, and Lawsuits of a Legendary Victorian*. New York: Doubleday, 2001.

Thompson, F. M. L. *The Rise of Respectable Society: A Social History of Victorian Britain 1830–1900*. Cambridge: Harvard UP, 1988.

Tilt, Edward John. *The Change of Life in Woman, in Health and Disease*. 4th ed. Philadelphia: P. Blakiston, 1883.

Todd, Barbara J. "The Remarrying Widow: A Stereotype Reconsidered." *Women in English Society 1500–1800*. London: Methuen, 1985.

Tosh, John. *Manliness and Masculinities in Nineteenth-Century Britain: Essays on Gender, Family and Empire*. Harlow, England: Pearson Longman, 2005.

Townsend, Meredith. "Will England Retain India?" *Contemporary Review* 53 (1888): 795–813.

Trollope, Anthony. *An Autobiography*. 1883. Ed. David Skilton. London: Penguin, 1996.

———. *An Old Man's Love*. 1884. 2 Vols. New York: Arno Press, 1981.

———. *Barchester Towers*. 1857. Oxford: Oxford UP, 1998.

———. *Can You Forgive Her?* 1864–65. Oxford: Oxford UP, 1991.

———. *Miss Mackenzie*. 1865. Oxford: Oxford UP, 1988.

———. *The Noble Jilt*. London: Constable & Company, 1923.

———. *North America*. London: Harper & Brothers, 1862.

———. *Phineas Finn*. 1867–69. Oxford: Oxford UP, 1973.

———. *Phineas Redux*. 1873–74. Oxford: Oxford UP, 1973.

———. *The Prime Minister*. 1875–76. Oxford: Oxford UP, 1983.

———. *The Small House at Allington*. 1862–64. New York: Oxford UP, 1980.

———. *South Africa*. 1878. Cape Town: A. A. Balkema, 1973.

———. "To [Adrian H. Joline]. 4 April 1879. *The Letters of Anthony Trollope*. Ed. N. John Hall. Stanford, CA: Stanford UP, 1983. 821.

———. *The Way We Live Now*. 1874–75. Oxford: Oxford UP, 1999.

———. "Work Sheet." Trollope Business Papers. The Bodleian Library.

Trollope, Frances. *The Widow Barnaby*. 1839. Phoenix Mill, Gloucestershire: Alan Sutton Publishing Limited, 1995.

———. *The Widow Married; a Sequel to the Widow Barnaby*. London: Henry Colburn, 1840.

———. *The Widow Wedded; or The Adventures of the Barnabys in America*. London: Ward and Lock, 1843.

Troyansky, David G. "The Eighteenth Century." *A History of Old Age*. Ed. Pat Thane. London: Thames & Hudson, 2005. 175–210.

———. "The Older Person in the Western World: From the Middle Ages to the Industrial Revolution." *Handbook of the Humanities and Aging*. Eds. Thomas R. Cole, David D. Van Tassel, and Robert Kastenbaum. New York: Springer Publishing Co., 1992. 40–61.

Tucker, Herbert F., ed. *A Companion To Victorian Literature and Culture*. Oxford: Blackwell Publishers, 1999.

Turner, E. S. *The Shocking History of Advertising*. Harmondsworth, Middlesex, England: Penguin, 1965.

Turner, Mark W. " 'Telling Of My Weekly Doings': The Material Culture of the Victorian Novel." *A Concise Companion to the Victorian Novel*. Ed. Francis O'Gorman. Oxford: Blackwell, 2005. 113–33.

———. *Trollope and the Magazines: Gendered Issues in Mid-Victorian Britain*. New York: St. Martin's P, 2000.

Vance, Norman. *The Sinews of the Spirit: The Ideal of Christian Manliness in Victorian Literature and Religious Thought*. Cambridge: Cambridge UP, 1985.

Walkowitz, Judith. *City of Dreadful Delight: Narratives of Sexual Danger in Late-Victorian London*. Chicago: U of Chicago P, 1992.

Walsh, Susan. "Bodies of Capital: *Great Expectations* and the Climacteric Economy." *Victorian Studies* 37.1 (1993): 73–98.

Walvin, James. "Symbols of Moral Superiority: Slavery, Sport and the Changing World Older, 1800–1940." *Manliness and Morality: Middle-Class Masculinity in Britain and America: 1800–1940*. Eds. J. A. Mangan and James Walvin. New York: St. Martin's P, 1987. 242–60.

Warren, Allen. "Popular Manliness: Baden-Powell, Scouting, and the Development of Manly Character." *Manliness and Morality: Middle-Class Masculinity in Britain and America: 1800–1940*. Eds. J. A. Mangan and James Walvin. New York: St. Martin's P, 1987. 199–219.

Weatherly, Lionel A. "Suffering and the Change of Life." 1882. *Women From Birth To Death: The Female Life Cycle in Britain 1830–1914*. Eds. Pat Jalland and John Hooper. Brighton: Harvester Press, 1986. 294–95.

Webster, J. C. "Character and Disposition at 'The Change.' " 1892. *Women From Birth To Death: The Female Life Cycle in Britain 1830–1914*. Eds. Pat Jalland and John Hooper. Brighton: Harvester Press, 1986. 295–97.

Welsh, Alexander. *From Copyright to Copperfield: The Identity of Dickens*. Cambridge: Harvard UP, 1987.

Wicke, Jennifer. *Advertising Fictions: Literature, Advertisement, and Social Reading*. New York: Columbia UP, 1988.

"The Widow Barnaby." Rev. *The Athenaeum* 584 (1839): 9–10.

"The Widow Barnaby, by Mrs. Trollope." Rev. *The London Times* 24 January 1839: 5.

Wilbush, Joel. "Climacteric Disorders—Historical Perspectives." *The Menopause.* Eds. John W. W. Studd and Malcolm I. Whitehead. Oxford: Blackwell Scientific, 1988.

———. "La Menespausie—The Birth of a Syndrome." *Maturitus* 1 (1979): 145–51.

Wilde, Oscar. *The Picture of Dorian Gray.* 1890. Oxford: Oxford UP, 1998.

Williams, Raymond. "Advertising: The Magic System." *Problems in Materialism and Culture.* London: NLB, 1980.

Williamson, Judith. *Decoding Advertisements: Ideology and Meaning in Advertising.* London: Boyars, 1978.

Winston, Elizabeth. "Revising *Miss Marjoribanks*." *Nineteenth Century Studies* 9 (1995): 85–97.

Woodward, Kathleen. "Against Wisdom: The Social Politics of Anger and Aging." *Cultural Critique* 51 (2002): 186–218.

———. *Aging and Its Discontents: Freud and Other Fictions.* Bloomington: Indiana UP, 1991.

———. "Instant Repulsion: Decrepitude, the Mirror Stage, and The Literary Imagination." *The Kenyon Review* 5.4 (Fall 1983): 43–66.

Wright, Ann L. "Variation in Navajo Menopause: Toward an Explanation." *Changing Perspectives on Menopause.* Eds. Ann M. Voda, Myra Dinnerstein, and Sheryl R. O'Donnell. Austin: U of Texas P, 1982.

Wrigley, E. A., and R. S. Schofield. *The Population History of England 1541–1871: A Reconstruction.* Cambridge: Harvard UP, 1981.

Yeazell, Ruth Bernard. *Fictions of Modesty: Women and Courtship in the English Novel.* Chicago: U Chicago P, 1991.

Index